A 1

D1321103

ALGORITHMIC INFORMATION THEORY

Cambridge Tracts in Theoretical Computer Science

Managing Editor: Professor C J van Rijsbergen, Computing Science Department, University of Glasgow, Glasgow, Scotland

Editorial Board:
S Abramsky, Department of Computing Science, Imperial College of Science and Technology
P H Aczel, Department of Computer Science, University of Manchester
J W de Bakker, Centrum voor Wiskunde en Informatica, Amsterdam
J A Goguen, SRI International, Menlo Park, CA
J V Tucker, Centre for Theoretical Computer Science, University of Leeds

Titles in the series

ALGORITHMIC
INFORMATION THEORY

GREGORY J. CHAITIN
IBM Thomas J. Watson Research Center
Yorktown Heights, New York

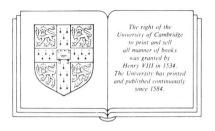

CAMBRIDGE UNIVERSITY PRESS

Cambridge

New York   New Rochelle

Melbourne   Sydney

Published by the Press Syndicate of the University of Cambridge
The Pitt Building, Trumpington Street, Cambridge CB2 1RP
32 East 57th Street, New York, NY 10022, USA
10 Stamford Road, Oakleigh, Melbourne 3166, Australia

First published 1987

Printed in Great Britain at the University Press, Cambridge

British Library cataloguing in publication data
Chaitin, Gregory J.

Algorithmic information theory. – (Cambridge tracts in theoretical computer science).
1. Electronic digital computers – Programming   2. Algorithms   3. Metamathematics
4. Incompleteness theorems
I. Title
05.1'2'028   QA76.6
Library of Congress cataloguing in publication data available

ISBN 0 521 34306 2

The author is pleased to acknowledge permission to make free use of previous publications:

Chapter 6 is based on his 1975 paper "A theory of program size formally identical to information theory" published in volume 22 of the *Journal of the ACM,* copyright © 1975, Association for Computing Machinery, Inc., reprinted by permission.

Chapters 7, 8, and 9 are based on his 1987 paper "Incompleteness theorems for random reals" published in volume 8 of *Advances in Applied Mathematics,* copyright © 1987 by Academic Press, Inc.

The author wishes to thank Ralph Gomory, Gordon Lasher, and the Physics Department of the Watson Research Center.

CONTENTS

FOREWORD

Turing's deep 1937 paper made it clear that Gödel's astonishing earlier results on arithmetic undecidability related in a very natural way to a class of computing automata, nonexistent at the time of Turing's paper, but destined to appear only a few years later, subsequently to proliferate as the ubiquitous stored-program computer of today. The appearance of computers, and the involvement of a large scientific community in elucidation of their properties and limitations, greatly enriched the line of thought opened by Turing. Turing's distinction between computational problems was rawly binary: some were solvable by algorithms, others not. Later work, of which an attractive part is elegantly developed in the present volume, refined this into a multiplicity of scales of computational difficulty, which is still developing as a fundamental theory of information and computation that plays much the same role in computer science that classical thermodynamics plays in physics: by defining the outer limits of the possible, it prevents designers of algorithms from trying to create computational structures which provably do not exist. It is not surprising that such a thermodynamics of information should be as rich in philosophical consequence as thermodynamics itself.

   This quantitative theory of description and computation, or Computational Complexity Theory as it has come to be known, studies the various kinds of resources required to describe and execute a computational process. Its most striking conclusion is that there exist computations and classes of computations having innocent-seeming definitions but nevertheless requiring inordinate quantities of some computational resource. Resources for which results of this kind have been established include:
(a) The mass of text required to describe an object;

(b) The volume of intermediate data which a computational process would need to generate;

(c) The time for which such a process will need to execute, either on a standard "serial" computer or on computational structures unrestricted in the degree of parallelism which they can employ.

Of these three resource classes, the first is relatively static, and pertains to the fundamental question of object describability; the others are dynamic since they relate to the resources required for a computation to execute. It is with the first kind of resource that this book is concerned. The crucial fact here is that there exist symbolic objects (i.e., texts) which are "algorithmically inexplicable," i.e., cannot be specified by any text shorter than themselves. Since texts of this sort have the properties associated with the random sequences of classical probability theory, the theory of describability developed in Part II of the present work yields a very interesting new view of the notion of randomness.

The first part of the book prepares in a most elegant, even playful, style for what follows; and the text as a whole reflects its author's wonderful enthusiasm for profundity and simplicity of thought in subject areas ranging over philosophy, computer technology, and mathematics.

J. T. Schwartz
Courant Institute
February, 1987

PREFACE

The aim of this book is to present the strongest possible version of Gödel's incompleteness theorem, using an information-theoretic approach based on the size of computer programs.

One half of the book is concerned with studying Ω, the halting probability of a universal computer if its program is chosen by tossing a coin. The other half of the book is concerned with encoding Ω as an algebraic equation in integers, a so-called exponential diophantine equation.

Gödel's original proof of his incompleteness theorem is essentially the assertion that one cannot always prove that a program will fail to halt. This is equivalent to asking whether it ever produces any output. He then converts this into an arithmetical assertion. Over the years this has been improved; it follows from the work on Hilbert's 10th problem that Gödel's theorem is equivalent to the assertion that one cannot always prove that a diophantine equation has no solutions if this is the case.

In our approach to incompleteness, we shall ask whether or not a program produces an infinite amount of output rather than asking whether it produces any; this is equivalent to asking whether or not a diophantine equation has infinitely many solutions instead of asking whether or not it is solvable.

If one asks whether or not a diophantine equation has a solution for N different values of a parameter, the N different answers to this question are not independent; in fact, they are only $\log_2 N$ bits of information. But if one asks whether or not there are infinitely many solutions for N different values of a parameter, then there are indeed cases in which the N different answers to these questions are independent mathematical facts, so that knowing one answer is no help in knowing any of the others. The equation encoding Ω has this property.

When mathematicians can't understand something they usually assume that it is their fault, but it may just be that there is no pattern or law to be discovered!

How to read this book: This entire monograph is essentially a proof of one theorem, Theorem D in Chapter 8. The exposition is completely self-contained. While the reader is assumed to be familiar with the basic concepts of recursive function or computability theory and probability theory, at a level easily acquired from DAVIS (1965) and FELLER (1970), we make no use of individual results from these fields that we do not reformulate and prove here. Familiarity with LISP programming is helpful but not necessary, because we give a self-contained exposition of the unusual version of pure LISP that we use, including a listing of an interpreter. For discussions of the history and significance of metamathematics, see DAVIS (1978), WEBB (1980), TYMOCZKO (1986), and RUCKER (1987).

Although the ideas in this book are not easy, we have tried to present the material in the most concrete and direct fashion possible. We give many examples, and computer programs for key algorithms. In particular, the theory of program-size in LISP presented in Chapter 5 and Appendix B, which has not appeared elsewhere, is intended as an illustration of the more abstract ideas in the following chapters.

FIGURES

CHAPTER 1

INTRODUCTION

More than half a century has passed since the famous papers GÖDEL (1931) and TURING (1937) that shed so much light on the foundations of mathematics, and that simultaneously promulgated mathematical formalisms for specifying algorithms, in one case via primitive recursive function definitions, and in the other case via Turing machines. The development of computer hardware and software technology during this period has been phenomenal, and as a result we now know much better how to do the high-level functional programming of Gödel, and how to do the low-level machine language programming found in Turing's paper. And we can actually run our programs on machines and debug them, which Gödel and Turing could not do.

I believe that the best way to actually program a universal Turing machine is John McCarthy's universal function EVAL. In 1960 McCarthy proposed LISP as a new mathematical foundation for the theory of computation [McCARTHY (1960)]. But by a quirk of fate LISP has largely been ignored by theoreticians and has instead become the standard programming language for work on artificial intelligence. I believe that pure LISP is in precisely the same role in computational mathematics that set theory is in theoretical mathematics, in that it provides a beautifully elegant and extremely powerful formalism which enables concepts such as that of numbers and functions to be defined from a handful of more primitive notions.

Simultaneously there have been profound theoretical advances. Gödel and Turing's fundamental undecidable proposition, the question of whether an algorithm ever halts, is equivalent to the question of whether it ever produces any output. In this monograph we will show that much more devastating undecidable propositions arise if one asks whether an algorithm produces an infinite amount of output or not.[1]

Gödel expended much effort to express his undecidable proposition as an arithmetical fact. Here too there has been considerable progress. In my opinion the most beautiful proof is the recent one of JONES and MATIJASEVIC (1984), based on three simple ideas:

1. the observation that $11^0 = 1$, $11^1 = 11$, $11^2 = 121$, $11^3 = 1331$, $11^4 = 14641$ reproduces Pascal's triangle, makes it possible to express binomial coefficients as the digits of powers of 11 written in high enough bases,

2. an appreciation of E. Lucas's remarkable hundred-year-old theorem that the binomial coefficient "n choose k" is odd if and only if each bit in the base-two numeral for k implies the corresponding bit in the base-two numeral for n,

3. the idea of using register machines rather than Turing machines, and of encoding computational histories via variables which are vectors giving the contents of a register as a function of time.

Their work gives a simple straightforward proof, using almost no number theory, that there is an exponential diophantine equation with one parameter p which has a solution if and only if the pth computer program (i.e., the program with Gödel number p) ever halts.

Similarly, one can use their method to arithmetize my undecidable proposition. The result is an exponential diophantine equation with the parameter n and the property that it has infinitely many solutions if and only if the nth bit of Ω is a 1. Here Ω is the halting probability of a universal Turing machine if an n-bit program has measure 2^{-n} [CHAITIN (1975b,1982b)]. Ω is an algorithmically random real number in the sense that the first N bits of the base-two expansion of Ω cannot be compressed into a program shorter than N bits, from which it follows that the successive bits of Ω cannot be distinguished from the result of independent tosses of a fair coin. We will also show in this monograph that an N-bit program cannot calculate the positions and values of more than N scattered bits of Ω, not just the first N bits.[2] This implies that there are exponential diophantine equations with one parameter n which have the property that no formal axiomatic theory can enable one to settle whether the number of solutions

---

[1]   These results are drawn from CHAITIN (1985b,1987).

[2]   This theorem was originally established in CHAITIN (1987).

of the equation is finite or infinite for more than a finite number of values of the parameter *n*.

What is gained by asking if there are infinitely many solutions rather than whether or not a solution exists? The question of whether or not an exponential diophantine equation has a solution is in general undecidable, but the answers to such questions are not independent. Indeed, if one considers such an equation with one parameter k, and asks whether or not there is a solution for $k = 0, 1, 2, \ldots, N - 1$, the N answers to these N questions really only constitute $\log_2 N$ bits of information. The reason for this is that we can in principle determine which equations have a solution if we know how many of them are solvable, for the set of solutions and of solvable equations is recursively enumerable (r.e.). On the other hand, if we ask whether the number of solutions is finite or infinite, then the answers can be independent, if the equation is constructed properly.

In view of the philosophical impact of exhibiting an algebraic equation with the property that the number of solutions jumps from finite to infinite at random as a parameter is varied, I have taken the trouble of explicitly carrying out the construction outlined by Jones and Matijasevic. That is to say, I have encoded the halting probability Ω into an exponential diophantine equation. To be able to actually do this, one has to start with a program for calculating Ω, and the only language I can think of in which actually writing such a program would not be an excruciating task is pure LISP.

It is in fact necessary to go beyond the ideas of McCarthy in three fundamental ways:

1. First of all, we simplify LISP by only allowing atoms to be one character long. (This is similar to McCarthy's "linear LISP.")
2. Secondly, EVAL must not lose control by going into an infinite loop. In other words, we need a safe EVAL that can execute garbage for a limited amount of time, and always results in an error message or a valid value of an expression. This is similar to the notion in modern operating systems that the supervisor should be able to give a user task a time slice of CPU, and that the supervisor should not abort if the user task has an abnormal error termination.
3. Lastly, in order to program such a safe time-limited EVAL, it greatly simplifies matters if we stipulate "permissive" LISP semantics with the property that the only way a syntactically valid LISP expression can fail to have a value is if it loops forever. Thus, for example, the head

(CAR) and tail (CDR) of an atom is defined to be the atom itself, and the value of an unbound variable is the variable.

Proceeding in this spirit, we have defined a class of abstract computers which, as in Jones and Matijasevic's treatment, are register machines. However, our machine's finite set of registers each contain a LISP S-expression in the form of a character string with balanced left and right parentheses to delimit the list structure. And we use a small set of machine instructions, instructions for testing, moving, erasing, and setting one character at a time. In order to be able to use subroutines more effectively, we have also added an instruction for jumping to a subroutine after putting into a register the return address, and an indirect branch instruction for returning to the address contained in a register. The complete register machine program for a safe time-limited LISP universal function (interpreter) EVAL is about 300 instructions long.

To test this LISP interpreter written for an abstract machine, we have written in 370 machine language a register machine simulator. We have also re-written this LISP interpreter directly in 370 machine language, representing LISP S-expressions by binary trees of pointers rather than as character strings, in the standard manner used in practical LISP implementations. We have then run a large suite of tests through the very slow interpreter on the simulated register machine, and also through the extremely fast 370 machine language interpreter, in order to make sure that identical results are produced by both implementations of the LISP interpreter.

Our version of pure LISP also has the property that in it we can write a short program to calculate Ω in the limit from below. The program for calculating Ω is only a few pages long, and by running it (on the 370 directly, not on the register machine!), we have obtained a lower bound of 127/128ths for the particular definition of Ω we have chosen, which depends on our choice of a self-delimiting universal computer.

The final step was to write a compiler that compiles a register machine program into an exponential diophantine equation. This compiler consists of about 700 lines of code in a very nice and easy to use programming language invented by Mike Cowlishaw called REXX. REXX is a pattern-matching string processing language which is implemented by means of a very efficient interpreter.[3] It takes the compiler only a few minutes to convert the 300-line LISP interpreter into a 900,000-character

---

[3]   See COWLISHAW (1985) and O'HARA and GOMBERG (1985).

17,000-variable universal exponential diophantine equation. The resulting equation is a little large, but the ideas used to produce it are simple and few, and the equation results from the straightforward application of these ideas.

Here we shall present the details of this adventure, but not the full equation.[4] My hope is that this monograph will convince mathematicians that randomness and unpredictability not only occur in nonlinear dynamics and quantum mechanics, but even in rather elementary branches of number theory.

In summary, the aim of this book is to construct a single equation involving only addition, multiplication, and exponentiation of non-negative integer constants and variables with the following remarkable property. One of the variables is considered to be a parameter. Take the parameter to be 0,1,2,... obtaining an infinite series of equations from the original one. Consider the question of whether each of the derived equations has finitely or infinitely many non-negative integer solutions. The original equation is constructed in such a manner that the answers to these questions about the derived equations mimic coin tosses and are an infinite series of independent mathematical facts, i.e., irreducible mathematical information that cannot be compressed into any finite set of axioms.

To produce this equation, we start with a universal Turing machine in the form of the LISP universal function EVAL written as a register machine program about 300 lines long. Then we "compile" this register machine program into a universal exponential diophantine equation. The resulting equation is about 900,000 characters long and has about 17,000 variables. Finally, we substitute for the program variable in the universal diophantine equation the binary representation of a LISP program for Ω, the halting probability of a universal Turing machine if n-bit programs have measure 2^{-n}.

---

[4]   The full equation is available from the author: "The Complete Arithmetization of EVAL," February 18th, 1987, 292 pp.

FORMALISMS FOR COMPUTATION:
REGISTER MACHINES,
EXPONENTIAL DIOPHANTINE EQUATIONS, &
PURE LISP

In Part I of this monograph, we do the bulk of the preparatory work that enables us in Part II to exhibit an exponential diophantine equation that encodes the successive bits of the halting probability Ω.

In Chapter 2 we present a method for compiling register machine programs into exponential diophantine equations. In Chapter 3 we present a stripped-down version of pure LISP. And in Chapter 4 we present a register machine interpreter for this LISP, and then compile it into a diophantine equation. The resulting equation, which unfortunately is too large to exhibit here in its entirety, has a solution, and only one, if the binary representation of a LISP expression that halts, i.e., that has a value, is substituted for a distinguished variable in it. It has no solution if the number substituted is the binary representation of a LISP expression without a value.

Having dealt with programming issues, we can then proceed in Part II to theoretical matters.

CHAPTER 2

THE ARITHMETIZATION OF REGISTER MACHINES

2.1. Introduction

In this chapter we present the beautiful work of JONES and MATIJASEVIC (1984), which is the culmination of a half century of development starting with GÖDEL (1931), and in which the paper of DAVIS, PUTNAM, and ROBINSON (1961) on Hilbert's tenth problem was such a notable milestone. The aim of this work is to encode computations arithmetically. As Gödel showed with his technique of Gödel numbering and primitive recursive functions, the metamathematical assertion that a particular proposition follows by certain rules of inference from a particular set of axioms, can be encoded as an arithmetical or number theoretic proposition. This shows that number theory well deserves its reputation as one of the hardest branches of mathematics, for any formalized mathematical assertion can be encoded as a statement about positive integers. And the work of Davis, Putnam, Robinson, and Matijasevic has shown that any computation can be encoded as a polynomial. The proof of this assertion, which shows that Hilbert's tenth problem is unsolvable, has been simplified over the years, but it is still fairly intricate and involves a certain amount of number theory; for a review see DAVIS, MATIJASEVIC, and ROBINSON (1976).

Formulas for primes: An illustration of the power and importance of these ideas is the fact that a trivial corollary of this work has been the construction of polynomials which generate or represent the set of primes; JONES et al. (1976) have performed the extra work to actually exhibit manageable polynomials having this property. This result, which would surely have amazed Fermat, Euler, and Gauss, actually has nothing to do with the primes, as it applies to any set of positive integers that can be generated by a computer program, that is, to any recursively enumerable set.

The recent proof of Jones and Matijasevic that any computation can be encoded in an exponential diophantine equation is quite remarkable. Their result is weaker in some ways, and stronger in others: the theorem deals with exponential diophantine equations rather than polynomial diophantine equations, but on the other hand diophantine equations are constructed which have unique solutions. But the most remarkable aspect of their proof is its directness and straightforwardness, and the fact that it involves almost no number theory! Indeed their proof is based on a curious property of the evenness or oddness of binomial coefficients, which follows immediately by considering Pascal's famous triangle of these coefficients.

In summary, I believe that the work on Hilbert's tenth problem stemming from Gödel is among the most important mathematics of this century, for it shows that all of mathematics, once formalized, is mirrored in properties of the whole numbers. And the proof of this fact, thanks to Jones and Matijasevic, is now within the reach of anyone. Their 1984 paper is only a few pages long; here we shall devote the better part of a hundred pages to a different proof, and one that is completely self-contained. While the basic mathematical ideas are the same, the programming is completely different, and we give many examples and actually exhibit the enormous diophantine equations that arise. Jones and Matijasevic make no use of LISP, which plays a central role here.

Let us now give a precise statement of the result which we shall prove. A predicate $P(a_1, \ldots, a_n)$ is said to be *recursively enumerable* (r.e.) if there is an algorithm which given the non-negative integers $a_1, \ldots, a_n$ will eventually discover that these numbers have the property P, if that is the case. This is weaker than the assertion that P is *recursive*, which means that there is an algorithm which will eventually discover that P is true or that it is false; P is recursive if and only if P and not P are both r.e. predicates. Consider functions $L(a_1, \ldots, a_n, x_1, \ldots, x_m)$ and $R(a_1, \ldots, a_n, x_1, \ldots, x_m)$ built up from the non-negative integer variables $a_1, \ldots, a_n, x_1, \ldots, x_m$ and from non-negative integer constants by using only the operations of addition $A + B$, multiplication $A \times B$, and exponentiation A^B. The predicate $P(a_1, \ldots, a_n)$ is said to be *exponential diophantine* if $P(a_1, \ldots, a_n)$ holds if and only if there exist non-negative integers $x_1, \ldots, x_m$ such that

$$L(a_1, \ldots, a_n, x_1, \ldots, x_m) = R(a_1, \ldots, a_n, x_1, \ldots, x_m).$$

Moreover, the exponential diophantine representation $L = R$ of P is said to be *singlefold* if $P(a_1, \ldots, a_n)$ implies that there is a unique m-tuple of non-negative integers $x_1, \ldots, x_m$ such that

$$L(a_1, \ldots, a_n, x_1, \ldots, x_m) = R(a_1, \ldots, a_n, x_1, \ldots, x_m)$$

Here the variables $a_1, \ldots, a_n$ are referred to as *parameters,* and the variables $x_1, \ldots, x_m$ are referred to as *unknowns.*

The most familiar example of an exponential diophantine equation is Fermat's so-called "last theorem." This is the famous conjecture that the equation

$$(x + 1)^{n+3} + (y + 1)^{n+3} = (z + 1)^{n+3}$$

has no solution in non-negative integers x, y, z and n. The reason that exponential diophantine equations as we define them have both a left-hand side and a right-hand side, is that we permit neither negative numbers nor subtraction. Thus it is not possible to collect all terms on one side of the equation.

The theorem of JONES and MATIJASEVIC (1984) states that a predicate is exponential diophantine if and only if it is r.e., and moreover, if a predicate is exponential diophantine, then it admits a singlefold exponential diophantine representation. That a predicate is exponential diophantine if and only if it is r.e. was first shown by DAVIS, PUTNAM, and ROBINSON (1961), but their proof is much more complicated and does not yield singlefold representations. It is known that the use of the exponential function A^B can be omitted, i.e., a predicate is in fact polynomial diophantine if and only if it is r.e., but it is not known whether singlefold representations are always possible without using exponentiation. Since singlefoldness is important in our applications of these results, and since the proof is so simple, it is most natural for us to use here the work on exponential diophantine representations rather than that on polynomial diophantine representations.

2.2. Pascal's Triangle Mod 2

Figure 1 shows Pascal's triangle up to

$$(x + y)^{16} = \sum_{k=0}^{16} \binom{16}{k} x^k y^{16-k}.$$

This table was calculated by using the formula

$$\binom{n + 1}{k + 1} = \binom{n}{k + 1} + \binom{n}{k}.$$

That is to say, each entry is the sum of two entries in the row above it: the entry in the same column, and the one in the column just to left. (This rule assumes that entries which are not explicitly shown in this table are all zero.)

Now let's replace each entry by a 0 if it is even, and let's replace it by a 1 if it is odd. That is to say, we retain only the rightmost bit in the base-two representation of each entry in the table in Figure 1. This gives us the table in Figure 2.

Figure 2 shows Pascal's triangle mod 2 up to $(x + y)^{64}$. This table was calculated by using the formula

$$\binom{n + 1}{k + 1} \equiv \binom{n}{k + 1} + \binom{n}{k} \quad (\text{mod } 2).$$

That is to say, each entry is the base-two sum without carry (the "EXCLUSIVE OR") of two entries in the row above it: the entry in the same column, and the one in the column just to left.

Erasing 0's makes it easier for one to appreciate the remarkable pattern in Figure 2. This gives us the table in Figure 3.

Fig 1. Pascal's Triangle

```
 0:  1
 1:  1   1
 2:  1   2    1
 3:  1   3    3    1
 4:  1   4    6    4     1
 5:  1   5   10   10     5     1
 6:  1   6   15   20    15     6     1
 7:  1   7   21   35    35    21     7     1
 8:  1   8   28   56    70    56    28     8     1
 9:  1   9   36   84   126   126    84    36     9     1
10:  1  10   45  120   210   252   210   120    45    10     1
11:  1  11   55  165   330   462   462   330   165    55    11     1
12:  1  12   66  220   495   792   924   792   495   220    66    12     1
13:  1  13   78  286   715  1287  1716  1716  1287   715   286    78    13     1
14:  1  14   91  364  1001  2002  3003  3432  3003  2002  1001   364    91    14    1
15:  1  15  105  455  1365  3003  5005  6435  6435  5005  3003  1365   455   105   15    1
16:  1  16  120  560  1820  4368  8008 11440 12870 11440  8008  4368  1820   560  120  16  1
```

Fig 2. Pascal's Triangle Mod 2

```
 0:  1
 1:  11
 2:  101
 3:  1111
 4:  10001
 5:  110011
 6:  1010101
 7:  11111111
 8:  100000001
 9:  1100000011
10:  10100000101
11:  111100001111
12:  1000100010001
13:  11001100110011
14:  101010101010101
15:  1111111111111111
16:  10000000000000001
17:  110000000000000011
18:  1010000000000000101
19:  11110000000000001111
20:  100010000000000010001
21:  1100110000000000110011
22:  10101010000000001010101
23:  111111110000000011111111
24:  1000000010000000100000001
25:  11000000110000001100000011
26:  101000001010000010100000101
27:  1111000011110000111100001111
28:  10001000100010001000100010001
29:  110011001100110011001100110011
30:  1010101010101010101010101010101
31:  11111111111111111111111111111111
32:  100000000000000000000000000000001
33:  1100000000000000000000000000000011
34:  10100000000000000000000000000000101
35:  111100000000000000000000000000001111
36:  1000100000000000000000000000000010001
37:  11001100000000000000000000000000110011
38:  101010100000000000000000000000001010101
39:  1111111100000000000000000000000011111111
40:  10000000100000000000000000000000100000001
41:  110000001100000000000000000000001100000011
42:  1010000010100000000000000000000010100000101
43:  11110000111100000000000000000000111100001111
44:  100010001000100000000000000000001000100010001
45:  1100110011001100000000000000000011001100110011
46:  10101010101010100000000000000000101010101010101
47:  111111111111111100000000000000001111111111111111
48:  1000000000000000100000000000000010000000000000001
49:  11000000000000001100000000000000110000000000000011
50:  101000000000000010100000000000001010000000000000101
51:  1111000000000000111100000000000011110000000000001111
52:  10001000000000001000100000000000100010000000000010001
53:  110011000000000011001100000000001100110000000000110011
54:  1010101000000000101010100000000010101010000000001010101
55:  11111111000000001111111100000000111111110000000011111111
56:  100000001000000010000000100000001000000010000000100000001
57:  1100000011000000110000001100000011000000110000001100000011
58:  10100000101000001010000010100000101000001010000010100000101
59:  111100001111000011110000111100001111000011110000111100001111
60:  1000100010001000100010001000100010001000100010001000100010001
61:  11001100110011001100110011001100110011001100110011001100110011
62:  101010101010101010101010101010101010101010101010101010101010101
63:  1111111111111111111111111111111111111111111111111111111111111111
64:  10000000000000000000000000000000000000000000000000000000000000001
```

Fig 3. Pascal's Triangle Mod 2 with 0's Replaced by Blanks: Note the fractal pattern with many parts similar to the whole. In fact, from a great distance this resembles the Sierpinski gasket described in MANDELBROT (1982), pp. 131, 142, 329.

```
 0: 1
 1: 11
 2: 1 1
 3: 1111
 4: 1   1
 5: 11  11
 6: 1 1 1 1
 7: 11111111
 8: 1       1
 9: 11      11
10: 1 1     1 1
11: 1111    1111
12: 1   1   1   1
13: 11  11  11  11
14: 1 1 1 1 1 1 1 1
15: 1111111111111111
16: 1               1
17: 11              11
18: 1 1             1 1
19: 1111            1111
20: 1   1           1   1
21: 11  11          11  11
22: 1 1 1 1         1 1 1 1
23: 11111111        11111111
24: 1       1       1       1
25: 11      11      11      11
26: 1 1     1 1     1 1     1 1
27: 1111    1111    1111    1111
28: 1   1   1   1   1   1   1   1
29: 11  11  11  11  11  11  11  11
30: 1 1 1 1 1 1 1 1 1 1 1 1 1 1 1 1
31: 11111111111111111111111111111111
*32: 1                               1
33: 11                              11
34: 1 1                             1 1
35: 1111                            1111
36: 1   1                           1   1
37: 11  11                          11  11
38: 1 1 1 1                         1 1 1 1
39: 11111111                        11111111
*40: 1       1                       1       1
41: 11      11                      11      11
*42: 1 1     1 1                     1 1     1 1
43: 1111    1111                    1111    1111
44: 1   1   1   1                   1   1   1   1
45: 11  11  11  11                  11  11  11  11
46: 1 1 1 1 1 1 1 1                 1 1 1 1 1 1 1 1
47: 1111111111111111                1111111111111111
48: 1               1               1               1
49: 11              11              11              11
50: 1 1             1 1             1 1             1 1
51: 1111            1111            1111            1111
52: 1   1           1   1           1   1           1   1
53: 11  11          11  11          11  11          11  11
54: 1 1 1 1         1 1 1 1         1 1 1 1         1 1 1 1
55: 11111111        11111111        11111111        11111111
56: 1       1       1       1       1       1       1       1
57: 11      11      11      11      11      11      11      11
58: 1 1     1 1     1 1     1 1     1 1     1 1     1 1     1 1
59: 1111    1111    1111    1111    1111    1111    1111    1111
60: 1   1   1   1   1   1   1   1   1   1   1   1   1   1   1   1
61: 11  11  11  11  11  11  11  11  11  11  11  11  11  11  11  11
62: 1 1 1 1 1 1 1 1 1 1 1 1 1 1 1 1 1 1 1 1 1 1 1 1 1 1 1 1 1 1 1 1
63: 1111111111111111111111111111111111111111111111111111111111111111
64: 1                                                               1
```

Note that moving one row down the table in Figure 3 corresponds to taking the EXCLUSIVE OR of the original row with a copy of it that has been shifted right one place. More generally, moving down the table 2^n rows corresponds to taking the EXCLUSIVE OR of the original row with a copy of it that has been shifted right 2^n places. This is easily proved by induction on n.

Consider the coefficients of x^k in the expansion of $(1 + x)^{42}$. Some are even and some are odd. There are eight odd coefficients: since $42 = 32 + 8 + 2$, the coefficients are odd for $k = (0 \text{ or } 32) + (0 \text{ or } 8) + (0 \text{ or } 2)$. (See the rows marked with an * in Figure 3.) Thus the coefficient of x^k in $(1 + x)^{42}$ is odd if and only if each bit in the base-two numeral for k "implies" (i.e., is less than or equal to) the corresponding bit in the base-two numeral for 42. More generally, the coefficient of x^k in $(1 + x)^n$ is odd if and only if each bit in the base-two numeral for k implies the corresponding bit in the base-two numeral for n.

Let us write $r \Rightarrow s$ if each bit in the base-two numeral for the non-negative integer r implies the corresponding bit in the base-two numeral for the non-negative integer s. We have seen that $r \Rightarrow s$ if and only if the binomial coefficient $\binom{s}{r}$ of x^r in $(1 + x)^s$ is odd. Let us express this as an exponential diophantine predicate.

We use the fact that the binomial coefficients are the digits of the number $(1 + t)^s$ written in base-t notation, if t is sufficiently large. For example, in base-ten we have

$$11^0 = 1$$
$$11^1 = 11$$
$$11^2 = 121$$
$$11^3 = 1331$$
$$11^4 = 14641$$

but for 11^5 a carry occurs when adding 6 and 4 and things break down. In fact, since the binomial coefficients of order s add up to 2^s, it is sufficient to take $t = 2^s$. Hence

$$t = 2^s$$

$r \Rightarrow s$ iff $u = \binom{s}{r}$ is odd iff
$$(1 + t)^s = v\, t^{r+1} + u\, t^r + w$$
$$w < t^r$$
$$u < t$$
$$u \text{ is odd.}$$

Thus $r \Rightarrow s$ if and only if there exist unique non-negative integers t, u, v, w, x, y, z such that

$$t = 2^s$$
$$(1 + t)^s = v\, t^{r+1} + u\, t^r + w$$
$$w + x + 1 = t^r$$
$$u + y + 1 = t$$
$$u = 2\, z + 1.$$

2.3. LISP Register Machines

Now let's look at register machines! These are machines which have a finite number of registers, each of which contains an arbitrarily large non-negative integer, and which have programs consisting of a finite list of labeled instructions. (Real computing machines of course have a large number of registers with finite capacity, rather than a small number of registers with infinite capacity.) Each of the registers is simultaneously considered to contain a LISP S-expression in the form of a finite string of characters. Each 8 bits of the base-two numeral for the contents of a register represent a particular character in the LISP alphabet, and the character string is in the register in reverse order. We reserve the 8-bit byte consisting entirely of 0's to mark the end of a character string.[5] Thus the rightmost 8 bits of a register are the first character in the S-expression, and replacing the contents of a register X by the integer part of the result of dividing it by 256 corresponds to removing the first character of the string. Similarly, if Y is between 1 and 255, replacing X by $256\, X + Y$ corresponds to adding the character Y at the beginning of the string X.

Figure 4 is a table giving all the register machine instructions. These are the fifteen different kinds of instructions permitted in register machine language. Note that there are only eleven different opcodes. All instructions must be labeled.

LABEL: HALT

    Halt execution.

LABEL: GOTO LABEL2

---

[5]   It is not really necessary to have a reserved end-of-string character, but this convention significantly simplifies the LISP interpreter that we present in Chapter 4.

This is an unconditional branch to *LABEL2*. (Normally, execution flows from each instruction to the next in sequential order.)

LABEL: JUMP REGISTER LABEL2

set *REGISTER* to "(*NEXT_LABEL*)" and go to *LABEL2*. Here "(*NEXT_LABEL*)" denotes the LISP S-expression consisting of the list of characters in the label of the next instruction in sequential order. This instruction is used to jump to a subroutine and simultaneously save the return address (i.e., where execution will resume after executing the subroutine) in a register.

LABEL: GOBACK REGISTER

Go to "(*LABEL*)" which is in *REGISTER*. This instruction is used in conjunction with the JUMP instruction to return from a subroutine. It is illegal if *REGISTER* does not contain the label of an instruction in the program between parentheses; i.e., the program is invalid.

LABEL: EQ REGISTER1 CONSTANT LABEL2

Fig 4. Register Machine Instructions: We use non-zero 8-bit bytes to represent a LISP character and we represent LISP S-expressions as reversed character strings in binary. I.e., registers contain LISP S-expressions with 8 bits per character and with the order of the characters reversed. See Figure 6 for the bit strings for each character. Thus the rightmost 8 bits of a register are the first character in an S-expression. $X \leftarrow 256X + Y$ $(0 < Y < 256)$ corresponds to adding the character Y to the beginning of an S-expression. $X \leftarrow$ the integer part of $X/256$ corresponds to removing the first character of an S-expression.

```
L: HALT                      Halt.
L: GOTO      L2              Unconditional branch to L2.
L: JUMP      R L2            (label) of next instruction into R &
                             goto L2.
L: GOBACK R                  Goto (label) which is in R.
L: EQ        R 0/255 L2      Compare the rightmost 8 bits of R
L: NEQ       R R2 L2         with an 8-bit constant
                             or with the rightmost 8 bits of R2
                             & branch to L2 for equal/not equal.
L: RIGHT     R               Shift R right 8 bits.
L: LEFT      R 0/255         Shift R left 8 bits & insert an 8-bit
             R R2            constant or insert the rightmost
                             8 bits of R2. In the latter case,
                             then shift R2 right 8 bits.
L: SET       R 0/255         Set the entire contents of R to be
             R R2            equal to that of R2 or to an 8-bit
                             constant (extended to the left with
                             infinitely many 0's).
L: OUT       R               Write string in R.
L: DUMP                      Dump all registers.
```

Conditional branch: The rightmost 8 bits of *REGISTER*1 are compared with an 8-bit *CONSTANT*. In other words, the first character in *REGISTER*1, which is the remainder of *REGISTER*1 divided by 256, is compared with a *CONSTANT* from 0 to 255. If they are equal, then execution continues at *LABEL*2. If they are not equal, then execution continues with the next instruction in sequential order.

LABEL: EQ REGISTER1 REGISTER2 LABEL2

Conditional branch: The rightmost 8 bits of *REGISTER*1 are compared with the rightmost 8 bits of *REGISTER*2. In other words, the first character in *REGISTER*1, which is the remainder of *REGISTER*1 divided by 256, is compared with the first character in *REGISTER*2, which is the remainder of *REGISTER*2 divided by 256. If they are equal, then execution continues at *LABEL*2. If they are not equal, then execution continues with the next instruction in sequential order.

LABEL: NEQ REGISTER1 CONSTANT LABEL2

Conditional branch: The rightmost 8 bits of *REGISTER*1 are compared with an 8-bit *CONSTANT*. In other words, the first character in *REGISTER*1, which is the remainder of *REGISTER*1 divided by 256, is compared with a *CONSTANT* from 0 to 255. If they are not equal, then execution continues at *LABEL*2. If they are equal, then execution continues with the next instruction in sequential order.

LABEL: NEQ REGISTER1 REGISTER2 LABEL2

Conditional branch: The rightmost 8 bits of *REGISTER*1 are compared with the rightmost 8 bits of *REGISTER*2. In other words, the first character in *REGISTER*1, which is the remainder of *REGISTER*1 divided by 256, is compared with the first character in *REGISTER*2, which is the remainder of *REGISTER*2 divided by 256. If they are not equal, then execution continues at *LABEL*2. If they are equal, then execution continues with the next instruction in sequential order.

LABEL: RIGHT REGISTER

Shift *REGISTER* right 8 bits. I.e., the contents of *REGISTER* is replaced by the integer part of *REGISTER* divided by 256. In other words, the first character in the S-expression in *REGISTER* is deleted.

LABEL: LEFT REGISTER1 CONSTANT

Shift *REGISTER*1 left 8 bits and add to it an 8-bit *CONSTANT*. I.e., the contents of *REGISTER*1 is multiplied by 256, and then a *CONSTANT* from 0 to 255 is added to it. In other words, the character string in *REGISTER* now consists of the character *CONSTANT* followed by the string of characters previously in *REGISTER*.

LABEL: LEFT REGISTER1 REGISTER2

Shift *REGISTER*1 left 8 bits, add to it the rightmost 8 bits of *REGISTER*2, and then shift *REGISTER*2 right 8 bits. I.e., the contents of *REGISTER*1 is multiplied by 256, the remainder of *REGISTER*2 divided by 256 is added to *REGISTER*1, and then *REGISTER*2 is replaced by the integer part of *REGISTER*2 divided by 256. In other words, the first character in *REGISTER*2 has been removed and added at the beginning of the character string in *REGISTER*1.

LABEL: SET REGISTER1 CONSTANT

Set the entire contents of *REGISTER*1 to an 8-bit *CONSTANT*. I.e., the contents of *REGISTER*1 is replaced by a *CONSTANT* from 0 to 255. In other words, the previous contents of *REGISTER*1 is discarded and replaced by a character string which is either a single character or the empty string.

LABEL: SET REGISTER1 REGISTER2

Set the entire contents of *REGISTER*1 to that of *REGISTER*2. I.e., the contents of *REGISTER*1 is replaced by the contents of *REGISTER*2 . In other words, the character string in *REGISTER*1 is discarded and replaced by a copy of the character string in *REGISTER*2.

LABEL: OUT REGISTER

The character string in *REGISTER* is written out (in the correct, not the reversed, order!). This instruction is not really necessary; it is used for debugging.

LABEL: DUMP

Each register's name and the character string that it contains are written out (with the characters in the correct, not the reversed, order!). This instruction is not really necessary; it is used for debugging.

Here *CONSTANT*, which denotes an 8-bit constant, is usually written as a single character enclosed in apostrophes preceded by a C, e.g., C'A', C'B', ... The apostrophe itself must be doubled: C'''' denotes the 8-bit constant which represents a single apostrophe. And X'00' denotes the 8-bit constant consisting entirely of 0's.

Figure 5 is an example of a register machine program. This program reverses the character string initially in register *A*. The contents of *A* is destroyed, the reversed string replaces the initial contents of register *B*, and then the program halts. This program depends on the fact that the byte consisting of 8 bits of 0's denotes the end of a character string and cannot occur inside a string. If register A starts with the string "abc", the program will eventually stop with A empty and with "cba" in register B.

From this program we shall construct an exponential diophantine equation with four parameters *input.A* , *input.B*, *output.A*, *output.B* that has a solution if and only if this program halts with *output.B* in B if it starts with *input.A* in A, that is to say, if and only if *output.B* is the reversal of *input.A* . The solution, if it exists, is a kind of chronological record of the entire history of a successful computation, i.e., one which reaches a HALT instruction without executing an illegal GOBACK after starting at the first instruction. Thus the solution, if it exists, is unique, because computers are deterministic and a computational history is uniquely determined by its input.

Note that if A initially contains "abc", a total of 8 instructions will be executed: *L1, L2, L3, L2, L3, L2, L3, L4.*

Let's start by giving the solution we want the equation to have, and then we shall construct an equation that forces this solution.

input.A = "abc"

is the initial contents of register A.

time = 8

is the total number of instructions executed.

number.of.instructions = 4

is the number of lines in the program.

The variable A encodes the contents of register A as a function of time in the form of a base-q number in which the digit corresponding to q^t is the contents of A at time t. Similarly, the variable B encodes the contents of register B as a function of time in the form of a base-q number in which the digit corresponding to q^t is the contents of B at time t:

Fig 5. A Register Machine Program to Reverse a Character String

```
L1:  SET   B  X'00'
L2:  LEFT  B  A
L3:  NEQ   A  X'00'  L2
L4:  HALT
```

$A = \Lambda, \Lambda, c, c, bc, bc, abc, abc_q$
$B = cba, cba, ba, ba, a, a, \Lambda, input.B_q.$

Here Λ denotes the empty string. More precisely, the rightmost digit gives the initial contents, the next digit gives the contents after the first instruction is executed, ... and the leftmost digit gives the contents after the next-to-the-last instruction is executed. (The last instruction executed must be HALT, which has no effect on the contents.) I.e., the digit corresponding to q^t $(0 \le t < time)$ gives the contents of a register **just before** the $(t + 1)$-th instruction is executed. q must be chosen large enough for everything to fit.

The base-q numbers $L1, L2, L3, L4$ encode the instruction being executed as a function of time; the digit corresponding to q^t in $LABEL$ is a 1 if $LABEL$ is executed at time t, and it is a 0 if $LABEL$ is not executed at time t.

$L1 = 00000001_q$
$L2 = 00101010_q$
$L3 = 01010100_q$
$L4 = 10000000_q.$

i is a base-q number consisting of *time* 1's:

$i = 11111111_q.$

Now let's construct from the program in Figure 5 an equation that forces this solution. This is rather like determining the boolean algebra for the logical design of a CPU chip. *number.of.instructions* is a constant, *input.A, input.B, output.A, output.B* are parameters, and *time, q, i, A, B, L1, L2, L3, L4,* are unknowns (nine of them).

Let's choose a big enough base:

$q = 256^{input.A + input.B + time + number.of.instructions}$

This implies that *number.of.instructions* is less than q, and also that the contents of registers A and B are both less than q throughout the entire course of the computation. Now we can define i:

$1 + (q - 1)\, i = q^{time}.$

This is the condition for starting execution at line $L1$:

$$1 \Rightarrow L1.$$

This is the condition for ending execution at line $L4$ after executing *time* instructions:

$$q^{time-1} = L4.$$

If there were several HALT instructions in the program, $L4$ would be replaced by the sum of the corresponding *LABEL*'s. The following conditions express the fact that at any given time one and only one instruction is being executed:

$$i = L1 + L2 + L3 + L4$$
$$L1 \Rightarrow i$$
$$L2 \Rightarrow i$$
$$L3 \Rightarrow i$$
$$L4 \Rightarrow i.$$

For these conditions to work, it is important that *number.of.instructions* , the number of lines in the program, be less than q, the base being used.

Now let us turn our attention to the contents of registers A and B as a function of time. First of all, the following conditions determine the right 8 bits of A and 8-bit right shift of A as a function of time:

$$256 \ shift.A \Rightarrow A$$
$$256 \ shift.A \Rightarrow (q - 1 - 255) \ i$$
$$A \Rightarrow 256 \ shift.A + 255 \ i$$
$$A = 256 \ shift.A + char.A$$

The following conditions determine whether or not the first 8 bits of register A are all 0's as a function of time:

$$eq.A.X'00' \Rightarrow i$$
$$256 \ eq.A.X'00' \Rightarrow 256 \ i - char.A$$
$$256 \ i - char.A \Rightarrow 256 \ eq.A.X'00' + 255 \ i$$

The following conditions determine when registers A and B are set, and to what values, as a function of time:

$set.B.L1 = 0$

$set.B.L2 \Rightarrow 256\ B + char.A$
$set.B.L2 \Rightarrow (q - 1)\ L2$
$256\ B + char.A \Rightarrow set.B.L2 + (q - 1)\ (i - L2)$

$set.A.L2 \Rightarrow shift.A$
$set.A.L2 \Rightarrow (q - 1)\ L2$
$shift.A \Rightarrow set.A.L2 + (q - 1)\ (i - L2)$

The following conditions determine the contents of registers A and B when they are not set:

$dont.set.A \Rightarrow A$
$dont.set.A \Rightarrow (q - 1)\ (i - L2)$
$A \Rightarrow dont.set.A + (q - 1)\ L2$

$dont.set.B \Rightarrow B$
$dont.set.B \Rightarrow (q - 1)\ (i - L1 - L2)$
$B \Rightarrow dont.set.B + (q - 1)\ (L1 + L2)$

Finally, the following conditions determine the contents of registers A and B as a function of time:

$A \Rightarrow (q - 1)\ i$
$B \Rightarrow (q - 1)\ i$
$A + output.A\ q^{time} = input.A + q\ (set.A.L2 + dont.set.A)$
$B + output.B\ q^{time} = input.B + q\ (set.B.L1 + set.B.L2 + dont.set.B)$

We also need conditions to express the manner in which control flows through the program, i.e., the sequence of execution of steps of the program. This is done as follows. $L1$ always goes to $L2$:

$q\ L1 \Rightarrow L2$

$L2$ always goes to $L3$:

$q\ L2 \Rightarrow L3$

$L3$ either goes to $L4$ or to $L2$:

$q\ L3 \Rightarrow L4 + L2$

If the right 8 bits of A are 0's then $L3$ does not go to $L2$:

$q\ L3 \Rightarrow L2 + q\ eq.A.X'00'$

There is no condition for $L4$ because it doesn't go anywhere.

Above there are 8 equations and 29 $\Rightarrow$'s, in 4 parameters (*input.A*, *input.B*, *output.A*, *output.B*) and 17 unknowns. Each condition $L \Rightarrow R$ above is expanded into the following 7 equations in 9 variables:

$$r = L$$
$$s = R$$
$$t = 2^s$$
$$(1 + t)^s = v\,t^{r+1} + u\,t^r + w$$
$$w + x + 1 = t^r$$
$$u + y + 1 = t$$
$$u = 2\,z + 1.$$

Each time this is done, the 9 variables $r, s, t, u, v, w, x, y, z$ must be renamed to unique variables in order to avoid a name clash. The result is $8 + 7 \times 29 = 211$ equations in 4 parameters and $17 + 9 \times 29 = 278$ unknowns. Minus signs are eliminated by transposing terms to the other side of the relevant equations $r = L$ or $s = R$. Then all the equations are combined into a single one by using the fact that

$$\sum (A_i - B_i)^2 = 0 \qquad \text{iff} \qquad A_i = B_i.$$

Here again, negative terms must be transposed to the other side of the composite equation. E.g., five equations can be combined into a single equation by using the fact that if $a, b, c, d, e, f, g, h, i, j$ are non-negative integers, then

$$a = b, \quad c = d, \quad e = f, \quad g = h, \quad i = j$$

if and only if

$$(a - b)^2 + (c - d)^2 + (e - f)^2 + (g - h)^2 + (i - j)^2 \;=\; 0,$$

that is, if and only if

$$a^2 + b^2 \;+\; c^2 + d^2 \;+\; e^2 + f^2 \;+\; g^2 + h^2 \;+\; i^2 + j^2$$
$$= \;2\,a\,b + 2\,c\,d + 2\,e\,f + 2\,g\,h + 2\,i\,j.$$

The result is a single (enormous!) exponential diophantine equation which has one solution for each successful computational history, i.e., for each one that finally halts.   Thus we have obtained a singlefold diophantine representation of the r.e. predicate "*output.B* is the character string reversal of *input.A* ".   The method that we have presented by working through this example is perfectly general: it applies to any predicate for which one can write a register machine computer program. In Chapter 4 we show that this is any r.e. predicate, by showing how powerful register machines are.

The names of auxiliary variables that we introduce are in lower-case with dots used for hyphenation, in order to avoid confusion with the names of labels and registers, which by convention are always in upper-case and use underscores for hyphenation.

Above, we encountered *eq.A.X'00'*. This is a somewhat special case; the general case of comparison for equality is a little bit harder. These are the conditions for *eq.A.B*, *ge.A.B*, and *ge.B.A*, which indicate whether the rightmost 8 bits of registers A and B are equal, greater than or equal, or less than or equal, respectively, as a function of time:

$$ge.A.B \Rrightarrow i$$
$$256\ ge.A.B \Rrightarrow 256\ i + (char.A - char.B)$$
$$256\ i + (char.A - char.B) \Rrightarrow 256\ ge.A.B + 255\ i$$

$$ge.B.A \Rrightarrow i$$
$$256\ ge.B.A \Rrightarrow 256\ i - (char.A - char.B)$$
$$256\ i - (char.A - char.B) \Rrightarrow 256\ ge.B.A + 255\ i$$

$$eq.A.B \Rrightarrow i$$
$$2\ eq.A.B \Rrightarrow ge.A.B + ge.B.A$$
$$ge.A.B + ge.B.A \Rrightarrow 2\ eq.A.B + i$$

Here we use the fact that the absolute value of the difference between two characters cannot exceed 255.

As for JUMP's and GOBACK's, the corresponding conditions are easily constructed using the above ideas, after introducing a variable *ic* to represent the instruction counter. Our program for character string reversal does not use JUMP or GOBACK, but if it did, the equation defining the instruction counter vector would be:

$$ic = C'(L1)'\ L1 + C'(L2)'\ L2 + C'(L3)'\ L3 + C'(L4)'\ L4$$

Here $C'(L1)'$ denotes the non-negative integer that represents the LISP S-expression $(L1)$, etc. Thus for the execution of this program that we considered above,

$$ic = (L4), (L3), (L2), (L3), (L2), (L3), (L2), (L1)_q$$

I.e., the digit corresponding to q^t in ic is a LISP S-expression for the list of the characters in the label of the instruction that is executed at time t. Note that if labels are very long, this may require the base q to be chosen a little larger, to ensure that the list of characters in a label always fits into a single base-q digit.

It is amusing to look at the size of the variables in a solution of these exponential diophantine equations. Rough estimates of the size of solutions simultaneously serve to fix in the mind how the equations work, and also to show just how very impractical they are. Here goes a very rough estimate. The dominant term determining the base q that is used is

$$q \approx 2^{8\ time}$$

where *time* is the total number of instructions executed during the computation, i.e., the amount of time it takes for the register machine to halt. This is because the LEFT instruction can increase the size of a character string in a register by one 8-bit character per "machine cycle", and q must be chosen so that the largest quantity that is ever in a register during the computation can fit into a single base-q digit. That's how big q is. How about the register variables? Well, they are vectors giving a chronological history of the contents of a register (in reverse order). I.e., each register variable is a vector of *time* elements, each of which is (8 *time*)-bits long, for a total of 8 $time^2$ bits altogether. Thus

$$\text{register variable} \approx 2^{8\ time^2}.$$

And how about the variables that arise when $\Rightarrow$'s are expanded into equations? Well, very roughly speaking, they can be of the order of 2 raised to a power which is itself a register variable! Thus

$$\text{expansion variable} \approx 2^{2^{8\ time^2}} \ !!$$

Considering how little a LISP register machine accomplishes in one step, non-trivial examples of computations will require on the order of tens or hundreds of thousands of steps, i.e., *time* ≈ 100,000.

For example, in Chapter 4 we shall consider a LISP interpreter and its implementation via a 306-instruction register machine program. To APPEND two lists consisting of two atoms each, takes the LISP interpreter 238908 machine cycles, and to APPEND two lists consisting of six atoms each, takes 1518884 machine cycles! This shows very clearly that these equations are only of theoretical interest, and certainly not a practical way of actually doing computations.

The register machine simulator that counted the number of machine cycles is written in 370 machine language. On the large 370 main-frame that I use, the elapsed time per million simulated register machine cycles is typically between 1 and 2 seconds, depending on the load on the machine. Fortunately, this same LISP can be directly implemented in 370 machine language using standard LISP implementation techniques. Then it runs extremely fast, typically one, two, or three orders of magnitude faster than on the register machine simulator. How much faster depends on the size of the character strings that the register machine LISP interpreter is constantly sweeping through counting parentheses in order to break lists into their component elements. Real LISP implementations avoid this by representing LISP S-expressions as binary trees of pointers instead of character strings, so that the decomposition of a list into its parts is immediate. They also replace the time-consuming search of the association list for variable bindings, by a direct table look-up. And they keep the interpreter stack in contiguous storage rather then representing it as a LISP S-expression.

We have written in REXX a "compiler" that automatically converts register machine programs into exponential diophantine equations in the manner described above. Solutions of the equation produced by this REXX compiler correspond to successful computational histories, and there are variables in the equation for the initial and final contents of each machine register. The equation compiled from a register machine program has no solution if the program never halts on given input, and it has exactly one solution if the program halts for that input.

Let's look at two simple examples to get a more concrete feeling for how the compiler works. But first we give in Section 2.4 a complete cast of characters, a dictionary of the different kinds of variables that appear in the compiled equations. Next we give the compiler a 16-instruction register machine program with every possible register machine instruction; this exercises all the capabilities of the compiler. Section 2.5 is the compiler's log explaining how it transformed the 16 register machine instructions into 17 equations and 111 ⇒'s. Note that the compiler uses a FORTRAN-like notation for equations in which multiplication is * and exponentiation is **.

We don't show the rest, but this is what the compiler does. First it expands the ⇒'s and obtains a total of $17 + 7 \times 111 = 794$ equations, and then it folds them together into a single equation. This equation is unfortunately too big to include here; as the summary information at the end of the compiler's log indicates, the left-hand side and right-hand side are each more than 20,000 characters long.

Next we take an even smaller register machine program, and this time we run it through the compiler and show all the steps up to the final equation. This example really works; it is the 4-instruction program for reversing a character string that we discussed above (Figure 5). Section 2.6 is the compiler's log explaining how it expands the 4-instruction program into 13 equations and 38 ⇒'s. This is slightly larger than the number of equations and ⇒'s that we obtained when we worked through this example by hand; the reason is that the compiler uses a more systematic approach.

In Section 2.7 the compiler shows how it eliminates all ⇒'s by expanding them into equations, seven for each ⇒. The original 13 equations and 38 ⇒'s produced from the program are flush at the left margin. The $13 + 7 \times 38 = 279$ equations that are generated from them are indented 6 spaces. When the compiler directly produces an equation, it appears twice, once flush left and then immediately afterwards indented 6 spaces. When the compiler produces a ⇒, it appears flush left, followed immediately by the seven equations that are generated from it, each indented six spaces. Note that the auxiliary variables generated to expand the nth ⇒ all end with the number n. By looking at the names of these variables one can determine the ⇒ in Section 2.6 that they came from, which will be numbered (imp.n), and see why the compiler generated them.

The last thing that the compiler does is to take each of the 279 equations that appear indented in Section 2.7 and fold it into the left-hand side and right-hand side of the final equation. This is done using the "sum of squares" technique: $x = y$ adds $x^2 + y^2$ to the left-hand side and $2\,x\,y$ to the right-hand side. Section 2.8 is the resulting left-hand side, and Section 2.9 is the right-hand side; the final equation is five pages long. More precisely, a 4-instruction register machine program has become an $8534 + 3 + 7418 = 15955$ character exponential diophantine equation. The "+ 3" is for the missing central equal sign surrounded by two blanks.

The equation in Sections 2.8 and 2.9 has exactly one solution in non-negative integers if *output.B* is the character-string reversal of *input.A*. It has no solution if *output.B* is not the reversal of *input.A*. One can jump into this equation, look at the names of the variables, and then with the help of Section 2.6 determine the corresponding part of the register machine program.

That concludes Chapter 2. In Chapter 3 we present a version of pure LISP. In Chapter 4 we program a register machine to interpret this LISP, and then compile the interpreter into a universal exponential diophantine equation, which will conclude our preparatory programming work and bring us to the theoretical half of this book.

2.4. Dictionary of Auxiliary Variables Used in Arithmetization—Dramatis Personae

i

    (vector) This is a base-q number with *time* digits all of which are 1's.

time

    (scalar) This is the time it takes the register machine to halt, and it is also the number of components in vectors, i.e., the number of base-q digits in variables which represent computational histories.

total.input

    (scalar) This is the sum of the initial contents of all machine registers.

q

    (scalar) This power of two is the base used in vectors which represent computational histories.

q.minus.1

    (scalar) This is $q - 1$.

ic

    (vector) This is a vector giving the label of the instruction being executed at any given time. I.e., if at time t the instruction *LABEL* is executed, then the base-q digit of *ic* corresponding to q^t is the binary representation of the S-expression (*LABEL*).

next.ic

    (vector) This is a vector giving the label of the next instruction to be executed. I.e., if at time $t + 1$ the instruction *LABEL* is executed, then the base-q digit of *ic* corresponding to q^t is the binary representation of the S-expression (*LABEL*).

longest.label

(scalar) This is the number of characters in the longest label of any instruction in the program.

number.of.instructions

(scalar) This is the total number of instructions in the program.

REGISTER

(vector) This is a vector giving the contents of *REGISTER* as a function of time. I.e., the base-q digit corresponding to q^t is the contents of *REGISTER* at time t.

LABEL

(logical vector) This is a vector giving the truth of the assertion that *LABEL* is the current instruction being executed as a function of time. I.e., the base-q digit corresponding to q^t is 1 if *LABEL* is executed at time t, and it is 0 if *LABEL* is not executed at time t.

char.REGISTER

(vector) This is a vector giving the first character (i.e., the rightmost 8 bits) in each register as a function of time. I.e., the base-q digit corresponding to q^t is the number between 0 and 255 that represents the first character in *REGISTER* at time t.

shift.REGISTER

(vector) This is a vector giving the 8-bit right shift of each register as a function of time. I.e., the base-q digit corresponding to q^t is the integer part of the result of dividing the contents of *REGISTER* at time t by 256.

input.REGISTER

(scalar) This is the initial contents of *REGISTER*.

output.REGISTER

(scalar) This is the final contents of *REGISTER*.

eq.REGISTER1.REGISTER2

(logical vector) This is a vector giving the truth of the assertion that the rightmost 8 bits of *REGISTER*1 and *REGISTER*2 are equal as a function of time. I.e., the base-q digit corresponding to q^t is 1 if the first characters in *REGISTER*1 and *REGISTER*2 are equal at time t, and it is 0 if the first characters in *REGISTER*1 and *REGISTER*2 are unequal at time t.

eq.REGISTER.CONSTANT

(logical vector) This is a vector giving the truth of the assertion that the rightmost 8 bits of *REGISTER* are equal to a *CONSTANT* as a function of time. I.e., the base-q digit corresponding to q^t is 1 if the first character in *REGISTER* and the *CONSTANT* are equal at time t, and it is 0 if the first character in *REGISTER* and the *CONSTANT* are unequal at time *t*.

ge.REGISTER1.REGISTER2

(logical vector) This is a vector giving the truth of the assertion that the rightmost 8 bits of *REGISTER*1 are greater than or equal to the rightmost 8 bits of *REGISTER*2 as a function of time. I.e., the base-*q* digit corresponding to q^t is 1 if the first character in *REGISTER*1 is greater than or equal to the first character in *REGISTER*2 at time *t*, and it is 0 if the first character in *REGISTER*1 is less than the first character in *REGISTER*2 at time *t*.

ge.REGISTER.CONSTANT

(logical vector) This is a vector giving the truth of the assertion that the rightmost 8 bits of *REGISTER* are greater than or equal to a *CONSTANT* as a function of time. I.e., the base-*q* digit corresponding to q^t is 1 if the first character in *REGISTER* is greater than or equal to the *CONSTANT* at time *t*, and it is 0 if the first character in *REGISTER* is less than the *CONSTANT* at time *t*.

ge.CONSTANT.REGISTER

(logical vector) This is a vector giving the truth of the assertion that a *CONSTANT* is greater than or equal to the rightmost 8 bits of *REGISTER* as a function of time. I.e., the base-*q* digit corresponding to q^t is 1 if the *CONSTANT* is greater than or equal to the first character in *REGISTER* at time *t*, and it is 0 if the *CONSTANT* is less than the contents of *REGISTER* at time *t*.

goback.LABEL

(vector) This vector's *t*-th component (i.e., the base-*q* digit corresponding to q^t) is the same as the corresponding component of *next.ic* if the GOBACK instruction *LABEL* is executed at time *t*, and it is 0 otherwise.

set.REGISTER

(logical vector) This vector's *t*-th component (i.e., the base-*q* digit corresponding to q^t) is 1 if *REGISTER* is set at time *t*, and it is 0 otherwise.

set.REGISTER.LABEL

(vector) This vector's *t*-th component (i.e., the base-*q* digit corresponding to q^t) is the new contents of *REGISTER* resulting from executing *LABEL* if *LABEL* sets *REGISTER* and is executed at time *t*, and it is 0 otherwise.

dont.set.REGISTER

(vector) This vector's t-th component (i.e., the base-q digit corresponding to q^t) gives the previous contents of *REGISTER* if the instruction executed at time t does not set *REGISTER*, and it is 0 otherwise.

rNUMBER

The left-hand side of the *NUMBER*th implication.

sNUMBER

The right-hand side of the *NUMBER*th implication.

tNUMBER

The base used in expanding the *NUMBER*th implication.

uNUMBER

The binomial coefficient used in expanding the *NUMBER*th implication.

vNUMBER

A junk variable used in expanding the *NUMBER*th implication.

wNUMBER

A junk variable used in expanding the *NUMBER*th implication.

xNUMBER

A junk variable used in expanding the *NUMBER*th implication.

yNUMBER

A junk variable used in expanding the *NUMBER*th implication.

zNUMBER

A junk variable used in expanding the *NUMBER*th implication.

2.5. An Example of Arithmetization

```
Program:

L1:  GOTO L1
L2:  JUMP C L1
L3:  GOBACK C
L4:  NEQ A C'a' L1
L5:  NEQ A B L1
L6:  EQ A C'b' L1
L7:  EQ A B L1
L8:  OUT C
L9:  DUMP
L10: HALT
L11: SET A C'a'
L12: SET A B
L13: RIGHT C
L14: LEFT A C'b'
L15: LEFT A B
L16: HALT


Equations defining base q ...................................
```

```
(eq.1)          total.input = input.A + input.B + input.C
(eq.2)          number.of.instructions = 16
(eq.3)          longest.label = 3
(eq.4)          q = 256 ** ( total.input + time +
                number.of.instructions + longest.label + 3 )
(eq.5)          q.minus.1 + 1 = q
```

Equation defining i, all of whose base q digits are 1's:
```
(eq.6)          1 + q * i = i + q ** time
```

Basic Label Variable Equations ********************************

```
(imp.1)         L1 => i
(imp.2)         L2 => i
(imp.3)         L3 => i
(imp.4)         L4 => i
(imp.5)         L5 => i
(imp.6)         L6 => i
(imp.7)         L7 => i
(imp.8)         L8 => i
(imp.9)         L9 => i
(imp.10)        L10 => i
(imp.11)        L11 => i
(imp.12)        L12 => i
(imp.13)        L13 => i
(imp.14)        L14 => i
(imp.15)        L15 => i
(imp.16)        L16 => i
(eq.7)          i = L1 + L2 + L3 + L4 + L5 + L6 + L7 + L8 + L9 +
                L10 + L11 + L12 + L13 + L14 + L15 + L16
```

Equations for starting & halting:
```
(imp.17)        1 => L1
(eq.8)          q ** time = q * L10 + q * L16
```

Equations for Flow of Control ********************************

```
L1: GOTO L1

(imp.18)    q * L1 => L1

L2: JUMP C L1

(imp.19)    q * L2 => L1

L3: GOBACK C

(imp.20)    goback.L3 => C
(imp.21)    goback.L3 => q.minus.1 * L3
(imp.22)    C => goback.L3 + q.minus.1 * i - q.minus.1 * L3

(imp.23)    goback.L3 => next.ic
(imp.24)    goback.L3 => q.minus.1 * L3
(imp.25)    next.ic => goback.L3 + q.minus.1 * i - q.minus.1 *
            L3
```

L4: NEQ A C'a' L1

(imp.26)   *q * L4 => L5 + L1*
(imp.27)   *q * L4 => L1 + q * eq.A.C'a'*

L5: NEQ A B L1

(imp.28)   *q * L5 => L6 + L1*
(imp.29)   *q * L5 => L1 + q * eq.A.B*

L6: EQ A C'b' L1

(imp.30)   *q * L6 => L7 + L1*
(imp.31)   *q * L6 => L7 + q * eq.A.C'b'*

L7: EQ A B L1

(imp.32)   *q * L7 => L8 + L1*
(imp.33)   *q * L7 => L8 + q * eq.A.B*

L8: OUT C

(imp.34)   *q * L8 => L9*

L9: DUMP

(imp.35)   *q * L9 => L10*

L10: HALT

L11: SET A C'a'

(imp.36)   *q * L11 => L12*

L12: SET A B

(imp.37)   *q * L12 => L13*

L13: RIGHT C

(imp.38)   *q * L13 => L14*

L14: LEFT A C'b'

(imp.39)   *q * L14 => L15*

L15: LEFT A B

(imp.40)   *q * L15 => L16*

L16: HALT

Instruction Counter equations (needed for GOBACK's) ....

The ic vector is defined as follows:

$$C'(L1)' * L1 + C'(L2)' * L2 + C'(L3)' * L3 +$$
$$C'(L4)' * L4 + C'(L5)' * L5 + C'(L6)' * L6 +$$
$$C'(L7)' * L7 + C'(L8)' * L8 + C'(L9)' * L9 +$$
$$C'(L10)' * L10 + C'(L11)' * L11 + C'(L12)' * L12 +$$
$$C'(L13)' * L13 + C'(L14)' * L14 + C'(L15)' * L15 +$$
$$C'(L16)' * L16$$

In other words,

(eq.9) $ic = 1075605632 * L1 + 1083994240 * L2 +$
$1079799936 * L3 + 1088188544 * L4 + 1077702784 *$
$L5 + 1086091392 * L6 + 1081897088 * L7 +$
$1090285696 * L8 + 1073901696 * L9 + 278839193728 *$
$L10 + 275349532800 * L11 + 277497016448 * L12 +$
$276423274624 * L13 + 278570758272 * L14 +$
$275886403712 * L15 + 278033887360 * L16$

(imp.41) $q * next.ic => ic$
(imp.42) $ic => q * next.ic + q - 1$

Auxiliary Register Equations **********************************

(3 =>'s are produced whenever a register's value is set)
(6 =>'s for a LEFT that sets 2 registers)

L1: *GOTO L1*

L2: *JUMP C L1*

Note: $C'(L3)'$ *is* 1079799936

(imp.43) $set.C.L2 => 1079799936 * i$
(imp.44) $set.C.L2 => q.minus.1 * L2$
(imp.45) $1079799936 * i => set.C.L2 + q.minus.1 * i -$
            $q.minus.1 * L2$

L3: *GOBACK C*

L4: *NEQ A C'a' L1*

L5: *NEQ A B L1*

L6: *EQ A C'b' L1*

L7: *EQ A B L1*

L8: *OUT C*

L9: *DUMP*

L10: *HALT*

L11: *SET A C'a'*

(imp.46) $set.A.L11 => 184 * i$
(imp.47) $set.A.L11 => q.minus.1 * L11$

```
(imp.48)      184 * i => set.A.L11 + q.minus.1 * i - q.minus.1 *
              L11
```

L12: *SET A B*

```
(imp.49)      set.A.L12 => B
(imp.50)      set.A.L12 => q.minus.1 * L12
(imp.51)      B => set.A.L12 + q.minus.1 * i - q.minus.1 * L12
```

L13: *RIGHT C*

```
(imp.52)      set.C.L13 => shift.C
(imp.53)      set.C.L13 => q.minus.1 * L13
(imp.54)      shift.C => set.C.L13 + q.minus.1 * i - q.minus.1 *
              L13
```

L14: *LEFT A C'b'*

```
(imp.55)      set.A.L14 => 256 * A + 120 * i
(imp.56)      set.A.L14 => q.minus.1 * L14
(imp.57)      256 * A + 120 * i => set.A.L14 + q.minus.1 * i -
              q.minus.1 * L14
```

L15: *LEFT A B*

```
(imp.58)      set.A.L15 => 256 * A + char.B
(imp.59)      set.A.L15 => q.minus.1 * L15
(imp.60)      256 * A + char.B => set.A.L15 + q.minus.1 * i -
              q.minus.1 * L15

(imp.61)      set.B.L15 => shift.B
(imp.62)      set.B.L15 => q.minus.1 * L15
(imp.63)      shift.B => set.B.L15 + q.minus.1 * i - q.minus.1 *
              L15
```

L16: *HALT*

Main Register Equations ************************************

Register A ....

```
(imp.64)      A => q.minus.1 * i
(eq.10)       A + output.A * q ** time = input.A + q * set.A.L11
              + q * set.A.L12 + q * set.A.L14 + q * set.A.L15 +
              q * dont.set.A

(eq.11)       set.A = L11 + L12 + L14 + L15
(imp.65)      dont.set.A => A
(imp.66)      dont.set.A => q.minus.1 * i - q.minus.1 * set.A
(imp.67)      A => dont.set.A + q.minus.1 * set.A

(imp.68)      256 * shift.A => A
(imp.69)      256 * shift.A => q.minus.1 * i - 255 * i
(imp.70)      A => 256 * shift.A + 255 * i
(eq.12)       A = 256 * shift.A + char.A
```

Register B ....

```
(imp.71)     B => q.minus.1 * i
(eq.13)      B + output.B * q ** time = input.B + q * set.B.L15
             + q * dont.set.B

(eq.14)      set.B = L15
(imp.72)     dont.set.B => B
(imp.73)     dont.set.B => q.minus.1 * i - q.minus.1 * set.B
(imp.74)     B => dont.set.B + q.minus.1 * set.B

(imp.75)     256 * shift.B => B
(imp.76)     256 * shift.B => q.minus.1 * i - 255 * i
(imp.77)     B => 256 * shift.B + 255 * i
(eq.15)      B = 256 * shift.B + char.B
```

Register C ....

```
(imp.78)     C => q.minus.1 * i
(eq.16)      C + output.C * q ** time = input.C + q * set.C.L2
             + q * set.C.L13 + q * dont.set.C

(eq.17)      set.C = L2 + L13
(imp.79)     dont.set.C => C
(imp.80)     dont.set.C => q.minus.1 * i - q.minus.1 * set.C
(imp.81)     C => dont.set.C + q.minus.1 * set.C

(imp.82)     256 * shift.C => C
(imp.83)     256 * shift.C => q.minus.1 * i - 255 * i
(imp.84)     C => 256 * shift.C + 255 * i
```

Equations for Compares ***************************************

Compare A C'a' ....

Note: C'a' is 184

```
(imp.85)     ge.A.C'a' => i
(imp.86)     256 * ge.A.C'a' => 256 * i + char.A - 184 * i
(imp.87)     256 * i + char.A - 184 * i => 256 * ge.A.C'a' +
             255 * i

(imp.88)     ge.C'a'.A => i
(imp.89)     256 * ge.C'a'.A => 256 * i + 184 * i - char.A
(imp.90)     256 * i + 184 * i - char.A => 256 * ge.C'a'.A +
             255 * i

(imp.91)     eq.A.C'a' => i
(imp.92)     2 * eq.A.C'a' => ge.A.C'a' + ge.C'a'.A
(imp.93)     ge.A.C'a' + ge.C'a'.A => 2 * eq.A.C'a' + i
```

Compare A B ....

```
(imp.94)     ge.A.B => i
(imp.95)     256 * ge.A.B => 256 * i + char.A - char.B
(imp.96)     256 * i + char.A - char.B => 256 * ge.A.B + 255 *
             i
```

```
(imp.97)     ge.B.A => i
(imp.98)     256 * ge.B.A => 256 * i + char.B - char.A
(imp.99)     256 * i + char.B - char.A => 256 * ge.B.A + 255 *
             i

(imp.100)    eq.A.B => i
(imp.101)    2 * eq.A.B => ge.A.B + ge.B.A
(imp.102)    ge.A.B + ge.B.A => 2 * eq.A.B + i
```

Compare A C'b' ....

Note: C'b' is 120

```
(imp.103)    ge.A.C'b' => i
(imp.104)    256 * ge.A.C'b' => 256 * i + char.A - 120 * i
(imp.105)    256 * i + char.A - 120 * i => 256 * ge.A.C'b' +
             255 * i

(imp.106)    ge.C'b'.A => i
(imp.107)    256 * ge.C'b'.A => 256 * i + 120 * i - char.A
(imp.108)    256 * i + 120 * i - char.A => 256 * ge.C'b'.A +
             255 * i

(imp.109)    eq.A.C'b' => i
(imp.110)    2 * eq.A.C'b' => ge.A.C'b' + ge.C'b'.A
(imp.111)    ge.A.C'b' + ge.C'b'.A => 2 * eq.A.C'b' + i
```

Summary Information **************************************

Number of labels in program..... 16
Number of registers in program.. 3

Number of equations generated... 17
Number of =>'s generated........ 111
Number of auxiliary variables... 43

Equations added to expand =>'s.. 777   (7 per =>)
Variables added to expand =>'s.. 999   (9 per =>)

Characters in left-hand side.... 24968
Characters in right-hand side... 21792

Register variables:
        A B C

Label variables:
        L1 L10 L11 L12 L13 L14 L15 L16 L2 L3 L4 L5 L6 L7
        L8 L9

Auxiliary variables:
        char.A char.B dont.set.A dont.set.B dont.set.C
        eq.A.B eq.A.C'a' eq.A.C'b' ge.A.B ge.A.C'a'
        ge.A.C'b' ge.B.A ge.C'a'.A ge.C'b'.A goback.L3 i
        ic input.A input.B input.C longest.label next.ic
        number.of.instructions output.A output.B output.C
```
```

q q.minus.1 set.A set.A.L11 set.A.L12 set.A.L14
set.A.L15 set.B set.B.L15 set.C set.C.L13 set.C.L2
shift.A shift.B shift.C time total.input

Variables added to expand =>'s:
r1 s1 t1 u1 v1 w1 x1 y1 z1 ... z111

Elapsed time is 22.732864 *seconds.*

2.6. A Complete Example of Arithmetization

Program:

```
L1: SET B X'00'
L2: LEFT B A
L3: NEQ A X'00' L2
L4: HALT
```

Equations defining base q ....

(eq.1)   total.input = input.A + input.B
(eq.2)   number.of.instructions = 4
(eq.3)   longest.label = 2
(eq.4)   q = 256 ** (total.input + time +
              number.of.instructions + longest.label + 3)
(eq.5)   q.minus.1 + 1 = q

Equation defining i, all of whose base q digits are 1's:
(eq.6)   1 + q * i = i + q ** time

Basic Label Variable Equations ********************************

(imp.1)   L1 => i
(imp.2)   L2 => i
(imp.3)   L3 => i
(imp.4)   L4 => i
(eq.7)   i = L1 + L2 + L3 + L4

Equations for starting & halting:
(imp.5)   1 => L1
(eq.8)   q ** time = q * L4

Equations for Flow of Control ********************************

L1: *SET B X'00'*

(imp.6)   q * L1 => L2

L2: *LEFT B A*

(imp.7)   q * L2 => L3

L3: *NEQ A X'00' L2*

```
(imp.8)      q * L3 => L4 + L2
(imp.9)      q * L3 => L2 + q * eq.A.X'00'
```

`L4: HALT`

Auxiliary Register Equations `*******************************`

```
(3 =>'s are produced whenever a register's value is set)
(6 =>'s for a LEFT that sets 2 registers)
```

`L1: SET B X'00'`

```
(imp.10)     set.B.L1 => 0 * i
(imp.11)     set.B.L1 => q.minus.1 * L1
(imp.12)     0 * i => set.B.L1 + q.minus.1 * i - q.minus.1 * L1
```

`L2: LEFT B A`

```
(imp.13)     set.B.L2 => 256 * B + char.A
(imp.14)     set.B.L2 => q.minus.1 * L2
(imp.15)     256 * B + char.A => set.B.L2 + q.minus.1 * i -
             q.minus.1 * L2

(imp.16)     set.A.L2 => shift.A
(imp.17)     set.A.L2 => q.minus.1 * L2
(imp.18)     shift.A => set.A.L2 + q.minus.1 * i - q.minus.1 *
             L2
```

`L3: NEQ A X'00' L2`

`L4: HALT`

Main Register Equations `*************************************`

Register A `................................................`

```
(imp.19)     A => q.minus.1 * i
(eq.9)       A + output.A * q ** time = input.A + q * set.A.L2
             + q * dont.set.A

(eq.10)      set.A = L2
(imp.20)     dont.set.A => A
(imp.21)     dont.set.A => q.minus.1 * i - q.minus.1 * set.A
(imp.22)     A => dont.set.A + q.minus.1 * set.A

(imp.23)     256 * shift.A => A
(imp.24)     256 * shift.A => q.minus.1 * i - 255 * i
(imp.25)     A => 256 * shift.A + 255 * i
(eq.11)      A = 256 * shift.A + char.A
```

Register B `................................................`

```
(imp.26)     B => q.minus.1 * i
(eq.12)      B + output.B * q ** time = input.B + q * set.B.L1
             + q * set.B.L2 + q * dont.set.B
```

```
(eq.13)      set.B = L1 + L2
(imp.27)     dont.set.B => B
(imp.28)     dont.set.B => q.minus.1 * i - q.minus.1 * set.B
(imp.29)     B => dont.set.B + q.minus.1 * set.B
```

Equations for Compares **************************************

Compare A X'00' ....

Note: X'00' is 0

```
(imp.30)     ge.A.X'00' => i
(imp.31)     256 * ge.A.X'00' => 256 * i + char.A - 0 * i
(imp.32)     256 * i + char.A - 0 * i => 256 * ge.A.X'00' + 255
             * i

(imp.33)     ge.X'00'.A => i
(imp.34)     256 * ge.X'00'.A => 256 * i + 0 * i - char.A
(imp.35)     256 * i + 0 * i - char.A => 256 * ge.X'00'.A + 255
             * i

(imp.36)     eq.A.X'00' => i
(imp.37)     2 * eq.A.X'00' => ge.A.X'00' + ge.X'00'.A
(imp.38)     ge.A.X'00' + ge.X'00'.A => 2 * eq.A.X'00' + i
```

Summary Information **************************************

```
Number of labels in program.....   4
Number of registers in program..   2

Number of equations generated...   13
Number of =>'s generated.......    38
Number of auxiliary variables...   23

Equations added to expand =>'s..   266     (7 per =>)
Variables added to expand =>'s..   342     (9 per =>)

Characters in left-hand side....   8534
Characters in right-hand side...   7418
```

Register variables:
  A B

Label variables:
  L1 L2 L3 L4

Auxiliary variables:
  char.A dont.set.A dont.set.B eq.A.X'00' ge.A.X'00'
  ge.X'00'.A i input.A input.B longest.label
  number.of.instructions output.A output.B q
  q.minus.1 set.A set.A.L2 set.B set.B.L1 set.B.L2
  shift.A time total.input

Variables added to expand =>'s:
  r1 s1 t1 u1 v1 w1 x1 y1 z1 ... z38

Elapsed time is 9.485622 *seconds.*

2.7. A Complete Example of Arithmetization: Expansion of ⇒'s

```
total.input = input.A + input.B
      total.input = input.A+input.B
number.of.instructions = 4
      number.of.instructions = 4
longest.label = 2
      longest.label = 2
q = 256 ** ( total.input + time + number.of.instructions + lon
gest.label + 3 )
      q = 256**(total.input+time+number.of.instructions+longe
      st.label+3)
q.minus.1 + 1 = q
      q.minus.1+1 = q
1 + q * i = i + q ** time
      1+q*i = i+q**time
L1 => i
      r1 = L1
      s1 = i
      t1 = 2**s1
      (1+t1)**s1 = v1*t1**(r1+1) + u1*t1**r1 + w1
      w1+x1+1 = t1**r1
      u1+y1+1 = t1
      u1 = 2*z1+ 1
L2 => i
      r2 = L2
      s2 = i
      t2 = 2**s2
      (1+t2)**s2 = v2*t2**(r2+1) + u2*t2**r2 + w2
      w2+x2+1 = t2**r2
      u2+y2+1 = t2
      u2 = 2*z2+ 1
L3 => i
      r3 = L3
      s3 = i
      t3 = 2**s3
      (1+t3)**s3 = v3*t3**(r3+1) + u3*t3**r3 + w3
      w3+x3+1 = t3**r3
      u3+y3+1 = t3
      u3 = 2*z3+ 1
L4 => i
      r4 = L4
      s4 = i
      t4 = 2**s4
      (1+t4)**s4 = v4*t4**(r4+1) + u4*t4**r4 + w4
      w4+x4+1 = t4**r4
      u4+y4+1 = t4
      u4 = 2*z4+ 1
i = L1 + L2 + L3 + L4
      i = L1+L2+L3+L4
1 => L1
      r5 = 1
```

$$s5 = L1$$
$$t5 = 2**s5$$
$$(1+t5)**s5 = v5*t5**(r5+1) + u5*t5**r5 + w5$$
$$w5+x5+1 = t5**r5$$
$$u5+y5+1 = t5$$
$$u5 = 2*z5+ 1$$
$$q ** time = q * L4$$
$$q**time = q*L4$$
$$q * L1 => L2$$
$$r6 = q*L1$$
$$s6 = L2$$
$$t6 = 2**s6$$
$$(1+t6)**s6 = v6*t6**(r6+1) + u6*t6**r6 + w6$$
$$w6+x6+1 = t6**r6$$
$$u6+y6+1 = t6$$
$$u6 = 2*z6+ 1$$
$$q * L2 => L3$$
$$r7 = q*L2$$
$$s7 = L3$$
$$t7 = 2**s7$$
$$(1+t7)**s7 = v7*t7**(r7+1) + u7*t7**r7 + w7$$
$$w7+x7+1 = t7**r7$$
$$u7+y7+1 = t7$$
$$u7 = 2*z7+ 1$$
$$q * L3 => L4 + L2$$
$$r8 = q*L3$$
$$s8 = L4+L2$$
$$t8 = 2**s8$$
$$(1+t8)**s8 = v8*t8**(r8+1) + u8*t8**r8 + w8$$
$$w8+x8+1 = t8**r8$$
$$u8+y8+1 = t8$$
$$u8 = 2*z8+ 1$$
$$q * L3 => L2 + q * eq.A.X'00'$$
$$r9 = q*L3$$
$$s9 = L2+q*eq.A.X'00'$$
$$t9 = 2**s9$$
$$(1+t9)**s9 = v9*t9**(r9+1) + u9*t9**r9 + w9$$
$$w9+x9+1 = t9**r9$$
$$u9+y9+1 = t9$$
$$u9 = 2*z9+ 1$$
$$set.B.L1 => 0 * i$$
$$r10 = set.B.L1$$
$$s10 = 0*i$$
$$t10 = 2**s10$$
$$(1+t10)**s10 = v10*t10**(r10+1) + u10*t10**r10 + w10$$
$$w10+x10+1 = t10**r10$$
$$u10+y10+1 = t10$$
$$u10 = 2*z10+ 1$$
$$set.B.L1 => q.minus.1 * L1$$
$$r11 = set.B.L1$$
$$s11 = q.minus.1*L1$$
$$t11 = 2**s11$$
$$(1+t11)**s11 = v11*t11**(r11+1) + u11*t11**r11 + w11$$
$$w11+x11+1 = t11**r11$$
$$u11+y11+1 = t11$$
$$u11 = 2*z11+ 1$$
$$0 * i => set.B.L1 + q.minus.1 * i - q.minus.1 * L1$$

```
      r12 = 0*i
      s12+q.minus.1*L1 = set.B.L1+q.minus.1*i
      t12 = 2**s12
      (1+t12)**s12 = v12*t12**(r12+1) + u12*t12**r12 + w12
      w12+x12+1 = t12**r12
      u12+y12+1 = t12
      u12 = 2*z12+ 1
set.B.L2 => 256 * B + char.A
      r13 = set.B.L2
      s13 = 256*B+char.A
      t13 = 2**s13
      (1+t13)**s13 = v13*t13**(r13+1) + u13*t13**r13 + w13
      w13+x13+1 = t13**r13
      u13+y13+1 = t13
      u13 = 2*z13+ 1
set.B.L2 => q.minus.1 * L2
      r14 = set.B.L2
      s14 = q.minus.1*L2
      t14 = 2**s14
      (1+t14)**s14 = v14*t14**(r14+1) + u14*t14**r14 + w14
      w14+x14+1 = t14**r14
      u14+y14+1 = t14
      u14 = 2*z14+ 1
256 * B + char.A => set.B.L2 + q.minus.1 * i - q.minus.1 * L2
      r15 = 256*B+char.A
      s15+q.minus.1*L2 = set.B.L2+q.minus.1*i
      t15 = 2**s15
      (1+t15)**s15 = v15*t15**(r15+1) + u15*t15**r15 + w15
      w15+x15+1 = t15**r15
      u15+y15+1 = t15
      u15 = 2*z15+ 1
set.A.L2 => shift.A
      r16 = set.A.L2
      s16 = shift.A
      t16 = 2**s16
      (1+t16)**s16 = v16*t16**(r16+1) + u16*t16**r16 + w16
      w16+x16+1 = t16**r16
      u16+y16+1 = t16
      u16 = 2*z16+ 1
set.A.L2 => q.minus.1 * L2
      r17 = set.A.L2
      s17 = q.minus.1*L2
      t17 = 2**s17
      (1+t17)**s17 = v17*t17**(r17+1) + u17*t17**r17 + w17
      w17+x17+1 = t17**r17
      u17+y17+1 = t17
      u17 = 2*z17+ 1
shift.A => set.A.L2 + q.minus.1 * i - q.minus.1 * L2
      r18 = shift.A
      s18+q.minus.1*L2 = set.A.L2+q.minus.1*i
      t18 = 2**s18
      (1+t18)**s18 = v18*t18**(r18+1) + u18*t18**r18 + w18
      w18+x18+1 = t18**r18
      u18+y18+1 = t18
      u18 = 2*z18+ 1
A => q.minus.1 * i
      r19 = A
```

```
      s19 = q.minus.1*i
      t19 = 2**s19
      (1+t19)**s19 = v19*t19**(r19+1) + u19*t19**r19 + w19
      w19+x19+1 = t19**r19
      u19+y19+1 = t19
      u19 = 2*z19+ 1
A + output.A * q ** time = input.A + q * set.A.L2 + q * dont.s
et.A
      A+output.A*q**time = input.A+q*set.A.L2+q*dont.set.A
set.A = L2
      set.A = L2
dont.set.A => A
      r20 = dont.set.A
      s20 = A
      t20 = 2**s20
      (1+t20)**s20 = v20*t20**(r20+1) + u20*t20**r20 + w20
      w20+x20+1 = t20**r20
      u20+y20+1 = t20
      u20 = 2*z20+ 1
dont.set.A => q.minus.1 * i - q.minus.1 * set.A
      r21 = dont.set.A
      s21+q.minus.1*set.A = q.minus.1*i
      t21 = 2**s21
      (1+t21)**s21 = v21*t21**(r21+1) + u21*t21**r21 + w21
      w21+x21+1 = t21**r21
      u21+y21+1 = t21
      u21 = 2*z21+ 1
A => dont.set.A + q.minus.1 * set.A
      r22 = A
      s22 = dont.set.A+q.minus.1*set.A
      t22 = 2**s22
      (1+t22)**s22 = v22*t22**(r22+1) + u22*t22**r22 + w22
      w22+x22+1 = t22**r22
      u22+y22+1 = t22
      u22 = 2*z22+ 1
256 * shift.A => A
      r23 = 256*shift.A
      s23 = A
      t23 = 2**s23
      (1+t23)**s23 = v23*t23**(r23+1) + u23*t23**r23 + w23
      w23+x23+1 = t23**r23
      u23+y23+1 = t23
      u23 = 2*z23+ 1
256 * shift.A => q.minus.1 * i - 255 * i
      r24 = 256*shift.A
      s24+255*i = q.minus.1*i
      t24 = 2**s24
      (1+t24)**s24 = v24*t24**(r24+1) + u24*t24**r24 + w24
      w24+x24+1 = t24**r24
      u24+y24+1 = t24
      u24 = 2*z24+ 1
A => 256 * shift.A + 255 * i
      r25 = A
      s25 = 256*shift.A+255*i
      t25 = 2**s25
      (1+t25)**s25 = v25*t25**(r25+1) + u25*t25**r25 + w25
      w25+x25+1 = t25**r25
```

```
        u25+y25+1 = t25
        u25 = 2*z25+ 1
A  = 256 * shift.A + char.A
        A = 256*shift.A+char.A
B => q.minus.1 * i
        r26 = B
        s26 = q.minus.1*i
        t26 = 2**s26
        (1+t26)**s26 = v26*t26**(r26+1) + u26*t26**r26 + w26
        w26+x26+1 = t26**r26
        u26+y26+1 = t26
        u26 = 2*z26+ 1
B + output.B * q ** time = input.B + q * set.B.L1 + q * set.B.
L2 + q * dont.set.B
        B+output.B*q**time = input.B+q*set.B.L1+q*set.B.L2+q*do
        nt.set.B
set.B = L1 + L2
        set.B = L1+L2
dont.set.B => B
        r27 = dont.set.B
        s27 = B
        t27 = 2**s27
        (1+t27)**s27 = v27*t27**(r27+1) + u27*t27**r27 + w27
        w27+x27+1 = t27**r27
        u27+y27+1 = t27
        u27 = 2*z27+ 1
dont.set.B => q.minus.1 * i - q.minus.1 * set.B
        r28 = dont.set.B
        s28+q.minus.1*set.B = q.minus.1*i
        t28 = 2**s28
        (1+t28)**s28 = v28*t28**(r28+1) + u28*t28**r28 + w28
        w28+x28+1 = t28**r28
        u28+y28+1 = t28
        u28 = 2*z28+ 1
B => dont.set.B + q.minus.1 * set.B
        r29 = B
        s29 = dont.set.B+q.minus.1*set.B
        t29 = 2**s29
        (1+t29)**s29 = v29*t29**(r29+1) + u29*t29**r29 + w29
        w29+x29+1 = t29**r29
        u29+y29+1 = t29
        u29 = 2*z29+ 1
ge.A.X'00' => i
        r30 = ge.A.X'00'
        s30 = i
        t30 = 2**s30
        (1+t30)**s30 = v30*t30**(r30+1) + u30*t30**r30 + w30
        w30+x30+1 = t30**r30
        u30+y30+1 = t30
        u30 = 2*z30+ 1
256 * ge.A.X'00' => 256 * i + char.A - 0 * i
        r31 = 256*ge.A.X'00'
        s31+0*i = 256*i+char.A
        t31 = 2**s31
        (1+t31)**s31 = v31*t31**(r31+1) + u31*t31**r31 + w31
        w31+x31+1 = t31**r31
        u31+y31+1 = t31
```

```
        u31 = 2*z31+ 1
256 *  i + char.A - 0 * i => 256 * ge.A.X'00' + 255 * i
        r32+0*i = 256*i+char.A
        s32 = 256*ge.A.X'00'+255*i
        t32 = 2**s32
        (1+t32)**s32 = v32*t32**(r32+1) + u32*t32**r32 + w32
        w32+x32+1 = t32**r32
        u32+y32+1 = t32
        u32 = 2*z32+ 1
ge.X'00'.A =>  i
        r33 = ge.X'00'.A
        s33 = i
        t33 = 2**s33
        (1+t33)**s33 = v33*t33**(r33+1) + u33*t33**r33 + w33
        w33+x33+1 = t33**r33
        u33+y33+1 = t33
        u33 = 2*z33+ 1
256 * ge.X'00'.A => 256 *  i + 0 *  i - char.A
        r34 = 256*ge.X'00'.A
        s34+char.A = 256*i+0*i
        t34 = 2**s34
        (1+t34)**s34 = v34*t34**(r34+1) + u34*t34**r34 + w34
        w34+x34+1 = t34**r34
        u34+y34+1 = t34
        u34 = 2*z34+ 1
256 *  i + 0 *  i - char.A => 256 * ge.X'00'.A + 255 * i
        r35+char.A = 256*i+0*i
        s35 = 256*ge.X'00'.A+255*i
        t35 = 2**s35
        (1+t35)**s35 = v35*t35**(r35+1) + u35*t35**r35 + w35
        w35+x35+1 = t35**r35
        u35+y35+1 = t35
        u35 = 2*z35+ 1
eq.A.X'00' =>  i
        r36 = eq.A.X'00'
        s36 = i
        t36 = 2**s36
        (1+t36)**s36 = v36*t36**(r36+1) + u36*t36**r36 + w36
        w36+x36+1 = t36**r36
        u36+y36+1 = t36
        u36 = 2*z36+ 1
2 * eq.A.X'00' => ge.A.X'00' + ge.X'00'.A
        r37 = 2*eq.A.X'00'
        s37 = ge.A.X'00'+ge.X'00'.A
        t37 = 2**s37
        (1+t37)**s37 = v37*t37**(r37+1) + u37*t37**r37 + w37
        w37+x37+1 = t37**r37
        u37+y37+1 = t37
        u37 = 2*z37+ 1
ge.A.X'00' + ge.X'00'.A => 2 * eq.A.X'00' + i
        r38 = ge.A.X'00'+ge.X'00'.A
        s38 = 2*eq.A.X'00'+i
        t38 = 2**s38
        (1+t38)**s38 = v38*t38**(r38+1) + u38*t38**r38 + w38
        w38+x38+1 = t38**r38
        u38+y38+1 = t38
        u38 = 2*z38+ 1
```

2.8. A Complete Example of Arithmetization: Left-Hand Side

```
(total.input)**2+(input.A+input.B)**2 + (number.of.instruction
s)**2+(4)**2 + (longest.label)**2+(2)**2 + (q)**2+(256**(total
.input+time+number.of.instructions+longest.label+3))**2 + (q.m
inus.1+1)**2+(q)**2 + (1+q*i)**2+(i+q**time)**2 + (r1)**2+(L1)
**2 + (s1)**2+(i)**2 + (t1)**2+(2**s1)**2 + ((1+t1)**s1)**2+(v
1*t1**(r1+1)+u1*t1**r1+w1)**2 + (w1+x1+1)**2+(t1**r1)**2 + (u1
+y1+1)**2+(t1)**2 + (u1)**2+(2*z1+1)**2 + (r2)**2+(L2)**2 + (s
2)**2+(i)**2 + (t2)**2+(2**s2)**2 + ((1+t2)**s2)**2+(v2*t2**(r
2+1)+u2*t2**r2+w2)**2 + (w2+x2+1)**2+(t2**r2)**2 + (u2+y2+1)**
2+(t2)**2 + (u2)**2+(2*z2+1)**2 + (r3)**2+(L3)**2 + (s3)**2+(i
)**2 + (t3)**2+(2**s3)**2 + ((1+t3)**s3)**2+(v3*t3**(r3+1)+u3*
t3**r3+w3)**2 + (w3+x3+1)**2+(t3**r3)**2 + (u3+y3+1)**2+(t3)**
2 + (u3)**2+(2*z3+1)**2 + (r4)**2+(L4)**2 + (s4)**2+(i)**2 + (
t4)**2+(2**s4)**2 + ((1+t4)**s4)**2+(v4*t4**(r4+1)+u4*t4**r4+w
4)**2 + (w4+x4+1)**2+(t4**r4)**2 + (u4+y4+1)**2+(t4)**2 + (u4)
**2+(2*z4+1)**2 + (i)**2+(L1+L2+L3+L4)**2 + (r5)**2+(1)**2 + (
s5)**2+(L1)**2 + (t5)**2+(2**s5)**2 + ((1+t5)**s5)**2+(v5*t5**
(r5+1)+u5*t5**r5+w5)**2 + (w5+x5+1)**2+(t5**r5)**2 + (u5+y5+1)
**2+(t5)**2 + (u5)**2+(2*z5+1)**2 + (q**time)**2+(q*L4)**2 + (
r6)**2+(q*L1)**2 + (s6)**2+(L2)**2 + (t6)**2+(2**s6)**2 + ((1+
t6)**s6)**2+(v6*t6**(r6+1)+u6*t6**r6+w6)**2 + (w6+x6+1)**2+(t6
**r6)**2 + (u6+y6+1)**2+(t6)**2 + (u6)**2+(2*z6+1)**2 + (r7)**
2+(q*L2)**2 + (s7)**2+(L3)**2 + (t7)**2+(2**s7)**2 + ((1+t7)**
s7)**2+(v7*t7**(r7+1)+u7*t7**r7+w7)**2 + (w7+x7+1)**2+(t7**r7)
**2 + (u7+y7+1)**2+(t7)**2 + (u7)**2+(2*z7+1)**2 + (r8)**2+(q*
L3)**2 + (s8)**2+(L4+L2)**2 + (t8)**2+(2**s8)**2 + ((1+t8)**s8
)**2+(v8*t8**(r8+1)+u8*t8**r8+w8)**2 + (w8+x8+1)**2+(t8**r8)**
2 + (u8+y8+1)**2+(t8)**2 + (u8)**2+(2*z8+1)**2 + (r9)**2+(q*L3
)**2 + (s9)**2+(L2+q*eq.A.X'00')**2 + (t9)**2+(2**s9)**2 + ((1
+t9)**s9)**2+(v9*t9**(r9+1)+u9*t9**r9+w9)**2 + (w9+x9+1)**2+(t
9**r9)**2 + (u9+y9+1)**2+(t9)**2 + (u9)**2+(2*z9+1)**2 + (r10)
**2+(set.B.L1)**2 + (s10)**2+(0*i)**2 + (t10)**2+(2**s10)**2 +
 ((1+t10)**s10)**2+(v10*t10**(r10+1)+u10*t10**r10+w10)**2 + (w
10+x10+1)**2+(t10**r10)**2 + (u10+y10+1)**2+(t10)**2 + (u10)**
2+(2*z10+1)**2 + (r11)**2+(set.B.L1)**2 + (s11)**2+(q.minus.1*
L1)**2 + (t11)**2+(2**s11)**2 + ((1+t11)**s11)**2+(v11*t11**(r
11+1)+u11*t11**r11+w11)**2 + (w11+x11+1)**2+(t11**r11)**2 + (u
11+y11+1)**2+(t11)**2 + (u11)**2+(2*z11+1)**2 + (r12)**2+(0*i)
**2 + (s12+q.minus.1*L1)**2+(set.B.L1+q.minus.1*i)**2 + (t12)*
*2+(2**s12)**2 + ((1+t12)**s12)**2+(v12*t12**(r12+1)+u12*t12**
r12+w12)**2 + (w12+x12+1)**2+(t12**r12)**2 + (u12+y12+1)**2+(t
12)**2 + (u12)**2+(2*z12+1)**2 + (r13)**2+(set.B.L2)**2 + (s13
)**2+(256*B+char.A)**2 + (t13)**2+(2**s13)**2 + ((1+t13)**s13)
**2+(v13*t13**(r13+1)+u13*t13**r13+w13)**2 + (w13+x13+1)**2+(t
13**r13)**2 + (u13+y13+1)**2+(t13)**2 + (u13)**2+(2*z13+1)**2
+ (r14)**2+(set.B.L2)**2 + (s14)**2+(q.minus.1*L2)**2 + (t14)*
*2+(2**s14)**2 + ((1+t14)**s14)**2+(v14*t14**(r14+1)+u14*t14**
r14+w14)**2 + (w14+x14+1)**2+(t14**r14)**2 + (u14+y14+1)**2+(t
14)**2 + (u14)**2+(2*z14+1)**2 + (r15)**2+(256*B+char.A)**2 +
(s15+q.minus.1*L2)**2+(set.B.L2+q.minus.1*i)**2 + (t15)**2+(2*
```

$*s15)**2 + ((1+t15)**s15)**2+(v15*t15**(r15+1)+u15*t15**r15+w1$
$5)**2 + (w15+x15+1)**2+(t15**r15)**2 + (u15+y15+1)**2+(t15)**2$
$+ (u15)**2+(2*z15+1)**2 + (r16)**2+(set.A.L2)**2 + (s16)**2+($
$shift.A)**2 + (t16)**2+(2**s16)**2 + ((1+t16)**s16)**2+(v16*t1$
$6**(r16+1)+u16*t16**r16+w16)**2 + (w16+x16+1)**2+(t16**r16)**2$
$+ (u16+y16+1)**2+(t16)**2 + (u16)**2+(2*z16+1)**2 + (r17)**2+$
$(set.A.L2)**2 + (s17)**2+(q.minus.1*L2)**2 + (t17)**2+(2**s17)$
$**2 + ((1+t17)**s17)**2+(v17*t17**(r17+1)+u17*t17**r17+w17)**2$
$+ (w17+x17+1)**2+(t17**r17)**2 + (u17+y17+1)**2+(t17)**2 + (u$
$17)**2+(2*z17+1)**2 + (r18)**2+(shift.A)**2 + (s18+q.minus.1*L$
$2)**2+(set.A.L2+q.minus.1*i)**2 + (t18)**2+(2**s18)**2 + ((1+t$
$18)**s18)**2+(v18*t18**(r18+1)+u18*t18**r18+w18)**2 + (w18+x18$
$+1)**2+(t18**r18)**2 + (u18+y18+1)**2+(t18)**2 + (u18)**2+(2*z$
$18+1)**2 + (r19)**2+(A)**2 + (s19)**2+(q.minus.1*i)**2 + (t19)$
$**2+(2**s19)**2 + ((1+t19)**s19)**2+(v19*t19**(r19+1)+u19*t19*$
$*r19+w19)**2 + (w19+x19+1)**2+(t19**r19)**2 + (u19+y19+1)**2+($
$t19)**2 + (u19)**2+(2*z19+1)**2 + (A+output.A*q**time)**2+(inp$
$ut.A+q*set.A.L2+q*dont.set.A)**2 + (set.A)**2+(L2)**2 + (r20)*$
$*2+(dont.set.A)**2 + (s20)**2+(A)**2 + (t20)**2+(2**s20)**2 +$
$((1+t20)**s20)**2+(v20*t20**(r20+1)+u20*t20**r20+w20)**2 + (w2$
$0+x20+1)**2+(t20**r20)**2 + (u20+y20+1)**2+(t20)**2 + (u20)**2$
$+(2*z20+1)**2 + (r21)**2+(dont.set.A)**2 + (s21+q.minus.1*set.$
$A)**2+(q.minus.1*i)**2 + (t21)**2+(2**s21)**2 + ((1+t21)**s21)$
$**2+(v21*t21**(r21+1)+u21*t21**r21+w21)**2 + (w21+x21+1)**2+(t$
$21**r21)**2 + (u21+y21+1)**2+(t21)**2 + (u21)**2+(2*z21+1)**2$
$+ (r22)**2+(A)**2 + (s22)**2+(dont.set.A+q.minus.1*set.A)**2 +$
$(t22)**2+(2**s22)**2 + ((1+t22)**s22)**2+(v22*t22**(r22+1)+u2$
$2*t22**r22+w22)**2 + (w22+x22+1)**2+(t22**r22)**2 + (u22+y22+1$
$)**2+(t22)**2 + (u22)**2+(2*z22+1)**2 + (r23)**2+(256*shift.A)$
$**2 + (s23)**2+(A)**2 + (t23)**2+(2**s23)**2 + ((1+t23)**s23)*$
$*2+(v23*t23**(r23+1)+u23*t23**r23+w23)**2 + (w23+x23+1)**2+(t2$
$3**r23)**2 + (u23+y23+1)**2+(t23)**2 + (u23)**2+(2*z23+1)**2 +$
$(r24)**2+(256*shift.A)**2 + (s24+255*i)**2+(q.minus.1*i)**2 +$
$(t24)**2+(2**s24)**2 + ((1+t24)**s24)**2+(v24*t24**(r24+1)+u2$
$4*t24**r24+w24)**2 + (w24+x24+1)**2+(t24**r24)**2 + (u24+y24+1$
$)**2+(t24)**2 + (u24)**2+(2*z24+1)**2 + (r25)**2+(A)**2 + (s25$
$)**2+(256*shift.A+255*i)**2 + (t25)**2+(2**s25)**2 + ((1+t25)*$
$*s25)**2+(v25*t25**(r25+1)+u25*t25**r25+w25)**2 + (w25+x25+1)*$
$*2+(t25**r25)**2 + (u25+y25+1)**2+(t25)**2 + (u25)**2+(2*z25+1$
$)**2 + (A)**2+(256*shift.A+char.A)**2 + (r26)**2+(B)**2 + (s26$
$)**2+(q.minus.1*i)**2 + (t26)**2+(2**s26)**2 + ((1+t26)**s26)*$
$*2+(v26*t26**(r26+1)+u26*t26**r26+w26)**2 + (w26+x26+1)**2+(t2$
$6**r26)**2 + (u26+y26+1)**2+(t26)**2 + (u26)**2+(2*z26+1)**2 +$
$(B+output.B*q**time)**2+(input.B+q*set.B.L1+q*set.B.L2+q*dont$
$.set.B)**2 + (set.B)**2+(L1+L2)**2 + (r27)**2+(dont.set.B)**2$
$+ (s27)**2+(B)**2 + (t27)**2+(2**s27)**2 + ((1+t27)**s27)**2+($
$v27*t27**(r27+1)+u27*t27**r27+w27)**2 + (w27+x27+1)**2+(t27**r$
$27)**2 + (u27+y27+1)**2+(t27)**2 + (u27)**2+(2*z27+1)**2 + (r2$
$8)**2+(dont.set.B)**2 + (s28+q.minus.1*set.B)**2+(q.minus.1*i)$
$**2 + (t28)**2+(2**s28)**2 + ((1+t28)**s28)**2+(v28*t28**(r28+$
$1)+u28*t28**r28+w28)**2 + (w28+x28+1)**2+(t28**r28)**2 + (u28+$
$y28+1)**2+(t28)**2 + (u28)**2+(2*z28+1)**2 + (r29)**2+(B)**2 +$
$(s29)**2+(dont.set.B+q.minus.1*set.B)**2 + (t29)**2+(2**s29)*$
$*2 + ((1+t29)**s29)**2+(v29*t29**(r29+1)+u29*t29**r29+w29)**2$
$+ (w29+x29+1)**2+(t29**r29)**2 + (u29+y29+1)**2+(t29)**2 + (u2$
$9)**2+(2*z29+1)**2 + (r30)**2+(ge.A.X'00')**2 + (s30)**2+(i)**$
$2 + (t30)**2+(2**s30)**2 + ((1+t30)**s30)**2+(v30*t30**(r30+1)$

```
+u30*t30**r30+w30)**2 + (w30+x30+1)**2+(t30**r30)**2 + (u30+y3
0+1)**2+(t30)**2 + (u30)**2+(2*z30+1)**2 + (r31)**2+(256*ge.A.
X'00')**2 + (s31+0*i)**2+(256*i+char.A)**2 + (t31)**2+(2**s31)
**2 + ((1+t31)**s31)**2+(v31*t31**(r31+1)+u31*t31**r31+w31)**2
 + (w31+x31+1)**2+(t31**r31)**2 + (u31+y31+1)**2+(t31)**2 + (u
31)**2+(2*z31+1)**2 + (r32+0*i)**2+(256*i+char.A)**2 + (s32)**
2+(256*ge.A.X'00'+255*i)**2 + (t32)**2+(2**s32)**2 + ((1+t32)*
*s32)**2+(v32*t32**(r32+1)+u32*t32**r32+w32)**2 + (w32+x32+1)*
*2+(t32**r32)**2 + (u32+y32+1)**2+(t32)**2 + (u32)**2+(2*z32+1
)**2 + (r33)**2+(ge.X'00'.A)**2 + (s33)**2+(i)**2 + (t33)**2+(
2**s33)**2 + ((1+t33)**s33)**2+(v33*t33**(r33+1)+u33*t33**r33+
w33)**2 + (w33+x33+1)**2+(t33**r33)**2 + (u33+y33+1)**2+(t33)*
*2 + (u33)**2+(2*z33+1)**2 + (r34)**2+(256*ge.X'00'.A)**2 + (s
34+char.A)**2+(256*i+0*i)**2 + (t34)**2+(2**s34)**2 + ((1+t34)
**s34)**2+(v34*t34**(r34+1)+u34*t34**r34+w34)**2 + (w34+x34+1)
**2+(t34**r34)**2 + (u34+y34+1)**2+(t34)**2 + (u34)**2+(2*z34+
1)**2 + (r35+char.A)**2+(256*i+0*i)**2 + (s35)**2+(256*ge.X'00
'.A+255*i)**2 + (t35)**2+(2**s35)**2 + ((1+t35)**s35)**2+(v35*
t35**(r35+1)+u35*t35**r35+w35)**2 + (w35+x35+1)**2+(t35**r35)*
*2 + (u35+y35+1)**2+(t35)**2 + (u35)**2+(2*z35+1)**2 + (r36)**
2+(eq.A.X'00')**2 + (s36)**2+(i)**2 + (t36)**2+(2**s36)**2 + (
(1+t36)**s36)**2+(v36*t36**(r36+1)+u36*t36**r36+w36)**2 + (w36
+x36+1)**2+(t36**r36)**2 + (u36+y36+1)**2+(t36)**2 + (u36)**2+
(2*z36+1)**2 + (r37)**2+(2*eq.A.X'00')**2 + (s37)**2+(ge.A.X'0
0'+ge.X'00'.A)**2 + (t37)**2+(2**s37)**2 + ((1+t37)**s37)**2+(
v37*t37**(r37+1)+u37*t37**r37+w37)**2 + (w37+x37+1)**2+(t37**r
37)**2 + (u37+y37+1)**2+(t37)**2 + (u37)**2+(2*z37+1)**2 + (r3
8)**2+(ge.A.X'00'+ge.X'00'.A)**2 + (s38)**2+(2*eq.A.X'00'+i)**
2 + (t38)**2+(2**s38)**2 + ((1+t38)**s38)**2+(v38*t38**(r38+1)
+u38*t38**r38+w38)**2 + (w38+x38+1)**2+(t38**r38)**2 + (u38+y3
8+1)**2+(t38)**2 + (u38)**2+(2*z38+1)**2
```

2.9. A Complete Example of Arithmetization: Right-Hand Side

```
2*(total.input)*(input.A+input.B) + 2*(number.of.instructions)
*(4) + 2*(longest.label)*(2) + 2*(q)*(256**(total.input+time+n
umber.of.instructions+longest.label+3)) + 2*(q.minus.1+1)*(q)
+ 2*(1+q*i)*(i+q**time) + 2*(r1)*(L1) + 2*(s1)*(i) + 2*(t1)*(2
**s1) + 2*((1+t1)**s1)*(v1*t1**(r1+1)+u1*t1**r1+w1) + 2*(w1+x1
+1)*(t1**r1) + 2*(u1+y1+1)*(t1) + 2*(u1)*(2*z1+1) + 2*(r2)*(L2
) + 2*(s2)*(i) + 2*(t2)*(2**s2) + 2*((1+t2)**s2)*(v2*t2**(r2+1
)+u2*t2**r2+w2) + 2*(w2+x2+1)*(t2**r2) + 2*(u2+y2+1)*(t2) + 2*
(u2)*(2*z2+1) + 2*(r3)*(L3) + 2*(s3)*(i) + 2*(t3)*(2**s3) + 2*
((1+t3)**s3)*(v3*t3**(r3+1)+u3*t3**r3+w3) + 2*(w3+x3+1)*(t3**r
3) + 2*(u3+y3+1)*(t3) + 2*(u3)*(2*z3+1) + 2*(r4)*(L4) + 2*(s4)
*(i) + 2*(t4)*(2**s4) + 2*((1+t4)**s4)*(v4*t4**(r4+1)+u4*t4**r
4+w4) + 2*(w4+x4+1)*(t4**r4) + 2*(u4+y4+1)*(t4) + 2*(u4)*(2*z4
+1) + 2*(i)*(L1+L2+L3+L4) + 2*(r5)*(1) + 2*(s5)*(L1) + 2*(t5)*
(2**s5) + 2*((1+t5)**s5)*(v5*t5**(r5+1)+u5*t5**r5+w5) + 2*(w5+
x5+1)*(t5**r5) + 2*(u5+y5+1)*(t5) + 2*(u5)*(2*z5+1) + 2*(q**ti
me)*(q*L4) + 2*(r6)*(q*L1) + 2*(s6)*(L2) + 2*(t6)*(2**s6) + 2*
((1+t6)**s6)*(v6*t6**(r6+1)+u6*t6**r6+w6) + 2*(w6+x6+1)*(t6**r
6) + 2*(u6+y6+1)*(t6) + 2*(u6)*(2*z6+1) + 2*(r7)*(q*L2) + 2*(s
7)*(L3) + 2*(t7)*(2**s7) + 2*((1+t7)**s7)*(v7*t7**(r7+1)+u7*t7
```

$**r7+w7) + 2*(w7+x7+1)*(t7**r7) + 2*(u7+y7+1)*(t7) + 2*(u7)*(2$
$*z7+1) + 2*(r8)*(q*L3) + 2*(s8)*(L4+L2) + 2*(t8)*(2**s8) + 2*($
$(1+t8)**s8)*(v8*t8**(r8+1)+u8*t8**r8+w8) + 2*(w8+x8+1)*(t8**r8$
$) + 2*(u8+y8+1)*(t8) + 2*(u8)*(2*z8+1) + 2*(r9)*(q*L3) + 2*(s9$
$)*(L2+q*eq.A.X'00') + 2*(t9)*(2**s9) + 2*((1+t9)**s9)*(v9*t9**$
$(r9+1)+u9*t9**r9+w9) + 2*(w9+x9+1)*(t9**r9) + 2*(u9+y9+1)*(t9)$
$+ 2*(u9)*(2*z9+1) + 2*(r10)*(set.B.L1) + 2*(s10)*(0*i) + 2*(t$
$10)*(2**s10) + 2*((1+t10)**s10)*(v10*t10**(r10+1)+u10*t10**r10$
$+w10) + 2*(w10+x10+1)*(t10**r10) + 2*(u10+y10+1)*(t10) + 2*(u1$
$0)*(2*z10+1) + 2*(r11)*(set.B.L1) + 2*(s11)*(q.minus.1*L1) + 2$
$*(t11)*(2**s11) + 2*((1+t11)**s11)*(v11*t11**(r11+1)+u11*t11**$
$r11+w11) + 2*(w11+x11+1)*(t11**r11) + 2*(u11+y11+1)*(t11) + 2*$
$(u11)*(2*z11+1) + 2*(r12)*(0*i) + 2*(s12+q.minus.1*L1)*(set.B.$
$L1+q.minus.1*i) + 2*(t12)*(2**s12) + 2*((1+t12)**s12)*(v12*t12$
$**(r12+1)+u12*t12**r12+w12) + 2*(w12+x12+1)*(t12**r12) + 2*(u1$
$2+y12+1)*(t12) + 2*(u12)*(2*z12+1) + 2*(r13)*(set.B.L2) + 2*(s$
$13)*(256*B+char.A) + 2*(t13)*(2**s13) + 2*((1+t13)**s13)*(v13*$
$t13**(r13+1)+u13*t13**r13+w13) + 2*(w13+x13+1)*(t13**r13) + 2*$
$(u13+y13+1)*(t13) + 2*(u13)*(2*z13+1) + 2*(r14)*(set.B.L2) + 2$
$*(s14)*(q.minus.1*L2) + 2*(t14)*(2**s14) + 2*((1+t14)**s14)*(v$
$14*t14**(r14+1)+u14*t14**r14+w14) + 2*(w14+x14+1)*(t14**r14) +$
$2*(u14+y14+1)*(t14) + 2*(u14)*(2*z14+1) + 2*(r15)*(256*B+char$
$.A) + 2*(s15+q.minus.1*L2)*(set.B.L2+q.minus.1*i) + 2*(t15)*(2$
$**s15) + 2*((1+t15)**s15)*(v15*t15**(r15+1)+u15*t15**r15+w15)$
$+ 2*(w15+x15+1)*(t15**r15) + 2*(u15+y15+1)*(t15) + 2*(u15)*(2*$
$z15+1) + 2*(r16)*(set.A.L2) + 2*(s16)*(shift.A) + 2*(t16)*(2**$
$s16) + 2*((1+t16)**s16)*(v16*t16**(r16+1)+u16*t16**r16+w16) +$
$2*(w16+x16+1)*(t16**r16) + 2*(u16+y16+1)*(t16) + 2*(u16)*(2*z1$
$6+1) + 2*(r17)*(set.A.L2) + 2*(s17)*(q.minus.1*L2) + 2*(t17)*($
$2**s17) + 2*((1+t17)**s17)*(v17*t17**(r17+1)+u17*t17**r17+w17)$
$+ 2*(w17+x17+1)*(t17**r17) + 2*(u17+y17+1)*(t17) + 2*(u17)*(2$
$*z17+1) + 2*(r18)*(shift.A) + 2*(s18+q.minus.1*L2)*(set.A.L2+q$
$.minus.1*i) + 2*(t18)*(2**s18) + 2*((1+t18)**s18)*(v18*t18**(r$
$18+1)+u18*t18**r18+w18) + 2*(w18+x18+1)*(t18**r18) + 2*(u18+y1$
$8+1)*(t18) + 2*(u18)*(2*z18+1) + 2*(r19)*(A) + 2*(s19)*(q.minu$
$s.1*i) + 2*(t19)*(2**s19) + 2*((1+t19)**s19)*(v19*t19**(r19+1)$
$+u19*t19**r19+w19) + 2*(w19+x19+1)*(t19**r19) + 2*(u19+y19+1)*$
$(t19) + 2*(u19)*(2*z19+1) + 2*(A+output.A*q**time)*(input.A+q*$
$set.A.L2+q*dont.set.A) + 2*(set.A)*(L2) + 2*(r20)*(dont.set.A)$
$+ 2*(s20)*(A) + 2*(t20)*(2**s20) + 2*((1+t20)**s20)*(v20*t20*$
$*(r20+1)+u20*t20**r20+w20) + 2*(w20+x20+1)*(t20**r20) + 2*(u20$
$+y20+1)*(t20) + 2*(u20)*(2*z20+1) + 2*(r21)*(dont.set.A) + 2*($
$s21+q.minus.1*set.A)*(q.minus.1*i) + 2*(t21)*(2**s21) + 2*((1+$
$t21)**s21)*(v21*t21**(r21+1)+u21*t21**r21+w21) + 2*(w21+x21+1)$
$*(t21**r21) + 2*(u21+y21+1)*(t21) + 2*(u21)*(2*z21+1) + 2*(r22$
$)*(A) + 2*(s22)*(dont.set.A+q.minus.1*set.A) + 2*(t22)*(2**s22$
$) + 2*((1+t22)**s22)*(v22*t22**(r22+1)+u22*t22**r22+w22) + 2*($
$w22+x22+1)*(t22**r22) + 2*(u22+y22+1)*(t22) + 2*(u22)*(2*z22+1$
$) + 2*(r23)*(256*shift.A) + 2*(s23)*(A) + 2*(t23)*(2**s23) + 2$
$*((1+t23)**s23)*(v23*t23**(r23+1)+u23*t23**r23+w23) + 2*(w23+x$
$23+1)*(t23**r23) + 2*(u23+y23+1)*(t23) + 2*(u23)*(2*z23+1) + 2$
$*(r24)*(256*shift.A) + 2*(s24+255*i)*(q.minus.1*i) + 2*(t24)*($
$2**s24) + 2*((1+t24)**s24)*(v24*t24**(r24+1)+u24*t24**r24+w24)$
$+ 2*(w24+x24+1)*(t24**r24) + 2*(u24+y24+1)*(t24) + 2*(u24)*(2$
$*z24+1) + 2*(r25)*(A) + 2*(s25)*(256*shift.A+255*i) + 2*(t25)*$
$(2**s25) + 2*((1+t25)**s25)*(v25*t25**(r25+1)+u25*t25**r25+w25$
$) + 2*(w25+x25+1)*(t25**r25) + 2*(u25+y25+1)*(t25) + 2*(u25)*($

```
2*z25+1) + 2*(A)*(256*shift.A+char.A) + 2*(r26)*(B) + 2*(s26)*
(q.minus.1*i) + 2*(t26)*(2**s26) + 2*((1+t26)**s26)*(v26*t26**
(r26+1)+u26*t26**r26+w26) + 2*(w26+x26+1)*(t26**r26) + 2*(u26+
y26+1)*(t26) + 2*(u26)*(2*z26+1) + 2*(B+output.B*q**time)*(inp
ut.B+q*set.B.L1+q*set.B.L2+q*dont.set.B) + 2*(set.B)*(L1+L2) +
  2*(r27)*(dont.set.B) + 2*(s27)*(B) + 2*(t27)*(2**s27) + 2*((1
+t27)**s27)*(v27*t27**(r27+1)+u27*t27**r27+w27) + 2*(w27+x27+1
)*(t27**r27) + 2*(u27+y27+1)*(t27) + 2*(u27)*(2*z27+1) + 2*(r2
8)*(dont.set.B) + 2*(s28+q.minus.1*set.B)*(q.minus.1*i) + 2*(t
28)*(2**s28) + 2*((1+t28)**s28)*(v28*t28**(r28+1)+u28*t28**r28
+w28) + 2*(w28+x28+1)*(t28**r28) + 2*(u28+y28+1)*(t28) + 2*(u2
8)*(2*z28+1) + 2*(r29)*(B) + 2*(s29)*(dont.set.B+q.minus.1*set
.B) + 2*(t29)*(2**s29) + 2*((1+t29)**s29)*(v29*t29**(r29+1)+u2
9*t29**r29+w29) + 2*(w29+x29+1)*(t29**r29) + 2*(u29+y29+1)*(t2
9) + 2*(u29)*(2*z29+1) + 2*(r30)*(ge.A.X'00') + 2*(s30)*(i) +
2*(t30)*(2**s30) + 2*((1+t30)**s30)*(v30*t30**(r30+1)+u30*t30*
*r30+w30) + 2*(w30+x30+1)*(t30**r30) + 2*(u30+y30+1)*(t30) + 2
*(u30)*(2*z30+1) + 2*(r31)*(256*ge.A.X'00') + 2*(s31+0*i)*(256
*i+char.A) + 2*(t31)*(2**s31) + 2*((1+t31)**s31)*(v31*t31**(r3
1+1)+u31*t31**r31+w31) + 2*(w31+x31+1)*(t31**r31) + 2*(u31+y31
+1)*(t31) + 2*(u31)*(2*z31+1) + 2*(r32+0*i)*(256*i+char.A) + 2
*(s32)*(256*ge.A.X'00'+255*i) + 2*(t32)*(2**s32) + 2*((1+t32)*
*s32)*(v32*t32**(r32+1)+u32*t32**r32+w32) + 2*(w32+x32+1)*(t32
**r32) + 2*(u32+y32+1)*(t32) + 2*(u32)*(2*z32+1) + 2*(r33)*(ge
.X'00'.A) + 2*(s33)*(i) + 2*(t33)*(2**s33) + 2*((1+t33)**s33)*
(v33*t33**(r33+1)+u33*t33**r33+w33) + 2*(w33+x33+1)*(t33**r33)
 + 2*(u33+y33+1)*(t33) + 2*(u33)*(2*z33+1) + 2*(r34)*(256*ge.X
'00'.A) + 2*(s34+char.A)*(256*i+0*i) + 2*(t34)*(2**s34) + 2*((
1+t34)**s34)*(v34*t34**(r34+1)+u34*t34**r34+w34) + 2*(w34+x34+
1)*(t34**r34) + 2*(u34+y34+1)*(t34) + 2*(u34)*(2*z34+1) + 2*(r
35+char.A)*(256*i+0*i) + 2*(s35)*(256*ge.X'00'.A+255*i) + 2*(t
35)*(2**s35) + 2*((1+t35)**s35)*(v35*t35**(r35+1)+u35*t35**r35
+w35) + 2*(w35+x35+1)*(t35**r35) + 2*(u35+y35+1)*(t35) + 2*(u3
5)*(2*z35+1) + 2*(r36)*(eq.A.X'00') + 2*(s36)*(i) + 2*(t36)*(2
**s36) + 2*((1+t36)**s36)*(v36*t36**(r36+1)+u36*t36**r36+w36)
+ 2*(w36+x36+1)*(t36**r36) + 2*(u36+y36+1)*(t36) + 2*(u36)*(2*
z36+1) + 2*(r37)*(2*eq.A.X'00') + 2*(s37)*(ge.A.X'00'+ge.X'00'
.A) + 2*(t37)*(2**s37) + 2*((1+t37)**s37)*(v37*t37**(r37+1)+u3
7*t37**r37+w37) + 2*(w37+x37+1)*(t37**r37) + 2*(u37+y37+1)*(t3
7) + 2*(u37)*(2*z37+1) + 2*(r38)*(ge.A.X'00'+ge.X'00'.A) + 2*(
s38)*(2*eq.A.X'00'+i) + 2*(t38)*(2**s38) + 2*((1+t38)**s38)*(v
38*t38**(r38+1)+u38*t38**r38+w38) + 2*(w38+x38+1)*(t38**r38) +
 2*(u38+y38+1)*(t38) + 2*(u38)*(2*z38+1)
```

CHAPTER 3

A VERSION OF PURE LISP

3.1. Introduction

In this chapter we present a "permissive" simplified version of pure LISP designed especially for metamathematical applications. Aside from the rule that an S-expression must have balanced ()'s, the only way that an expression can fail to have a value is by looping forever. This is important because algorithms that simulate other algorithms chosen at random, must be able to run garbage safely.

This version of LISP developed from one originally designed for teaching [CHAITIN (1976a)]. The language was reduced to its essence and made as easy to learn as possible, and was actually used in several university courses. Like APL, this version of LISP is so concise that one can write it as fast as one thinks. This LISP is so simple that an interpreter for it can be coded in three hundred and fifty lines of **REXX**.

How to read this chapter: This chapter can be quite difficult to understand, especially if one has never programmed in LISP before. The correct approach is to read it several times, and to try to work through all the examples in detail. Initially the material will seem completely incomprehensible, but all of a sudden the pieces will snap together into a coherent whole. Alternatively, one can skim Chapters 3, 4, and 5, which depend heavily on the details of this LISP, and proceed directly to the more theoretical material in Chapter 6, which could be based on Turing machines or any other formalism for computation.

The purpose of Chapters 3 and 4 is to show how easy it is to implement an extremely powerful and theoretically attractive programming language on the abstract register machines that we presented in Chapter 2. If one takes this for granted, then it is not necessary to study Chapters 3 and 4 in detail. On the other hand, if one has never experienced LISP before and wishes to master it thoroughly, one should write a LISP interpreter and run it on one's favorite computer; that is how the author learned LISP.

3.2. Definition of LISP

LISP is an unusual programming language created around 1960 by John McCarthy [McCARTHY (1960,1962,1981)]. It and its descendants are frequently used in research on artificial intelligence [ABELSON, SUSSMAN and SUSSMAN (1985), WINSTON and HORN (1984)]. And it stands out for its simple design and for its precisely defined syntax and semantics.

However LISP more closely resembles such fundamental subjects as set theory and logic than its does a programming language [see LEVIN (1974)].

Fig 6. The LISP Character Set: These are the 128 characters that are used in LISP S-expressions: the left and right parentheses and the 126 one-character atoms. The place that a character appears in this list of all 128 of them is important; it defines the binary representation for that character. In this monograph we use two different representations:

1. The first binary representation uses 8 bits per character, with the characters in reverse order. The 8-bit string corresponding to a character is obtained by taking the 1-origin ordinal number of its position in the list, which ranges from 1 to 128, writing this number as an 8-bit string in base-two, and then reversing this 8-bit string. This is the representation used in the exponential diophantine version of the LISP interpreter in Part I.
2. The second binary representation uses 7 bits per character, with the characters in the normal order. The 7-bit string corresponding to a character is obtained by taking the 0-origin ordinal number of its position in the list, which ranges from 0 to 127, writing this number as a 7-bit string in base-two, and then reversing this 7-bit string. This is the representation that is used to define a program-size complexity measure in Part II.

```
()
ABCDEFGHIJKLMNOPQRSTUVWXYZ
abcdefghijklmnopqrstuvwxyz0123456789
¢.<+|&!$*;¬-/,%_>?∧¨∨:#@'="~↑↓≤⌈⌊→⎕
⊃⊂○←¯∩∪⊥≥∘⍺∊⍳⍴⍵×\÷∇∆⊤≠⌽⍉⍒⍋⌶⍟⍎
```

As a result LISP is easy to learn with little previous knowledge. Contrariwise, those who know other programming languages may have difficulty learning to think in the completely different fashion required by LISP.

LISP is a functional programming language, not an imperative language like FORTRAN. In FORTRAN the question is "In order to do something what operations must be carried out, and in what order?" In LISP the question is "How can this function be defined?" The LISP formalism consists of a handful of primitive functions and certain rules for defining more complex functions from the initially given ones. In a LISP run, after defining functions one requests their values for specific arguments of interest. It is the LISP interpreter's task to deduce these values using the function's definitions.

LISP functions are technically known as partial recursive functions. "Partial" because in some cases they may not have a value (this situation is analogous to division by zero or an infinite loop). "Recursive" because functions re-occur in their own definitions. The following definition of factorial n is the most familiar example of a recursive function: if $n = 0$, then its value is 1, else its value is n by factorial $n - 1$. From this definition one deduces that factorial 3 = (3 by factorial 2) = (3 by 2 by factorial 1) = (3 by 2 by 1 by factorial 0) = (3 by 2 by 1 by 1) = 6.

A LISP function whose value is always true or false is called a predicate. By means of predicates the LISP formalism encompasses relations such as "x is less than y."

Data and function definitions in LISP consist of S-expressions (S stands for "symbolic"). S-expressions are made up of characters called atoms that are grouped into lists by means of pairs of parentheses. The atoms are most of the characters except blank, left parenthesis, right parenthesis, left bracket, and right bracket in the largest font of mathematical symbols that I could find, the APL character set. The simplest kind of S-expression is an atom all by itself. All other S-expressions are lists. A list consists of a left parenthesis followed by zero or more elements (which may be atoms or sublists) followed by a right parenthesis. Also, the empty list () is considered to be an atom.

Here are two examples of S-expressions. c is an atom. $(d(ef)d((a)))$ is a list with four elements. The first and third elements are the atom d. The second element is a list whose elements are the atoms e and f, in that order. The fourth element is a list with a single element, which is a list with a single element, which is the atom a.

The formal definition is as follows. The class of S-expressions is the union of the class of atoms and the class of lists. A list consists of a left parenthesis followed by zero or more S-expressions followed by a right parenthesis. There is one list that is also an atom, the empty list (). All other atoms are found in Figure 6, which gives the complete 128-character set used in writing S-expressions, consisting of the 126 one-character atoms and the left and right parenthesis. The total number of characters is chosen to be a power of two in order to simplify the theoretical analysis of LISP in Part II.

In LISP the atom 1 stands for "true" and the atom 0 stands for "false." Thus a LISP predicate is a function whose value is always 0 or 1.

It is important to note that we do not identify 0 and (). It is usual in LISP to identify falsehood and the empty list; both are usually called NIL. This would complicate our LISP and make it harder to write the LISP interpreter that we give in Chapter 4, because it would be harder to determine if two S-expressions are equal. This would also be a serious mistake from an information-theoretic point of view, because it would make large numbers of S-expressions into synonyms. And wasting the expressive power of S-expressions in this manner would invalidate large portions of Chapter 5 and Appendix B. Thus there is no single-character synonym in our LISP for the empty list (); 2 characters are required.

The fundamental semantical concept in LISP is that of the value of an S-expression in a given environment. An environment consists of a so-called "association list" in which variables (atoms) and their values (S-expressions) alternate. If a variable appears several times, only its first value is significant. If a variable does not appear in the environment, then it itself is its value, so that it is in effect a literal constant. $(xa\ x(a)\ x((a))$ $F(\triangledown(x)(\rightarrow(\circ x)x(F(\uparrow x)))))$ is a typical environment. In this environment the value of x is a, the value of F is $(\triangledown(x)(\rightarrow(\circ x)x(F(\uparrow x))))$, and any other atom, for example Q, has itself as value.

Thus the value of an atomic S-expression is obtained by searching odd elements of the environment for that atom. What is the value of a non-atomic S-expression, that is, of a non-empty list? In this case the value is defined recursively, in terms of the values of the elements of the S-expression in the same environment. The value of the first element of the S-expression is the function, and the function's arguments are the values of the remaining elements of the expression. Thus in LISP the notation $(fxyz)$ is used for what in FORTRAN would be written $f(x,y,z)$. Both denote the function f applied to the arguments xyz.

There are two kinds of functions: primitive functions and defined functions. The ten primitive functions are the atoms `∘ = ↑ ↓ , ⎕ ' → ⍎` and `⍕`. A defined function is a three-element list (traditionally called a LAMBDA expression) of the form `(∇vb)`, where *v* is a list of variables. By definition the result of applying a defined function to arguments is the value of the body of the function *b* in the environment resulting from concatenating a list of the form (variable1 argument1 variable2 argument2...) and the environment of the original S-expression, in that order. The concatenation of an *n*-element list and an *m*-element list is defined to be the $(n + m)$-element list whose elements are those of the first list followed by those of the second list.

The primitive functions are now presented. In the examples of their use the environment in Figure 7 is assumed.

Name	Atom
Symbol	`∘`
Arguments	1
Explanation	The result of applying this function to an argument is true or false depending on whether or not the argument is an atom.
Examples	`(∘x)` has value `1` `(∘y)` has value `0`

Name	Equal
Symbol	`=`
Arguments	2
Explanation	The result of applying this function to two arguments is true or false depending on whether or not they are the same S-expression.
Examples	`(=wx)` has value `1` `(=yz)` has value `0`

Name	Head/First/Take 1/CAR
Symbol	`↑`
Arguments	1
Explanation	The result of applying this function to an atom is the atom itself. The result of applying this function to a non-empty list is the first element of the list.

Fig 7. A LISP Environment

```
(t1 f0 wa xa y(bcd) z((ef)))
```

Examples	(↑*x*) has value *a*
	(↑*y*) has value *b*
	(↑*z*) has value (*ef*)

Name	Tail/Rest/Drop 1/CDR
Symbol	↓
Arguments	1
Explanation	The result of applying this function to an atom is the atom itself. The result of applying this function to a non-empty list is what remains if its first element is erased. Thus the tail of an (*n* + 1)-element list is an *n*-element list.
Examples	(↓*x*) has value *a*
	(↓*y*) has value (*cd*)
	(↓*z*) has value ()

Name	Join/CONS
Symbol	,
Arguments	2
Explanation	If the second argument is not a list, then the result of applying this function is the first argument. If the second argument is an *n*-element list, then the result of applying this function is the (*n* + 1)-element list whose head is the first argument and whose tail is the second argument.
Examples	(,*xx*) has value *a*
	(,*x*()) has value (*a*)
	(,*xy*) has value (*abcd*)
	(,*xz*) has value (*a*(*ef*))
	(,*yz*) has value ((*bcd*)(*ef*))

Name	Output
Symbol	☐
Arguments	1
Explanation	The result of applying this function is its argument, in other words, this is an identity function. The side-effect is to display the argument. This function is used to display intermediate results. It is the only primitive function that has a side-effect.
Examples	Evaluation of (↓(☐(↓(☐(↓*y*))))) displays (*cd*) and (*d*) and yields value ()

Name	Quote

Symbol	'
Arguments	1
Explanation	The result of applying this function is the unevaluated argument expression.
Examples	('*x*) has value *x*
	(' (, *xy*)) has value (, *xy*)

Name	If-then-else
Symbol	→
Arguments	3
Explanation	If the first argument is not false, then the result is the second argument. If the first argument is false, then the result is the third argument. The argument that is not selected is not evaluated.
Examples	(→*zxy*) has value *a*
	(→*txy*) has value *a*
	(→*fxy*) has value (*bcd*)
	Evaluation of (→*tx*(□*y*)) does not have the side-effect of displaying (*bcd*)

Name	Eval
Symbol	⊛
Arguments	1
Explanation	The expression that is the value of the argument is evaluated in an empty environment. This is the only primitive function that is a partial rather than a total function.
Examples	(⊛('*x*)) has value *x* instead of *a*, because *x* is evaluated in an empty environment.
	(⊛('(∘*x*))) has value 1
	(⊛('(('(∇(*f*)(*f*)))('(∇()(*f*))))))) has no value.

Name	Safe Eval/Depth-limited Eval
Symbol	⚲
Arguments	2
Explanation	The expression that is the value of the second argument is evaluated in an empty environment. If the evaluation is completed within "time" given by the first argument, the value returned is a list whose sole element is the value of the value of the second argument. If the evaluation is not completed within "time" given by the first argument, the

value returned is the atom ?. More precisely, the "time limit" is given by the number of elements of the first argument, and is zero if the first argument is not a list. The "time limit" actually limits the depth of the call stack, more precisely, the maximum number of defined functions whose evaluation has been started but has not yet been completed. The key property of ⊉ is that it is a total function, i.e., is defined for all values of its arguments, and that $(\overline{\ast}x)$ is defined if and only if $(\underline{\ast}tx)$ is not equal to ? for all sufficiently large values of t. (See Section 3.6 for a more precise definition of ⊉.)

Examples $(\underline{\ast}0('x))$ has value (x)

$(\underline{\ast}0('(('(\nabla(x)x))a)))$ has value ?

$(\underline{\ast}('(1))('(('(\nabla(x)x))a)))$ has value (a)

The argument of ' and the unselected argument of → are exceptions to the rule that the evaluation of an S-expression that is a non-empty list requires the previous evaluation of all its elements. When evaluation of the elements of a list is required, this is always done one element at a time, from left to right.

M-expressions (M stands for "meta") are S-expressions in which the parentheses grouping together primitive functions and their arguments are omitted as a convenience for the LISP programmer. See Figure 8. For these purposes, ∇ ("function/del/LAMBDA/define") is treated as if it were a primitive function with two arguments, and ← ("LET/is") is treated as if it were a primitive function with three arguments.   ← is another meta-notational abbreviation, but may be thought of as an additional primitive function.   ←*vde* denotes the value of *e* in an environment in which *v* evaluates to the current value of *d*, and ←*(fxyz)de* denotes the value of *e* in an environment in which *f* evaluates to $(\nabla(xyz)d)$. More precisely, the M-expression ←*vde* denotes the S-expression $(('(\nabla(v)e))d)$, and the M-expression   ←*(fxyz)de*   denotes   the   S-expression $(('(\nabla(f)e))('(\nabla(xyz)d)))$, and similarly for functions with a different number of arguments.

A " is written before a self-contained portion of an M-expression to indicate that the convention regarding invisible parentheses and the meaning of ← does not apply within it, i.e., that there follows an S-expression "as is".

Input to the LISP interpreter consists of a list of M-expressions. All blanks are ignored, and comments may be inserted anywhere by placing them between balanced ⌜'s and ⌝'s, so that comments may include other comments. Two kinds of M-expressions are read by the interpreter: expressions to be evaluated, and others that indicate the environment to be used for these evaluations. The initial environment is the empty list ().

Each M-expression is transformed into the corresponding S-expression and displayed:

1. If the S-expression is of the form (∇*xe*) where *x* is an atom and *e* is an S-expression, then (*xv*) is concatenated with the current environment to obtain a new environment, where *v* is the value of *e*. Thus (∇*xe*) is used to define the value of a variable *x* to be equal to the value of an S-expression *e*.

2. If the S-expression is of the form (∇(*fxyz*)*d*) where *fxyz* is one or more atoms and *d* is an S-expression, then (*f*(∇(*xyz*)*d*)) is concatenated with the current environment to obtain a new environment. Thus (∇(*fxyz*)*d*) is used to establish function definitions, in this case the function *f* of the variables *xyz*.

3. If the S-expression is not of the form (∇...) then it is evaluated in the current environment and its value is displayed. The primitive function ⎕ may cause the interpreter to display additional S-expressions before this value.

3.3. Examples

Here are five elementary examples of expressions and their values.

The M-expression
>   ,a,b,c()

denotes the S-expression
>   (,a(,b(,c())))

whose value is the S-expression
>   (abc).

The M-expression
>   ↑↓↓↓'(abcde)

denotes the S-expression
>   (↑(↓(↓(↓('(abcde)))))).

Fig 8. Atoms with Implicit Parentheses

Atom	∘	=	↑	↓	,	⎕	'	→	⊤	♁	∇	←
Arguments	1	2	1	1	2	1	1	3	1	2	2	3

whose value is the S-expression

    d.

The M-expression

    `,"+,"=,"-()`

denotes the S-expression

    `(,+(,=(,-()))) `

whose value is the S-expression

    `(+=-).`

The M-expression

    `('∇(xyz),z,y,x()abc)`

denotes the S-expression

    `(('(∇(xyz)(,z(,y(,x()))))))abc)`

whose value is the S-expression

    `(cba).`

The M-expression

    `+(Cxy)+∘xy,+x(C+xy)(C'(abcdef)'(ghijkl))`

denotes the S-expression

    `(('(∇(C)(C('(abcdef)))('(ghijkl)))))`
     `('(∇(xy)(+(∘x)y(,(+x)(C(+x)y)))))))`

whose value is the S-expression

    `(abcdefghijkl).`

In this example c is the concatenation function. It is instructive to state the definition of concatenation, usually called **APPEND**, in words: "Let concatenation be a function of two variables x and y defined as follows: if x is an atom, then the value is y; otherwise join the head of x to the concatenation of the tail of x with y."

    In the remaining three sections of this chapter we give three serious examples of programs written in this LISP: three increasingly sophisticated versions of EVAL, the traditional definition of LISP in LISP, which is of course just the LISP equivalent of a universal Turing machine. I.e., EVAL is a universal partial recursive function.

    The program in Section 3.4 is quite simple; it is a stripped down version of EVAL for our version of LISP, greatly simplified because it does not handle ᛜ and ꙮ. What is interesting about this example is that it was run on the register machine LISP interpreter of Chapter 4, and one of the evaluations took 720 million simulated register machine cycles![6]

The program in Section 3.5 defines a conventional LISP with atoms that may be any number of characters long. This example makes an important point, which is that if our LISP with one-character atoms can simulate a normal LISP with multi-character atoms, then the restriction on the size of names is not of theoretical importance: any function that can be defined using long names can also be defined using our one-character names. In other words, Section 3.5 proves that our LISP is computationally universal, and can define any computable function. In practice the one-character restriction is not too serious, because one style of using names is to give them only local significance, and then names can be reused within a large function definition.[7]

The third and final example of LISP in LISP in this chapter, Section 3.6, is the most serious one of all. It is essentially a complete definition of the semantics of our version of pure LISP, including ᵴ and ᵴ. Almost, but not quite. We cheat in two ways:

1. First of all, the top level of our LISP does not run under a time limit, and the definition of LISP in LISP in Section 3.6 omits this, and always imposes time limits on evaluations. We ought to reserve a special internal time limit value to mean no limit; the LISP interpreter given in Chapter 4 uses the underscore sign for this purpose.

2. Secondly, Section 3.6 reserves a special value, the dollar sign, as an error value. This is of course cheating; we ought to return an atom if there is an error, and the good value wrapped in parentheses if there is no error, but this would complicate the definition of LISP in LISP given in Section 3.6. The LISP interpreter in Chapter 4 uses an illegal S-expression consisting of a single right parenthesis as the internal error value; no valid S-expression can begin with a right parenthesis.

But except for these two "cheats," we take Section 3.6 to be our official definition of the semantics of our LISP. One can immediately deduce from the definition given in Section 3.6 a number of important details about the way our LISP achieves its "permissiveness." Most important, extra arguments to functions are ignored, and empty lists are supplied for missing

---

[6]   All the other LISP interpreter runs shown in this book were run directly on a large main-frame computer, not on a simulated register machine; see Appendix A for details.

[7]   Allowing long names would make it harder to program the LISP interpreter on a register machine, which we do in Chapter 4.

arguments. E.g., parameters in a function definition which are not supplied with an argument expression when the function is applied will be bound to the empty list (). This works this way because when EVAL runs off the end of a list of arguments, it is reduced to the empty argument list, and head and tail applied to this empty list will continue to give the empty list. Also if an atom is repeated in the parameter list of a function definition, the binding corresponding to the first occurrence will shadow the later occurrences of the same variable. Section 3.6 is a complete definition of LISP semantics in the sense that there are no hidden error messages and error checks in it: it performs exactly as written on what would normally be considered "erroneous" expressions. Of course, in our LISP there are no erroneous expressions, only expressions that fail to have a value because the interpreter never finishes evaluating them: it goes into an infinite loop and never returns a value.

That concludes Chapter 3. What lies ahead in Chapter 4? In the next chapter we re-write the LISP program of Section 3.6 as a register machine program, and then compile it into an exponential diophantine equation. The one-page LISP function definition in Section 3.6 becomes a 306-instruction register machine LISP interpreter, and then a $306 + 19 + 446 + 16191 = 16962$-variable equation with a left-hand side and a right-hand side each about half a million characters long. This equation is a LISP interpreter, and in theory it can be used to get the values of S-expressions. In Part II the crucial property of this equation is that it has a variable *input.EXPRESSION*, it has exactly one solution if the LISP S-expression with binary representation[8] *input.EXPRESSION* has a value, and it has no solution if *input.EXPRESSION* does not have a value. We don't care what *output.VALUE* is; we just want to know if the evaluation eventually terminates.

3.4. LISP in LISP I

LISP Interpreter Run

```
[[[ LISP semantics defined in LISP ]]]

[ (Vse) = value of S-expression s in environment e.
  If a new environment is created it is displayed. ]
```

---

[8]   Recall that the binary representation of an S-expression has 8 bits per character with the characters in reverse order (see Figures 4 and 6).

```
∇ (Vse)
  →∘s →∘es →=s↑e↓↓e (Vs↓↓e)
  ('∇(f) [ f is the function ]
    →=f"' ↑↓s
    →=f"∘ ∘(V↑↓se)
    →=f"↑ ↑(V↑↓se)
    →=f"↓ ↓(V↑↓se)
    →=f"□ □(V↑↓se)
    →=f"= =(V↑↓se)(V↑↓↓se)
    →=f", ,(V↑↓se)(V↑↓↓se)
    →=f"→ →(V↑↓se)(V↑↓↓se)(V↑↓↓↓se)
      (V↑↓↓f□(N↑↓f↓se)) [ display new environment ]
  (V↑se)) [ evaluate function f ]

V:          (∇(se)(→(∘s)(→(∘e)s(→(=s(↑e))(↑(↓e))(Vs(↓(↓e))))))(
            ('(∇(f)(→(=f')(↑(↓s)))(→(=f∘)(∘(V(↑(↓s))e))(→(=f↑)(
            ↑(V(↑(↓s))e))(→(=f↓)(↓(V(↑(↓s))e))(→(=f□)(□(V(↑(↓s
            ))e))(→(=f=)(=(V(↑(↓s))e)(V(↑(↓(↓s)))e))(→(=f,)(,((
            V(↑(↓s))e)(V(↑(↓(↓s)))e))(→(=f→)(→(V(↑(↓s))e)(V(↑(
            ↓(↓s)))e)(V(↑(↓(↓(↓s))))e))(V(↑(↓(↓(↓f)))(□(N(↑(↓f))
            (↓s)e)))))))))))))))(V(↑s)e))))
```

```
[ (Nxae) = new environment created from list of
  variables x, list of unevaluated arguments a, and
  previous environment e. ]
∇ (Nxae) →∘xe ,↑x,(V↑ae)(N↓x↓ae)
```

```
N:          (∇(xae)(→(∘x)e(,(↑x)(,(V(↑a)e)(N(↓x)(↓a)e)))))
```

```
[ Test function (Fx) = first atom in the S-expression x. ]
∇ (Fx)→∘xx(F↑x)          [ end of definitions ]
```

```
F:          (∇(x)(→(∘x)x(F(↑x))))
```

```
(F'(((ab)c)d))               [ direct evaluation ]

expression  (F('(((ab)c)d)))
value       a
cycles      1435288
```

```
(V'(F'(((ab)c)d)),'F,F()) [ same thing but using V ]

expression  (V('(F('(((ab)c)d))))(,('F)(,F())))
display     (x(((ab)c)d)F(∇(x)(→(∘x)x(F(↑x)))))
display     (x((ab)c)x(((ab)c)d)F(∇(x)(→(∘x)x(F(↑x)))))
display     (x(ab)x((ab)c)x(((ab)c)d)F(∇(x)(→(∘x)x(F(↑x)))))
display     (xax(ab)x((ab)c)x(((ab)c)d)F(∇(x)(→(∘x)x(F(↑x)))))
value       a
cycles      719669821
```

```
End of LISP Run
```

Elapsed time is 856.554706 *seconds.*

3.5. LISP in LISP II

LISP Interpreter Run

```
[[[ Normal LISP semantics defined in "Sub-Atomic" LISP ]]]

[ (Vse) = value of S-expression s in environment e.
  If a new environment is created it is displayed. ]
∇ (Vse)
  →∘↑s           →=s↑e↑↓e (Vs↓↓e)
  →=↑s'(QUOTE) ↑↓s
  →=↑s'(ATOM)   →∘↑(V↑↓se)'(T)'(NIL)
  →=↑s'(CAR)    ↑(V↑↓se)
  →=↑s'(CDR)    ← x ↓(V↑↓se) →∘x'(NIL)x
  →=↑s'(OUT)    □(V↑↓se)
  →=↑s'(EQ)     →=(V↑↓se)(V↑↓↓se)'(T)'(NIL)
  →=↑s'(CONS)   ← x (V↑↓se) ← y (V↑↓↓se) →=y'(NIL) ,x() ,xy
  →=↑s'(COND)   →='(NIL)(V↑↓↓se) (V,↑s↓↓se) (V↑↓↓↓se)
  ← f  →∘↑↑s(V↑se)↑s      [ f is ((LAMBDA)((X)(Y))(BODY)) ]
  (V↑↓↓f□(N↑↓f↓se))       [ display new environment ]
```

```
V:        (∇(se)(→(∘(↑s))(→(=s(↑e))(↑(↓e))(Vs(↓(↓e))))(→(=(↑
          s)('(QUOTE)))(↑(↓s))(→(=(↑s)('(ATOM)))(→(∘(↑(V(↑(↓
          s))e)))('(T))('(NIL)))(→(=(↑s)('(CAR)))(↑(V(↑(↓s))
          e))(→(=(↑s)('(CDR)))(('(∇(x)(→(∘x)('(NIL))x)))(↓(V
          (↑(↓s))e)))(→(=(↑s)('(OUT)))(□(V(↑(↓s))e))(→(=(↑s)
          ('(EQ)))(→(=(V(↑(↓s))e)(V(↑(↓(↓s)))e))('(T))('(NIL
          )))(→(=(↑s)('(CONS)))(('(∇(x)(('(∇(y)(→(=y('(NIL))
          )(,x())(,xy))))(V(↑(↓(↓s)))e))))(V(↑(↓s))e))(→(=(↑
          s)('(COND)))(→(=(('(NIL))(V(↑(↑(↓s)))e))(V(,(↑s)(↓(
          ↓s)))e)(V(↑(↓(↑(↓s))))e))(('(∇(f)(V(↑(↓(↓f)))(□(N(
          ↑(↓f))(↓s)e)))))(→(∘(↑(↑s)))(V(↑s)e)(↑s)))))))))))
          ))
```

```
[ (Nxae) = new environment created from list of
  variables x, list of unevaluated arguments a, and
  previous environment e. ]
∇ (Nxae) →∘xe ,↑x,(V↑ae)(N↓x↓ae)
```

```
N:        (∇(xae)(→(∘x)e(,(↑x)(,(V(↑a)e)(N(↓x)(↓a)e)))))
```

```
[ FIRSTATOM
    ( LAMBDA  ( X )
       ( COND  (( ATOM    X ) X )
               (( QUOTE    T ) ( FIRSTATOM ( CAR   X )))))
]
∇ F '
((FIRSTATOM)
   ((LAMBDA) ((X))
```

```
        ((COND) (((ATOM)  (X)) (X))
              (((QUOTE) (T)) ((FIRSTATOM) ((CAR) (X))))))
)
```

expression   `('((FIRSTATOM)((LAMBDA)((X))((COND)(((ATOM)(X))(X)`
               `)(((QUOTE)(T))((FIRSTATOM)((CAR)(X))))))))`
F: `((FIRSTATOM)((LAMBDA)((X))((COND)(((ATOM)(X))(X))(`
               `((QUOTE)(T))((FIRSTATOM)((CAR)(X)))))))`


```
[ APPEND
    ( LAMBDA  ( X  Y )  ( COND  (( ATOM   X )  Y )
     (( QUOTE   T )  ( CONS  ( CAR   X )
                            ( APPEND  ( CDR  X )  Y )))))
]
∇ C '
((APPEND)
     ((LAMBDA)  ((X)(Y))  ((COND)  (((ATOM)  (X))  (Y))
     (((QUOTE)  (T))  ((CONS)  ((CAR)  (X))
                            ((APPEND)  ((CDR)  (X))  (Y))))))
)
```

expression   `('((APPEND)((LAMBDA)((X)(Y))((COND)(((ATOM)(X))(Y)`
               `)(((QUOTE)(T))((CONS)((CAR)(X))((APPEND)((CDR)(X))`
               `(Y)))))))))`
C: `((APPEND)((LAMBDA)((X)(Y))((COND)(((ATOM)(X))(Y))(`
               `((QUOTE)(T))((CONS)((CAR)(X))((APPEND)((CDR)(X))(Y`
               `)))))))`


```
(V'
((FIRSTATOM)  ((QUOTE)  ((((A)(B))(C))(D))))
F)
```

expression   `(V('((FIRSTATOM)((QUOTE)((((A)(B))(C))(D)))))F)`
display   `((X)((((A)(B))(C))(D))(FIRSTATOM)((LAMBDA)((X))((C`
               `OND)(((ATOM)(X))(X))(((QUOTE)(T))((FIRSTATOM)((CAR`
               `)(X)))))))`
display   `((X)(((A)(B))(C))(X)((((A)(B))(C))(D))(FIRSTATOM)(`
               `(LAMBDA)((X))((COND)(((ATOM)(X))(X))(((QUOTE)(T))(`
               `(FIRSTATOM)((CAR)(X)))))))`
display   `((X)((A)(B))(X)(((A)(B))(C))(X)((((A)(B))(C))(D))(`
               `FIRSTATOM)((LAMBDA)((X))((COND)(((ATOM)(X))(X))(((`
               `QUOTE)(T))((FIRSTATOM)((CAR)(X)))))))`
display   `((X)(A)(X)((A)(B))(X)(((A)(B))(C))(X)((((A)(B))(C)`
               `)(D))(FIRSTATOM)((LAMBDA)((X))((COND)(((ATOM)(X))(`
               `X))(((QUOTE)(T))((FIRSTATOM)((CAR)(X)))))))`
value   `(A)`


```
(V'
((APPEND)  ((QUOTE)((A)(B)(C)))  ((QUOTE)((D)(E)(F))))
C)
```

expression   `(V('((APPEND)((QUOTE)((A)(B)(C)))((QUOTE)((D)(E)(F`
               `)))))C)`
display   `((X)((A)(B)(C))(Y)((D)(E)(F))(APPEND)((LAMBDA)((X)`

```
            (Y))((COND)(((ATOM)(X))(Y))(((QUOTE)(T))((CONS)((C
            AR)(X))((APPEND)((CDR)(X))(Y))))))))
display     ((X)((B)(C))(Y)((D)(E)(F))(X)((A)(B)(C))(Y)((D)(E)
            (F))(APPEND)((LAMBDA)((X)(Y))((COND)(((ATOM)(X))(Y
            ))(((QUOTE)(T))((CONS)((CAR)(X))((APPEND)((CDR)(X)
            )(Y)))))))
display     ((X)((C))(Y)((D)(E)(F))(X)((B)(C))(Y)((D)(E)(F))(X
            )((A)(B)(C))(Y)((D)(E)(F))(APPEND)((LAMBDA)((X)(Y)
            )((COND)(((ATOM)(X))(Y))(((QUOTE)(T))((CONS)((CAR)
            (X))((APPEND)((CDR)(X))(Y)))))))
display     ((X)(NIL)(Y)((D)(E)(F))(X)((C))(Y)((D)(E)(F))(X)((
            B)(C))(Y)((D)(E)(F))(X)((A)(B)(C))(Y)((D)(E)(F))(A
            PPEND)((LAMBDA)((X)(Y))((COND)(((ATOM)(X))(Y))(((Q
            UOTE)(T))((CONS)((CAR)(X))((APPEND)((CDR)(X))(Y)))
            ))))
value       ((A)(B)(C)(D)(E)(F))

End of LISP Run

Elapsed time is 9.336304 seconds.
```

3.6. LISP in LISP III

LISP Interpreter Run

```
[[[ LISP semantics defined in LISP ]]]
[
  Permissive LISP:
  head & tail of atom = atom,
  join of x with nonzero atom = x,
  initially all atoms evaluate to self,
  only depth exceeded failure!

  (Vsed) =
  value of S-expression s in environment e within depth d.
  If a new environment is created it is displayed.

  d is a natural number which must be decremented
  at each call.  And if it reaches zero, evaluation aborts.
  If depth is exceeded, V returns a special failure value $.
  Evaluation cannot fail any other way!
  Normally, when get value v, if bad will return it as is:
  →=$vv
  To stop unwinding,
  one must convert $ to ? & wrap good v in ()'s.
]
∇ (Vsed)
  →∘ s ← (Ae)  →∘e s →=s↑e↑↓e (A↓↓e)
                [ A is "Assoc" ]
        (Ae)       [ evaluate atom; if not in e, evals to self ]
  ← f (V↑sed)      [ evaluate the function f ]
  →=$ff            [ if evaluation of function failed, give up ]
  →=f"'  ↑↓s       [ do "quote" ]
  →=f"→  ← p (V↑↓sed) →=$pp →=0p (V↑↓↓↓sed) (V↑↓↓sed)
```

```
                    [ do "if" ]
  ←  (Wl)  →∘ll ← x (V↑led) →=$xx ← y (W↓l) →=$yy ,xy
                    [ W is "Evalst" ]
  ← a (W↓s)        [ a is the list of argument values ]
  →=$aa            [ evaluation of arguments failed, give up ]
  ← x ↑a           [ pick up first argument ]
  ← y ↑↓a          [ pick up second argument ]
  →=f"⊼ (Vx()d)    [ do "eval"; use fresh environment ]
  →=f"⚩            [ do "depth-limited eval" ]
     ← (≤ij)  →∘i1 →∘j0 (≤↓i↓j)
                    [ natural # i is less than or equal to j ]
     →(≤dx) ← v (Vy()d) →=$vv ,v()
                    [ old depth more limiting; keep unwinding ]
            ← v (Vy()x) →=$v? ,v()
                    [ new depth limit more limiting;
                      stop unwinding ]
  →=f"∘ ∘x         [ do "atom"  ]
  →=f"↑ ↑x         [ do "head"  ]
  →=f"↓ ↓x         [ do "tail"  ]
  →=f"□ □x         [ do "out"   ]
  →=f"= =xy        [ do "eq"    ]
  →=f", ,xy        [ do "join"  ]
                    [ do function definition ]
  →∘d   $          [ fail if depth already zero ]
  ← (Bxa) →∘xe ,↑x,↑a(B↓x↓a)
                    [ B is "Bind" ]
  (V↑↓↓f□(B↑↓fa)↓d)  [ decrement d & display new environment ]
```

```
V:            (∇(sed)(→(∘s)(('(∇(A)(Ae)))('(∇(e)(→(∘e)s(→(=s(↑e)
              )(↑(↓e))(A(↓(↓e)))))))))(('(∇(f)(→(=$f)f(→(=f')(↑(↓
              s))(→(=f→)(('(∇(p)(→(=$p)p(→(=0p)(V(↑(↓(↓(↓s))))ed
              )(V(↑(↓(↓s)))ed)))))(V(↑(↓s))ed))(('(∇(W)(('(∇(a)(
              →(=$a)a(('(∇(x)(('(∇(y)(→(=f⊼)(Vx()d)(→(=f⚩)(('(∇(
              ≤)(→(≤dx)(('(∇(v)(→(=$v)v(,v())))))(Vy()d))(('(∇(v)
              (→(=$v)?(,v())))))(Vy()x)))))('(∇(ij)(→(∘i)1(→(∘j)0
              (≤(↓i)(↓j)))))))))(→(=f∘)(∘x)(→(=f↑)(↑x)(→(=f↓)(↓x)(
              →(=f□)(□x)(→(=f=)(=xy)(→(=f,)(,xy)(→(∘d)$(('(∇(B)(
              V(↑(↓(↓f)))(□(B(↑(↓f))a))(↓d))))('(∇(xa)(→(∘x)e(,(
              ↑x)(,(↑a)(B(↓x)(↓a)))))))))))))))))))))))(↑(↓a))))(↑a
              )))))(W(↓s)))))('(∇(l)(→(∘l)1((('(∇(x)(→(=$x)x(('(∇
              (y)(→(=$y)y(,xy))))(W(↓l))))))(V(↑l)ed))))))))))))))(
              V(↑s)ed))))
```

```
[ Test function (Cxy) = concatenate list x and list y. ]

[ Define environment for concatenation. ]
∇ E '( C ∇(xy) →∘xy ,↑x(C↓xy) )

expression  ('(C(∇(xy)(→(∘x)y(,(↑x)(C(↓x)y))))))))
E:          (C(∇(xy)(→(∘x)y(,(↑x)(C(↓x)y)))))

(V '(C'(ab)'(cd)) E '())

expression  (V('(C('(ab))('(cd))))E('()))
value       $
```

```
(V '(C'(ab)'(cd)) E '(1))

expression  (V('(C('(ab))('(cd))))E('(1)))
display     (x(ab)y(cd)C(∇(xy)(→(∘x)y(,(↑x)(C(↓x)y)))))
value       $

(V '(C'(ab)'(cd)) E '(11))

expression  (V('(C('(ab))('(cd))))E('(11)))
display     (x(ab)y(cd)C(∇(xy)(→(∘x)y(,(↑x)(C(↓x)y)))))
display     (x(b)y(cd)x(ab)y(cd)C(∇(xy)(→(∘x)y(,(↑x)(C(↓x)y)))
            ))
value       $

(V '(C'(ab)'(cd)) E '(111))

expression  (V('(C('(ab))('(cd))))E('(111)))
display     (x(ab)y(cd)C(∇(xy)(→(∘x)y(,(↑x)(C(↓x)y)))))
display     (x(b)y(cd)x(ab)y(cd)C(∇(xy)(→(∘x)y(,(↑x)(C(↓x)y)))
            ))
display     (x()y(cd)x(b)y(cd)x(ab)y(cd)C(∇(xy)(→(∘x)y(,(↑x)(C
            (↓x)y)))))
value       (abcd)

End of LISP Run

Elapsed time is 7.858155 seconds.
```

CHAPTER 4

THE LISP INTERPRETER EVAL

In this chapter we convert the definition of LISP in LISP given in Section 3.6 into a register machine program. Then we compile this register machine program into an exponential diophantine equation.

4.1. Register Machine Pseudo-Instructions

The first step to program an interpreter for our version of pure LISP is to write subroutines for breaking S-expressions apart (SPLIT) and for putting them back together again (JOIN). The next step is to use SPLIT and JOIN to write routines that push and pop the interpreter stack. Then we can raise the level of discourse by defining register machine pseudo-instructions which are expanded by the assembler into calls to these routines; i.e., we extend register machine language with pseudo-machine instructions which expand into several real machine instructions. Thus we have four "microcode" subroutines: SPLIT, JOIN, PUSH, and POP. SPLIT and JOIN are leaf routines, and PUSH and POP call SPLIT and JOIN.

 Figure 9 is a table giving the twelve register machine pseudo-instructions.

 Now a few words about register usage; there are only 19 registers! First of all, the S-expression to be evaluated is input in EXPRESSION, and the value of this S-expression is output in VALUE. There are three large permanent data structures used by the interpreter:

1. the association list ALIST which contains all variable bindings,
2. the interpreter STACK used for saving and restoring information when the interpreter calls itself, and
3. the current remaining DEPTH limit on evaluations.

All other registers are either temporary scratch registers used by the interpreter (FUNCTION, ARGUMENTS, VARIABLES, X, and Y), or hidden registers used by the microcode rather than directly by the interpreter. These hidden registers include:

1. the two in-boxes and two out-boxes for micro-routines: SOURCE, SOURCE2, TARGET, and TARGET2,
2. the two scratch registers for pseudo-instruction expansion and micro-routines: WORK and PARENS, and
3. the three registers for return addresses from subroutine calls: LINKREG, LINKREG2, and LINKREG3

Section 4.2 is a complete listing of the register machine pseudo-code for the interpreter, and the 306 real register machine instructions that are generated by the assembler from the pseudo-code. A few words of explanation: Register machine pseudo-instructions that declare a register name or instruction label start flush left, and so do comments. Other pseudo-instructions are indented 2 spaces. The operands of pseudo-instructions are always separated by commas. The real register machine instructions generated from these pseudo-instructions are indented 6 spaces. Their operands are separated by spaces instead of commas. And real instructions always start with a label and a colon.

Section 4.3 is the summary information produced at the end of the compilation of the interpreter into an exponential diophantine equation, including the name of each of the 16962 variables in the equation. Section

Fig 9. Register Machine Pseudo-Instructions: In the table below source registers all start with an S, and target registers with a T. "Head," "tail," and "join" refer to the LISP primitive functions applied to the binary representations of S-expressions, as defined in Figure 4.

```
*  Comment              Comment is ignored; for documentation only.
R  REGISTER             Declare the name of a machine register.
L  LABEL                Declare the name of the next instruction.
   SPLIT    T1,T2,S     Put the head and tail of S into T1 and T2.
   HD       T,S         Put the head of S into T.
   TL       T,S         Put the tail of S into T.
   EMPTY    T           Set T to be the empty list ().
   ATOM     S,L         Branch to L if S contains an atom.
   JN       T,S1,S2     Join S1 to S2 and put the result into T.
   PUSH     S           Push S into the STACK.
                        (This is equivalent to JN STACK,S,STACK.)
   POP      T           Pop T from the STACK.
                        (This is equivalent to POPL T,STACK.)
   POPL     T,S         Pop T from the list S:
                        put the head of S into T and then
                        replace S by its tail.
```

4.4 is the first five thousand characters of the left-hand side of the resulting equation, and Section 4.5 is the last five thousand characters of the right-hand side of the equation. Unfortunately we are forced to only give these excerpts; the full compiler log and equation are available from the author.[9]

4.2. EVAL in Register Machine Language

```
*
* The LISP Machine! .....................................
*
* input in EXPRESSION, output in VALUE
  EMPTY ALIST                    initial association list
       L1: SET ALIST C')'
       L2: LEFT ALIST C'('
  SET STACK,ALIST                empty stack
       L3: SET STACK ALIST
  SET DEPTH,C'_'                 no depth limit
       L4: SET DEPTH C'_'
  JUMP LINKREG,EVAL              evaluate expression
       L5: JUMP LINKREG EVAL
  HALT                           finished !
       L6: HALT
*
* Recursive Return .................................
*
RETURNQ LABEL
  SET VALUE,C'?'
       RETURNQ: SET VALUE C'?'
  GOTO UNWIND
       L8: GOTO UNWIND
*
RETURN0 LABEL
  SET VALUE,C'0'
       RETURN0: SET VALUE C'0'
  GOTO UNWIND
       L10: GOTO UNWIND
*
RETURN1 LABEL
  SET VALUE,C'1'
       RETURN1: SET VALUE C'1'
*
UNWIND LABEL
  POP LINKREG                    pop return address
       UNWIND: JUMP LINKREG2 POP_ROUTINE
       L13: SET LINKREG TARGET
  GOBACK LINKREG
       L14: GOBACK LINKREG
*
* Recursive Call .................................
```

---

9   "The Complete Arithmetization of EVAL," February 18th, 1987, 292 pp.

```
*
EVAL LABEL
   PUSH LINKREG                    push return address
      EVAL: SET SOURCE LINKREG
      L16: JUMP LINKREG2 PUSH_ROUTINE
   ATOM EXPRESSION,EXPRESSION_IS_ATOM
      L17: NEQ EXPRESSION C'(' EXPRESSION_IS_ATOM
      L18: SET WORK EXPRESSION
      L19: RIGHT WORK
      L20: EQ WORK C')' EXPRESSION_IS_ATOM
   GOTO EXPRESSION_ISNT_ATOM
      L21: GOTO EXPRESSION_ISNT_ATOM
*
EXPRESSION_IS_ATOM LABEL
   SET X,ALIST                     copy alist
      EXPRESSION_IS_ATOM: SET X ALIST
ALIST_SEARCH LABEL
   SET VALUE,EXPRESSION            variable not in alist
      ALIST_SEARCH: SET VALUE EXPRESSION
   ATOM X,UNWIND                   evaluates to self
      L24: NEQ X C'(' UNWIND
      L25: SET WORK X
      L26: RIGHT WORK
      L27: EQ WORK C')' UNWIND
   POPL Y,X                        pick up variable
      L28: SET SOURCE X
      L29: JUMP LINKREG3 SPLIT_ROUTINE
      L30: SET Y TARGET
      L31: SET X TARGET2
   POPL VALUE,X                    pick up its value
      L32: SET SOURCE X
      L33: JUMP LINKREG3 SPLIT_ROUTINE
      L34: SET VALUE TARGET
      L35: SET X TARGET2
   EQ EXPRESSION,Y,UNWIND          right one ?
      L36: EQ EXPRESSION Y UNWIND
   GOTO ALIST_SEARCH
      L37: GOTO ALIST_SEARCH
*
EXPRESSION_ISNT_ATOM LABEL    expression is not atom
   SPLIT EXPRESSION,ARGUMENTS,EXPRESSION
*                               split into function & arguments
      EXPRESSION_ISNT_ATOM: SET SOURCE EXPRESSION
      L39: JUMP LINKREG3 SPLIT_ROUTINE
      L40: SET EXPRESSION TARGET
      L41: SET ARGUMENTS TARGET2
   PUSH ARGUMENTS                  push arguments
      L42: SET SOURCE ARGUMENTS
      L43: JUMP LINKREG2 PUSH_ROUTINE
   JUMP LINKREG,EVAL               evaluate function
      L44: JUMP LINKREG EVAL
   POP ARGUMENTS                   pop arguments
      L45: JUMP LINKREG2 POP_ROUTINE
      L46: SET ARGUMENTS TARGET
   EQ VALUE,C')',UNWIND            abort ?
      L47: EQ VALUE C')' UNWIND
   SET FUNCTION,VALUE              remember value of function
```

```
          L48: SET FUNCTION VALUE
*
* Quote ...........................................................
*
   NEQ FUNCTION,C'''',NOT_QUOTE
          L49: NEQ FUNCTION C'''' NOT_QUOTE
*                                    ' Quote
   HD VALUE,ARGUMENTS              return argument "as is"
          L50: SET SOURCE ARGUMENTS
          L51: JUMP LINKREG3 SPLIT_ROUTINE
          L52: SET VALUE TARGET
   GOTO UNWIND
          L53: GOTO UNWIND
*
NOT_QUOTE LABEL
*
* If .............................................................
*
   NEQ FUNCTION,C'→',NOT_IF_THEN_ELSE
          NOT_QUOTE: NEQ FUNCTION C'→' NOT_IF_THEN_ELSE
*                                    → If
   POPL EXPRESSION,ARGUMENTS  pick up "if" clause
          L55: SET SOURCE ARGUMENTS
          L56: JUMP LINKREG3 SPLIT_ROUTINE
          L57: SET EXPRESSION TARGET
          L58: SET ARGUMENTS TARGET2
   PUSH ARGUMENTS                remember "then" & "else" clauses
          L59: SET SOURCE ARGUMENTS
          L60: JUMP LINKREG2 PUSH_ROUTINE
   JUMP LINKREG,EVAL            evaluate predicate
          L61: JUMP LINKREG EVAL
   POP ARGUMENTS                pick up "then" & "else" clauses
          L62: JUMP LINKREG2 POP_ROUTINE
          L63: SET ARGUMENTS TARGET
   EQ VALUE,C')',UNWIND         abort ?
          L64: EQ VALUE C')' UNWIND
   NEQ VALUE,C'0',THEN_CLAUSE predicate considered true
*                                 if not 0
          L65: NEQ VALUE C'0' THEN_CLAUSE
   TL ARGUMENTS,ARGUMENTS       if false, skip "then" clause
          L66: SET SOURCE ARGUMENTS
          L67: JUMP LINKREG3 SPLIT_ROUTINE
          L68: SET ARGUMENTS TARGET2
THEN_CLAUSE LABEL
   HD EXPRESSION,ARGUMENTS      pick up "then" or "else" clause
          THEN_CLAUSE: SET SOURCE ARGUMENTS
          L70: JUMP LINKREG3 SPLIT_ROUTINE
          L71: SET EXPRESSION TARGET
   JUMP LINKREG,EVAL            evaluate it
          L72: JUMP LINKREG EVAL
   GOTO UNWIND                  return value "as is"
          L73: GOTO UNWIND
*
NOT_IF_THEN_ELSE LABEL
*
* Evaluate Arguments .........................................
*
```

```
    PUSH FUNCTION
        NOT_IF_THEN_ELSE: SET SOURCE FUNCTION
        L75: JUMP LINKREG2 PUSH_ROUTINE
    JUMP LINKREG,EVALST
        L76: JUMP LINKREG EVALST
    POP FUNCTION
        L77: JUMP LINKREG2 POP_ROUTINE
        L78: SET FUNCTION TARGET
    EQ VALUE,C')',UNWIND          abort ?
        L79: EQ VALUE C')' UNWIND
    SET ARGUMENTS,VALUE           remember argument values
        L80: SET ARGUMENTS VALUE
    SPLIT X,Y,ARGUMENTS           pick up first argument in x
        L81: SET SOURCE ARGUMENTS
        L82: JUMP LINKREG3 SPLIT_ROUTINE
        L83: SET X TARGET
        L84: SET Y TARGET2
    HD Y,Y                        & second argument in y
        L85: SET SOURCE Y
        L86: JUMP LINKREG3 SPLIT_ROUTINE
        L87: SET Y TARGET
*
* Eval ....................................................
*
    NEQ FUNCTION,C'₮',NOT_EVAL
        L88: NEQ FUNCTION C'₮' NOT_EVAL
*                                 ₮ Eval
    SET EXPRESSION,X              pick up argument
        L89: SET EXPRESSION X
    PUSH ALIST                   push alist
        L90: SET SOURCE ALIST
        L91: JUMP LINKREG2 PUSH_ROUTINE
    EMPTY ALIST                  fresh environment
        L92: SET ALIST C')'
        L93: LEFT ALIST C'('
    JUMP LINKREG,EVAL            evaluate argument again
        L94: JUMP LINKREG EVAL
    POP ALIST                    restore old environment
        L95: JUMP LINKREG2 POP_ROUTINE
        L96: SET ALIST TARGET
    GOTO UNWIND
        L97: GOTO UNWIND
*
NOT_EVAL LABEL
*
* Evald ...................................................
*
    NEQ FUNCTION,C'♠',NOT_EVALD
        NOT_EVAL: NEQ FUNCTION C'♠' NOT_EVALD
*                                 ♠ Eval depth limited
    SET VALUE,X                  pick up first argument
        L99: SET VALUE X
    SET EXPRESSION,Y             pick up second argument
        L100: SET EXPRESSION Y
* First argument of ♠ is in VALUE and
* second argument of ♠ is in EXPRESSION.
* First argument is new depth limit and
```

```
* second argument is expression to safely eval.
  PUSH ALIST                     save old environment
      L101: SET SOURCE ALIST
      L102: JUMP LINKREG2 PUSH_ROUTINE
  EMPTY ALIST                    fresh environment
      L103: SET ALIST C')'
      L104: LEFT ALIST C'('
* Decide whether old or new depth restriction is stronger
  SET X,DEPTH                    pick up old depth limit
      L105: SET X DEPTH
  SET Y,VALUE                    pick up new depth limit
      L106: SET Y VALUE
  EQ X,C'_',NEW_DEPTH            no previous limit,
*                                so switch to new one
      L107: EQ X C'_' NEW_DEPTH
CHOOSE LABEL
  ATOM X,OLD_DEPTH               old limit smaller, so keep it
      CHOOSE: NEQ X C'(' OLD_DEPTH
      L109: SET WORK X
      L110: RIGHT WORK
      L111: EQ WORK C')' OLD_DEPTH
  ATOM Y,NEW_DEPTH               new limit smaller, so switch
      L112: NEQ Y C'(' NEW_DEPTH
      L113: SET WORK Y
      L114: RIGHT WORK
      L115: EQ WORK C')' NEW_DEPTH
  TL X,X
      L116: SET SOURCE X
      L117: JUMP LINKREG3 SPLIT_ROUTINE
      L118: SET X TARGET2
  TL Y,Y
      L119: SET SOURCE Y
      L120: JUMP LINKREG3 SPLIT_ROUTINE
      L121: SET Y TARGET2
  GOTO CHOOSE
      L122: GOTO CHOOSE
*
NEW_DEPTH LABEL                  NEW depth limit more restrictive
  PUSH DEPTH                     push old depth
      NEW_DEPTH: SET SOURCE DEPTH
      L124: JUMP LINKREG2 PUSH_ROUTINE
  SET DEPTH,VALUE                pick up new depth
      L125: SET DEPTH VALUE
  NEQ DEPTH,C'_',DEPTH_OKAY
      L126: NEQ DEPTH C'_' DEPTH_OKAY
  SET DEPTH,C'0'                 only top level has no depth limit
      L127: SET DEPTH C'0'
DEPTH_OKAY LABEL
  JUMP LINKREG,EVAL              evaluate second argument
*                                of ⚫ again
      DEPTH_OKAY: JUMP LINKREG EVAL
  POP DEPTH                      restore old depth
      L129: JUMP LINKREG2 POP_ROUTINE
      L130: SET DEPTH TARGET
  POP ALIST                      restore environment
      L131: JUMP LINKREG2 POP_ROUTINE
      L132: SET ALIST TARGET
```

```
    EQ VALUE,C')',RETURNQ        convert "no value" to ?
        L133: EQ VALUE C')' RETURNQ
WRAP LABEL
  EMPTY SOURCE2
        WRAP: SET SOURCE2 C')'
        L135: LEFT SOURCE2 C'('
  JN VALUE,VALUE,SOURCE2          wrap good value in parentheses
        L136: SET SOURCE VALUE
        L137: JUMP LINKREG3 JN_ROUTINE
        L138: SET VALUE TARGET
    GOTO UNWIND
        L139: GOTO UNWIND
*
OLD_DEPTH LABEL                   OLD depth limit more restrictive
    JUMP LINKREG,EVAL            evaluate second argument
*                                of ⌑ again
        OLD_DEPTH: JUMP LINKREG EVAL
    POP ALIST                    restore environment
        L141: JUMP LINKREG2 POP_ROUTINE
        L142: SET ALIST TARGET
    EQ VALUE,C')',UNWIND          if bad value, keep unwinding
        L143: EQ VALUE C')' UNWIND
    GOTO WRAP                    wrap good value in parentheses
        L144: GOTO WRAP
*
NOT_EVALD LABEL
*
* Atom & Equal ...........................................
*
    NEQ FUNCTION,C'∘',NOT_ATOM
        NOT_EVALD: NEQ FUNCTION C'∘' NOT_ATOM
*                                    ∘ Atom
    ATOM X,RETURN1                if argument is atomic return true
        L146: NEQ X C'(' RETURN1
        L147: SET WORK X
        L148: RIGHT WORK
        L149: EQ WORK C')' RETURN1
    GOTO RETURN0                 otherwise return nil
        L150: GOTO RETURN0
*
NOT_ATOM LABEL
*
    NEQ FUNCTION,C'=',NOT_EQUAL
        NOT_ATOM: NEQ FUNCTION C'=' NOT_EQUAL
*                                    = Equal
COMPARE LABEL
  NEQ X,Y,RETURN0               not equal !
        COMPARE: NEQ X Y RETURN0
  RIGHT X
        L153: RIGHT X
  RIGHT Y
        L154: RIGHT Y
  NEQ X,X'00',COMPARE
        L155: NEQ X X'00' COMPARE
  GOTO RETURN1                 equal !
        L156: GOTO RETURN1
*
```

```
NOT_EQUAL LABEL
*
* Head, Tail & Join ........................................
*
  SPLIT TARGET,TARGET2,X      get head & tail of argument
      NOT_EQUAL: SET SOURCE X
      L158: JUMP LINKREG3 SPLIT_ROUTINE
  SET VALUE,TARGET
      L159: SET VALUE TARGET
  EQ FUNCTION,C'↑',UNWIND      ↑ pick Head
      L160: EQ FUNCTION C'↑' UNWIND
  SET VALUE,TARGET2
      L161: SET VALUE TARGET2
  EQ FUNCTION,C'↓',UNWIND      ↓ pick Tail
      L162: EQ FUNCTION C'↓' UNWIND
*
  JN VALUE,X,Y                , Join first argument
*                               to second argument
      L163: SET SOURCE X
      L164: SET SOURCE2 Y
      L165: JUMP LINKREG3 JN_ROUTINE
      L166: SET VALUE TARGET
  EQ FUNCTION,C',',UNWIND
      L167: EQ FUNCTION C',' UNWIND
*
* Output ...................................................
*
  NEQ FUNCTION,C'☐',NOT_OUTPUT
      L168: NEQ FUNCTION C'☐' NOT_OUTPUT
*                               ☐ Output
  OUT X                        write argument
      L169: OUT X
  SET VALUE,X                  identity function!
      L170: SET VALUE X
  GOTO UNWIND
      L171: GOTO UNWIND
*
NOT_OUTPUT LABEL
*
* Defined Function .........................................
*
* Decrement Depth Limit
*
  EQ DEPTH,C'_',NO_LIMIT
      NOT_OUTPUT: EQ DEPTH C'_' NO_LIMIT
  SET VALUE,C')'
      L173: SET VALUE C')'
  ATOM DEPTH,UNWIND            if limit exceeded, unwind
      L174: NEQ DEPTH C'(' UNWIND
      L175: SET WORK DEPTH
      L176: RIGHT WORK
      L177: EQ WORK C')' UNWIND
NO_LIMIT LABEL
  PUSH DEPTH                   push limit before decrementing it
      NO_LIMIT: SET SOURCE DEPTH
      L179: JUMP LINKREG2 PUSH_ROUTINE
  TL DEPTH,DEPTH               decrement it
```

```
          L180: SET SOURCE DEPTH
          L181: JUMP LINKREG3 SPLIT_ROUTINE
          L182: SET DEPTH TARGET2
*
*  Bind
*
   TL FUNCTION,FUNCTION            throw away ▽
          L183: SET SOURCE FUNCTION
          L184: JUMP LINKREG3 SPLIT_ROUTINE
          L185: SET FUNCTION TARGET2
   POPL VARIABLES,FUNCTION     pick up variables
*                              from function definition
          L186: SET SOURCE FUNCTION
          L187: JUMP LINKREG3 SPLIT_ROUTINE
          L188: SET VARIABLES TARGET
          L189: SET FUNCTION TARGET2
   PUSH ALIST                     save environment
          L190: SET SOURCE ALIST
          L191: JUMP LINKREG2 PUSH_ROUTINE
   JUMP LINKREG,BIND              new environment
*                                 (preserves function)
          L192: JUMP LINKREG BIND
*
*  Evaluate Body
*
   HD EXPRESSION,FUNCTION      pick up body of function
          L193: SET SOURCE FUNCTION
          L194: JUMP LINKREG3 SPLIT_ROUTINE
          L195: SET EXPRESSION TARGET
   JUMP LINKREG,EVAL              evaluate body
          L196: JUMP LINKREG EVAL
*
*  Unbind
*
   POP ALIST                      restore environment
          L197: JUMP LINKREG2 POP_ROUTINE
          L198: SET ALIST TARGET
   POP DEPTH                      restore previous depth limit
          L199: JUMP LINKREG2 POP_ROUTINE
          L200: SET DEPTH TARGET
   GOTO UNWIND
          L201: GOTO UNWIND
*
*  Evalst .................................................
*
*  input in ARGUMENTS, output in VALUE
EVALST LABEL                      loop to eval arguments
   PUSH LINKREG                   push return address
          EVALST: SET SOURCE LINKREG
          L203: JUMP LINKREG2 PUSH_ROUTINE
   SET VALUE,ARGUMENTS            null argument list has
          L204: SET VALUE ARGUMENTS
   ATOM ARGUMENTS,UNWIND          null list of values
          L205: NEQ ARGUMENTS C'(' UNWIND
          L206: SET WORK ARGUMENTS
          L207: RIGHT WORK
          L208: EQ WORK C')' UNWIND
```

```
POPL EXPRESSION,ARGUMENTS   pick up next argument
    L209: SET SOURCE ARGUMENTS
    L210: JUMP LINKREG3 SPLIT_ROUTINE
    L211: SET EXPRESSION TARGET
    L212: SET ARGUMENTS TARGET2
PUSH ARGUMENTS              push remaining arguments
    L213: SET SOURCE ARGUMENTS
    L214: JUMP LINKREG2 PUSH_ROUTINE
JUMP LINKREG,EVAL           evaluate first argument
    L215: JUMP LINKREG EVAL
POP ARGUMENTS              pop remaining arguments
    L216: JUMP LINKREG2 POP_ROUTINE
    L217: SET ARGUMENTS TARGET
EQ VALUE,C')',UNWIND        abort ?
    L218: EQ VALUE C')' UNWIND
PUSH VALUE                 push value of first argument
    L219: SET SOURCE VALUE
    L220: JUMP LINKREG2 PUSH_ROUTINE
JUMP LINKREG,EVALST         evaluate remaining arguments
    L221: JUMP LINKREG EVALST
POP X                      pop value of first argument
    L222: JUMP LINKREG2 POP_ROUTINE
    L223: SET X TARGET
EQ VALUE,C')',UNWIND        abort ?
    L224: EQ VALUE C')' UNWIND
JN VALUE,X,VALUE           add first value to rest
    L225: SET SOURCE X
    L226: SET SOURCE2 VALUE
    L227: JUMP LINKREG3 JN_ROUTINE
    L228: SET VALUE TARGET
GOTO UNWIND
    L229: GOTO UNWIND
*
* Bind ...................................................................
*
* input in VARIABLES, ARGUMENTS, ALIST, output in ALIST
BIND LABEL                 must not ruin FUNCTION
  PUSH LINKREG
    BIND: SET SOURCE LINKREG
    L231: JUMP LINKREG2 PUSH_ROUTINE
ATOM VARIABLES,UNWIND       any variables left to bind?
    L232: NEQ VARIABLES C'(' UNWIND
    L233: SET WORK VARIABLES
    L234: RIGHT WORK
    L235: EQ WORK C')' UNWIND
POPL X,VARIABLES           pick up variable
    L236: SET SOURCE VARIABLES
    L237: JUMP LINKREG3 SPLIT_ROUTINE
    L238: SET X TARGET
    L239: SET VARIABLES TARGET2
PUSH X                     save it
    L240: SET SOURCE X
    L241: JUMP LINKREG2 PUSH_ROUTINE
POPL X,ARGUMENTS           pick up argument value
    L242: SET SOURCE ARGUMENTS
    L243: JUMP LINKREG3 SPLIT_ROUTINE
    L244: SET X TARGET
```

```
    L245: SET ARGUMENTS TARGET2
PUSH X                          save it
    L246: SET SOURCE X
    L247: JUMP LINKREG2 PUSH_ROUTINE
JUMP LINKREG,BIND
    L248: JUMP LINKREG BIND
POP X                           pop value
    L249: JUMP LINKREG2 POP_ROUTINE
    L250: SET X TARGET
JN ALIST,X,ALIST                (value ALIST)
    L251: SET SOURCE X
    L252: SET SOURCE2 ALIST
    L253: JUMP LINKREG3 JN_ROUTINE
    L254: SET ALIST TARGET
POP X                           pop variable
    L255: JUMP LINKREG2 POP_ROUTINE
    L256: SET X TARGET
JN ALIST,X,ALIST                (variable value ALIST)
    L257: SET SOURCE X
    L258: SET SOURCE2 ALIST
    L259: JUMP LINKREG3 JN_ROUTINE
    L260: SET ALIST TARGET
GOTO UNWIND
    L261: GOTO UNWIND
*
* Push & Pop Stack .........................................
*
PUSH_ROUTINE LABEL              input in source
  JN STACK,SOURCE,STACK         stack = join source to stack
    PUSH_ROUTINE: SET SOURCE2 STACK
    L263: JUMP LINKREG3 JN_ROUTINE
    L264: SET STACK TARGET
  GOBACK LINKREG2
    L265: GOBACK LINKREG2
*
POP_ROUTINE LABEL               output in target
  SPLIT TARGET,STACK,STACK      target = head of stack
    POP_ROUTINE: SET SOURCE STACK
    L267: JUMP LINKREG3 SPLIT_ROUTINE
    L268: SET STACK TARGET2
  GOBACK LINKREG2               stack  = tail of stack
    L269: GOBACK LINKREG2
*
* Split S-exp into Head & Tail ..............................
*
SPLIT_ROUTINE LABEL             input in source,
*                               output in target & target2
  SET TARGET,SOURCE             is argument atomic ?
    SPLIT_ROUTINE: SET TARGET SOURCE
  SET TARGET2,SOURCE            if so, its head & its tail
    L271: SET TARGET2 SOURCE
  ATOM SOURCE,SPLIT_EXIT        are just the argument itself
    L272: NEQ SOURCE C'(' SPLIT_EXIT
    L273: SET WORK SOURCE
    L274: RIGHT WORK
    L275: EQ WORK C')' SPLIT_EXIT
  SET TARGET,X'00'
```

```
      L276: SET TARGET X'00'
   SET TARGET2,X'00'
      L277: SET TARGET2 X'00'
*
   RIGHT SOURCE                  skip initial ( of source
      L278: RIGHT SOURCE
   SET WORK,X'00'
      L279: SET WORK X'00'
   SET PARENS,X'00'              p = 0
      L280: SET PARENS X'00'
*
COPY_HD LABEL
   NEQ SOURCE,C'(',NOT_LPAR    if (
      COPY_HD: NEQ SOURCE C'(' NOT_LPAR
   LEFT PARENS,C'1'             then p = p + 1
      L282: LEFT PARENS C'1'
NOT_LPAR LABEL
   NEQ SOURCE,C')',NOT_RPAR    if )
      NOT_LPAR: NEQ SOURCE C')' NOT_RPAR
   RIGHT PARENS                 then p = p - 1
      L284: RIGHT PARENS
NOT_RPAR LABEL
   LEFT WORK,SOURCE             copy head of source
      NOT_RPAR: LEFT WORK SOURCE
   EQ PARENS,C'1',COPY_HD       continue if p ≠ 0
      L286: EQ PARENS C'1' COPY_HD
*
REVERSE_HD LABEL
   LEFT TARGET,WORK              reverse result into target
      REVERSE_HD: LEFT TARGET WORK
   NEQ WORK,X'00',REVERSE_HD
      L288: NEQ WORK X'00' REVERSE_HD
*
   SET WORK,C'('                initial ( of tail
      L289: SET WORK C'('
COPY_TL LABEL
   LEFT WORK,SOURCE             copy tail of source
      COPY_TL: LEFT WORK SOURCE
   NEQ SOURCE,X'00',COPY_TL
      L291: NEQ SOURCE X'00' COPY_TL
*
REVERSE_TL LABEL
   LEFT TARGET2,WORK            reverse result into target2
      REVERSE_TL: LEFT TARGET2 WORK
   NEQ WORK,X'00',REVERSE_TL
      L293: NEQ WORK X'00' REVERSE_TL
*
SPLIT_EXIT LABEL
   GOBACK LINKREG3              return
      SPLIT_EXIT: GOBACK LINKREG3
*
* Join X & Y ...............................................
*
JN_ROUTINE LABEL                 input in source & source2,
*                                output in target
   SET TARGET,SOURCE
      JN_ROUTINE: SET TARGET SOURCE
```

```
      NEQ SOURCE2,C'(',JN_EXIT    is source2 a list ?
          L296: NEQ SOURCE2 C'(' JN_EXIT
      SET TARGET,X'00'            if not, join is just source1
          L297: SET TARGET X'00'
*
      SET WORK,X'00'
          L298: SET WORK X'00'
      LEFT WORK,SOURCE2           copy ( at beginning of source2
          L299: LEFT WORK SOURCE2
*
COPY1 LABEL
      LEFT WORK,SOURCE            copy source1
          COPY1: LEFT WORK SOURCE
      NEQ SOURCE,X'00',COPY1
          L301: NEQ SOURCE X'00' COPY1
*
COPY2 LABEL
      LEFT WORK,SOURCE2           copy rest of source2
          COPY2: LEFT WORK SOURCE2
      NEQ SOURCE2,X'00',COPY2
          L303: NEQ SOURCE2 X'00' COPY2
*
REVERSE LABEL
      LEFT TARGET,WORK            reverse result
          REVERSE: LEFT TARGET WORK
      NEQ WORK,X'00',REVERSE
          L305: NEQ WORK X'00' REVERSE
*
JN_EXIT LABEL
      GOBACK LINKREG3             return
          JN_EXIT: GOBACK LINKREG3
*
* Declare Registers .......................................
*
EXPRESSION REGISTER
VALUE REGISTER
ALIST REGISTER
STACK REGISTER
DEPTH REGISTER
FUNCTION REGISTER
ARGUMENTS REGISTER
VARIABLES REGISTER
X REGISTER
Y REGISTER
SOURCE REGISTER
SOURCE2 REGISTER
TARGET REGISTER
TARGET2 REGISTER
WORK REGISTER
PARENS REGISTER
LINKREG REGISTER
LINKREG2 REGISTER
LINKREG3 REGISTER
*
```

4.3. The Arithmetization of EVAL: Summary Information

```
Number of labels in program.....   306
Number of registers in program..   19

Number of equations generated...   59
Number of =>'s generated.......    1799
Number of auxiliary variables...   446

Equations added to expand =>'s..   12593    (7 per =>)
Variables added to expand =>'s.    16191    (9 per =>)

Characters in left-hand side....   472906
Characters in right-hand side...   422298
```

Register variables:

> ALIST ARGUMENTS DEPTH EXPRESSION FUNCTION LINKREG
> LINKREG2 LINKREG3 PARENS SOURCE SOURCE2 STACK
> TARGET TARGET2 VALUE VARIABLES WORK X Y

Label variables:

> ALIST_SEARCH BIND CHOOSE COMPARE COPY_HD COPY_TL
> COPY1 COPY2 DEPTH_OKAY EVAL EVALST
> EXPRESSION_IS_ATOM EXPRESSION_ISNT_ATOM JN_EXIT
> JN_ROUTINE L1 L10 L100 L101 L102 L103 L104 L105
> L106 L107 L109 L110 L111 L112 L113 L114 L115 L116
> L117 L118 L119 L120 L121 L122 L124 L125 L126 L127
> L129 L13 L130 L131 L132 L133 L135 L136 L137 L138
> L139 L14 L141 L142 L143 L144 L146 L147 L148 L149
> L150 L153 L154 L155 L156 L158 L159 L16 L160 L161
> L162 L163 L164 L165 L166 L167 L168 L169 L17 L170
> L171 L173 L174 L175 L176 L177 L179 L18 L180 L181
> L182 L183 L184 L185 L186 L187 L188 L189 L19 L190
> L191 L192 L193 L194 L195 L196 L197 L198 L199 L2
> L20 L200 L201 L203 L204 L205 L206 L207 L208 L209
> L21 L210 L211 L212 L213 L214 L215 L216 L217 L218
> L219 L220 L221 L222 L223 L224 L225 L226 L227 L228
> L229 L231 L232 L233 L234 L235 L236 L237 L238 L239
> L24 L240 L241 L242 L243 L244 L245 L246 L247 L248
> L249 L25 L250 L251 L252 L253 L254 L255 L256 L257
> L258 L259 L26 L260 L261 L263 L264 L265 L267 L268
> L269 L27 L271 L272 L273 L274 L275 L276 L277 L278
> L279 L28 L280 L282 L284 L286 L288 L289 L29 L291
> L293 L296 L297 L298 L299 L3 L30 L301 L303 L305 L31
> L32 L33 L34 L35 L36 L37 L39 L4 L40 L41 L42 L43 L44
> L45 L46 L47 L48 L49 L5 L50 L51 L52 L53 L55 L56 L57
> L58 L59 L6 L60 L61 L62 L63 L64 L65 L66 L67 L68 L70
> L71 L72 L73 L75 L76 L77 L78 L79 L8 L80 L81 L82 L83
> L84 L85 L86 L87 L88 L89 L90 L91 L92 L93 L94 L95
> L96 L97 L99 NEW_DEPTH NO_LIMIT NOT_ATOM NOT_EQUAL
> NOT_EVAL NOT_EVALD NOT_IF_THEN_ELSE NOT_LPAR
> NOT_OUTPUT NOT_QUOTE NOT_RPAR OLD_DEPTH
> POP_ROUTINE PUSH_ROUTINE RETURNQ RETURN0 RETURN1
> REVERSE REVERSE_HD REVERSE_TL SPLIT_EXIT
> SPLIT_ROUTINE THEN_CLAUSE UNWIND WRAP

Auxiliary variables:

```
char.ARGUMENTS char.DEPTH char.EXPRESSION
char.FUNCTION char.PARENS char.SOURCE char.SOURCE2
char.VALUE char.VARIABLES char.WORK char.X char.Y
dont.set.ALIST dont.set.ARGUMENTS dont.set.DEPTH
dont.set.EXPRESSION dont.set.FUNCTION
dont.set.LINKREG dont.set.LINKREG2
dont.set.LINKREG3 dont.set.PARENS dont.set.SOURCE
dont.set.SOURCE2 dont.set.STACK dont.set.TARGET
dont.set.TARGET2 dont.set.VALUE dont.set.VARIABLES
dont.WORK dont.set.X dont.set.Y
eq.ARGUMENTS.C'(' eq.DEPTH.C'(' eq.DEPTH.C'_'
eq.EXPRESSION.C'(' eq.EXPRESSION.Y
eq.FUNCTION.C',' eq.FUNCTION.C''''
eq.FUNCTION.C'=' eq.FUNCTION.C'↑' eq.FUNCTION.C'↓'
eq.FUNCTION.C'→' eq.FUNCTION.C'□' eq.FUNCTION.C'∘'
eq.FUNCTION.C'⊼' eq.FUNCTION.C'≗' eq.PARENS.C'1'
eq.SOURCE.C'(' eq.SOURCE.C')' eq.SOURCE.X'00'
eq.SOURCE2.C'(' eq.SOURCE2.X'00' eq.VALUE.C')'
eq.VALUE.C'0' eq.VARIABLES.C'(' eq.WORK.C')'
eq.WORK.X'00' eq.X.C'(' eq.X.C'_' eq.X.X'00'
eq.X.Y eq.Y.C'(' ge.ARGUMENTS.C'('
ge.C'('.ARGUMENTS ge.C'('.DEPTH ge.C'('.EXPRESSION
ge.C'('.SOURCE ge.C'('.SOURCE2 ge.C'('.VARIABLES
ge.C'('.X ge.C'('.Y ge.C')'.SOURCE ge.C')'.VALUE
ge.C')'.WORK ge.C','.FUNCTION ge.C'_'.DEPTH
ge.C'_'.X ge.C''''.FUNCTION ge.C'='.FUNCTION
ge.C'↑'.FUNCTION ge.C'↓'.FUNCTION ge.C'→'.FUNCTION
ge.C'□'.FUNCTION ge.C'∘'.FUNCTION ge.C'⊼'.FUNCTION
ge.C'0'.VALUE ge.C'1'.PARENS ge.C'≗'.FUNCTION
ge.DEPTH.C'(' ge.DEPTH.C'_' ge.EXPRESSION.C'('
ge.EXPRESSION.Y ge.FUNCTION.C',' ge.FUNCTION.C''''
ge.FUNCTION.C'=' ge.FUNCTION.C'↑' ge.FUNCTION.C'↓'
ge.FUNCTION.C'→' ge.FUNCTION.C'□' ge.FUNCTION.C'∘'
ge.FUNCTION.C'⊼' ge.FUNCTION.C'≗' ge.PARENS.C'1'
ge.SOURCE.C'(' ge.SOURCE.C')' ge.SOURCE.X'00'
ge.SOURCE2.C'(' ge.SOURCE2.X'00' ge.VALUE.C')'
ge.VALUE.C'0' ge.VARIABLES.C'(' ge.WORK.C')'
ge.WORK.X'00' ge.X.C'(' ge.X.C'_' ge.X.X'00'
ge.X.Y ge.X'00'.SOURCE ge.X'00'.SOURCE2
ge.X'00'.WORK ge.X'00'.X ge.Y.C'(' ge.Y.EXPRESSION
ge.Y.X goback.JN_EXIT goback.L14 goback.L265
goback.L269 goback.SPLIT_EXIT i ic input.ALIST
input.ARGUMENTS input.DEPTH input.EXPRESSION
input.FUNCTION input.LINKREG input.LINKREG2
input.LINKREG3 input.PARENS input.SOURCE
input.SOURCE2 input.STACK input.TARGET
input.TARGET2 input.VALUE input.VARIABLES
input.WORK input.X input.Y longest.label next.ic
number.of.instructions output.ALIST
output.ARGUMENTS output.DEPTH output.EXPRESSION
output.FUNCTION output.LINKREG output.LINKREG2
output.LINKREG3 output.PARENS output.SOURCE
output.SOURCE2 output.STACK output.TARGET
output.TARGET2 output.VALUE output.VARIABLES
```

```
output.WORK output.X output.Y q q.minus.1
set.ALIST set.ALIST.L1 set.ALIST.L103
set.ALIST.L104 set.ALIST.L132 set.ALIST.L142
set.ALIST.L198 set.ALIST.L2 set.ALIST.L254
set.ALIST.L260 set.ALIST.L92 set.ALIST.L93
set.ALIST.L96 set.ARGUMENTS set.ARGUMENTS.L212
set.ARGUMENTS.L217 set.ARGUMENTS.L245
set.ARGUMENTS.L41 set.ARGUMENTS.L46
set.ARGUMENTS.L58 set.ARGUMENTS.L63
set.ARGUMENTS.L68 set.ARGUMENTS.L80 set.DEPTH
set.DEPTH.L125 set.DEPTH.L127 set.DEPTH.L130
set.DEPTH.L182 set.DEPTH.L200 set.DEPTH.L4
set.EXPRESSION set.EXPRESSION.L100
set.EXPRESSION.L195 set.EXPRESSION.L211
set.EXPRESSION.L40 set.EXPRESSION.L57
set.EXPRESSION.L71 set.EXPRESSION.L89 set.FUNCTION
set.FUNCTION.L185 set.FUNCTION.L189
set.FUNCTION.L48 set.FUNCTION.L78 set.LINKREG
set.LINKREG.DEPTH_OKAY set.LINKREG.L13
set.LINKREG.L192 set.LINKREG.L196 set.LINKREG.L215
set.LINKREG.L221 set.LINKREG.L248 set.LINKREG.L44
set.LINKREG.L5 set.LINKREG.L61 set.LINKREG.L72
set.LINKREG.L76 set.LINKREG.L94
set.LINKREG.OLD_DEPTH set.LINKREG2
set.LINKREG2.L102 set.LINKREG2.L124
set.LINKREG2.L129 set.LINKREG2.L131
set.LINKREG2.L141 set.LINKREG2.L16
set.LINKREG2.L179 set.LINKREG2.L191
set.LINKREG2.L197 set.LINKREG2.L199
set.LINKREG2.L203 set.LINKREG2.L214
set.LINKREG2.L216 set.LINKREG2.L220
set.LINKREG2.L222 set.LINKREG2.L231
set.LINKREG2.L241 set.LINKREG2.L247
set.LINKREG2.L249 set.LINKREG2.L255
set.LINKREG2.L43 set.LINKREG2.L45 set.LINKREG2.L60
set.LINKREG2.L62 set.LINKREG2.L75 set.LINKREG2.L77
set.LINKREG2.L91 set.LINKREG2.L95
set.LINKREG2.UNWIND set.LINKREG3 set.LINKREG3.L117
set.LINKREG3.L120 set.LINKREG3.L137
set.LINKREG3.L158 set.LINKREG3.L165
set.LINKREG3.L181 set.LINKREG3.L184
set.LINKREG3.L187 set.LINKREG3.L194
set.LINKREG3.L210 set.LINKREG3.L227
set.LINKREG3.L237 set.LINKREG3.L243
set.LINKREG3.L253 set.LINKREG3.L259
set.LINKREG3.L263 set.LINKREG3.L267
set.LINKREG3.L29 set.LINKREG3.L33 set.LINKREG3.L39
set.LINKREG3.L51 set.LINKREG3.L56 set.LINKREG3.L67
set.LINKREG3.L70 set.LINKREG3.L82 set.LINKREG3.L86
set.PARENS set.PARENS.L280 set.PARENS.L282
set.PARENS.L284 set.SOURCE set.SOURCE.BIND
set.SOURCE.COPY_TL set.SOURCE.COPY1
set.SOURCE.EVAL set.SOURCE.EVALST
set.SOURCE.EXPRESSION_ISNT_ATOM set.SOURCE.L101
set.SOURCE.L116 set.SOURCE.L119 set.SOURCE.L136
set.SOURCE.L163 set.SOURCE.L180 set.SOURCE.L183
set.SOURCE.L186 set.SOURCE.L190 set.SOURCE.L193
```

```
set.SOURCE.L209 set.SOURCE.L213 set.SOURCE.L219
set.SOURCE.L225 set.SOURCE.L236 set.SOURCE.L240
set.SOURCE.L242 set.SOURCE.L246 set.SOURCE.L251
set.SOURCE.L257 set.SOURCE.L278 set.SOURCE.L28
set.SOURCE.L32 set.SOURCE.L42 set.SOURCE.L50
set.SOURCE.L55 set.SOURCE.L59 set.SOURCE.L66
set.SOURCE.L81 set.SOURCE.L85 set.SOURCE.L90
set.SOURCE.NEW_DEPTH set.SOURCE.NO_LIMIT
set.SOURCE.NOT_EQUAL set.SOURCE.NOT_IF_THEN_ELSE
set.SOURCE.NOT_RPAR set.SOURCE.POP_ROUTINE
set.SOURCE.THEN_CLAUSE set.SOURCE2
set.SOURCE2.COPY2 set.SOURCE2.L135
set.SOURCE2.L164 set.SOURCE2.L226 set.SOURCE2.L252
set.SOURCE2.L258 set.SOURCE2.L299
set.SOURCE2.PUSH_ROUTINE set.SOURCE2.WRAP
set.STACK set.STACK.L264 set.STACK.L268
set.STACK.L3 set.TARGET set.TARGET.JN_ROUTINE
set.TARGET.L276 set.TARGET.L297 set.TARGET.REVERSE
set.TARGET.REVERSE_HD set.TARGET.SPLIT_ROUTINE
set.TARGET2 set.TARGET2.L271 set.TARGET2.L277
set.TARGET2.REVERSE_TL set.VALUE
set.VALUE.ALIST_SEARCH set.VALUE.L138
set.VALUE.L159 set.VALUE.L161 set.VALUE.L166
set.VALUE.L170 set.VALUE.L173 set.VALUE.L204
set.VALUE.L228 set.VALUE.L34 set.VALUE.L52
set.VALUE.L99 set.VALUE.RETURNQ set.VALUE.RETURN0
set.VALUE.RETURN1 set.VARIABLES set.VARIABLES.L188
set.VARIABLES.L239 set.WORK set.WORK.COPY_TL
set.WORK.COPY1 set.WORK.COPY2 set.WORK.L109
set.WORK.L110 set.WORK.L113 set.WORK.L114
set.WORK.L147 set.WORK.L148 set.WORK.L175
set.WORK.L176 set.WORK.L18 set.WORK.L19
set.WORK.L206 set.WORK.L207 set.WORK.L233
set.WORK.L234 set.WORK.L25 set.WORK.L26
set.WORK.L273 set.WORK.L274 set.WORK.L279
set.WORK.L289 set.WORK.L298 set.WORK.L299
set.WORK.NOT_RPAR set.WORK.REVERSE
set.WORK.REVERSE_HD set.WORK.REVERSE_TL set.X
set.X.EXPRESSION_IS_ATOM set.X.L105 set.X.L118
set.X.L153 set.X.L223 set.X.L238 set.X.L244
set.X.L250 set.X.L256 set.X.L31 set.X.L35
set.X.L83 set.Y set.Y.L106 set.Y.L121 set.Y.L154
set.Y.L30 set.Y.L84 set.Y.L87 shift.ARGUMENTS
shift.DEPTH shift.EXPRESSION shift.FUNCTION
shift.PARENS shift.SOURCE shift.SOURCE2
shift.VALUE shift.VARIABLES shift.WORK shift.X
shift.Y time total.input
```

```
Variables added to expand =>'s:
        r1 s1 t1 u1 v1 w1 x1 y1 z1 ... z1799
```

```
Elapsed time is 383.296124 seconds.
```

4.4. The Arithmetization of EVAL: Start of Left-Hand Side

$(total.input)**2+(input.ALIST+input.ARGUMENTS+input.DEPTH+inpu$
$t.EXPRESSION+input.FUNCTION+input.LINKREG+input.LINKREG2+input$
$.LINKREG3+input.PARENS+input.SOURCE+input.SOURCE2+input.STACK+$
$input.TARGET+input.TARGET2+input.VALUE+input.VARIABLES+input.W$
$ORK+input.X+input.Y)**2 + (number.of.instructions)**2+(306)**2$
$ + (longest.label)**2+(20)**2 + (q)**2+(256**(total.input+time$
$+number.of.instructions+longest.label+3))**2 + (q.minus.1+1)**$
$2+(q)**2 + (1+q*i)**2+(i+q**time)**2 + (r1)**2+(L1)**2 + (s1)$
$**2+(i)**2 + (t1)**2+(2**s1)**2 + ((1+t1)**s1)**2+(v1*t1**(r1+1$
$)+u1*t1**r1+w1)**2 + (w1+x1+1)**2+(t1**r1)**2 + (u1+y1+1)**2+($
$t1)**2 + (u1)**2+(2*z1+1)**2 + (r2)**2+(L2)**2 + (s2)**2+(i)**$
$2 + (t2)**2+(2**s2)**2 + ((1+t2)**s2)**2+(v2*t2**(r2+1)+u2*t2*$
$*r2+w2)**2 + (w2+x2+1)**2+(t2**r2)**2 + (u2+y2+1)**2+(t2)**2 +$
$ (u2)**2+(2*z2+1)**2 + (r3)**2+(L3)**2 + (s3)**2+(i)**2 + (t3)$
$**2+(2**s3)**2 + ((1+t3)**s3)**2+(v3*t3**(r3+1)+u3*t3**r3+w3)*$
$*2 + (w3+x3+1)**2+(t3**r3)**2 + (u3+y3+1)**2+(t3)**2 + (u3)**2$
$+(2*z3+1)**2 + (r4)**2+(L4)**2 + (s4)**2+(i)**2 + (t4)**2+(2**$
$s4)**2 + ((1+t4)**s4)**2+(v4*t4**(r4+1)+u4*t4**r4+w4)**2 + (w4$
$+x4+1)**2+(t4**r4)**2 + (u4+y4+1)**2+(t4)**2 + (u4)**2+(2*z4+1$
$)**2 + (r5)**2+(L5)**2 + (s5)**2+(i)**2 + (t5)**2+(2**s5)**2 +$
$ ((1+t5)**s5)**2+(v5*t5**(r5+1)+u5*t5**r5+w5)**2 + (w5+x5+1)**$
$2+(t5**r5)**2 + (u5+y5+1)**2+(t5)**2 + (u5)**2+(2*z5+1)**2 + ($
$r6)**2+(L6)**2 + (s6)**2+(i)**2 + (t6)**2+(2**s6)**2 + ((1+t6)$
$**s6)**2+(v6*t6**(r6+1)+u6*t6**r6+w6)**2 + (w6+x6+1)**2+(t6**r$
$6)**2 + (u6+y6+1)**2+(t6)**2 + (u6)**2+(2*z6+1)**2 + (r7)**2+($
$RETURNQ)**2 + (s7)**2+(i)**2 + (t7)**2+(2**s7)**2 + ((1+t7)**s$
$7)**2+(v7*t7**(r7+1)+u7*t7**r7+w7)**2 + (w7+x7+1)**2+(t7**r7)*$
$*2 + (u7+y7+1)**2+(t7)**2 + (u7)**2+(2*z7+1)**2 + (r8)**2+(L8)$
$**2 + (s8)**2+(i)**2 + (t8)**2+(2**s8)**2 + ((1+t8)**s8)**2+(v$
$8*t8**(r8+1)+u8*t8**r8+w8)**2 + (w8+x8+1)**2+(t8**r8)**2 + (u8$
$+y8+1)**2+(t8)**2 + (u8)**2+(2*z8+1)**2 + (r9)**2+(RETURN0)**2$
$ + (s9)**2+(i)**2 + (t9)**2+(2**s9)**2 + ((1+t9)**s9)**2+(v9*t$
$9**(r9+1)+u9*t9**r9+w9)**2 + (w9+x9+1)**2+(t9**r9)**2 + (u9+y9$
$+1)**2+(t9)**2 + (u9)**2+(2*z9+1)**2 + (r10)**2+(L10)**2 + (s1$
$0)**2+(i)**2 + (t10)**2+(2**s10)**2 + ((1+t10)**s10)**2+(v10*t$
$10**(r10+1)+u10*t10**r10+w10)**2 + (w10+x10+1)**2+(t10**r10)**$
$2 + (u10+y10+1)**2+(t10)**2 + (u10)**2+(2*z10+1)**2 + (r11)**2$
$+(RETURN1)**2 + (s11)**2+(i)**2 + (t11)**2+(2**s11)**2 + ((1+t$
$11)**s11)**2+(v11*t11**(r11+1)+u11*t11**r11+w11)**2 + (w11+x11$
$+1)**2+(t11**r11)**2 + (u11+y11+1)**2+(t11)**2 + (u11)**2+(2*z$
$11+1)**2 + (r12)**2+(UNWIND)**2 + (s12)**2+(i)**2 + (t12)**2+($
$2**s12)**2 + ((1+t12)**s12)**2+(v12*t12**(r12+1)+u12*t12**r12+$
$w12)**2 + (w12+x12+1)**2+(t12**r12)**2 + (u12+y12+1)**2+(t12)*$
$*2 + (u12)**2+(2*z12+1)**2 + (r13)**2+(L13)**2 + (s13)**2+(i)*$
$*2 + (t13)**2+(2**s13)**2 + ((1+t13)**s13)**2+(v13*t13**(r13+1$
$)+u13*t13**r13+w13)**2 + (w13+x13+1)**2+(t13**r13)**2 + (u13+y$
$13+1)**2+(t13)**2 + (u13)**2+(2*z13+1)**2 + (r14)**2+(L14)**2$
$+ (s14)**2+(i)**2 + (t14)**2+(2**s14)**2 + ((1+t14)**s14)**2+($
$v14*t14**(r14+1)+u14*t14**r14+w14)**2 + (w14+x14+1)**2+(t14**r$
$14)**2 + (u14+y14+1)**2+(t14)**2 + (u14)**2+(2*z14+1)**2 + (r1$
$5)**2+(EVAL)**2 + (s15)**2+(i)**2 + (t15)**2+(2**s15)**2 + ((1$
$+t15)**s15)**2+(v15*t15**(r15+1)+u15*t15**r15+w15)**2 + (w15+x$
$15+1)**2+(t15**r15)**2 + (u15+y15+1)**2+(t15)**2 + (u15)**2+(2$
$*z15+1)**2 + (r16)**2+(L16)**2 + (s16)**2+(i)**2 + (t16)**2+(2$
$**s16)**2 + ((1+t16)**s16)**2+(v16*t16**(r16+1)+u16*t16**r16+w$
$16)**2 + (w16+x16+1)**2+(t16**r16)**2 + (u16+y16+1)**2+(t16)**$

```
2 + (u16)**2+(2*z16+1)**2 + (r17)**2+(L17)**2 + (s17)**2+(i)**
2 + (t17)**2+(2**s17)**2 + ((1+t17)**s17)**2+(v17*t17**(r17+1)
+u17*t17**r17+w17)**2 + (w17+x17+1)**2+(t17**r17)**2 + (u17+y1
7+1)**2+(t17)**2 + (u17)**2+(2*z17+1)**2 + (r18)**2+(L18)**2 +
 (s18)**2+(i)**2 + (t18)**2+(2**s18)**2 + ((1+t18)**s18)**2+(v
18*t18**(r18+1)+u18*t18**r18+w18)**2 + (w18+x18+1)**2+(t18**r1
8)**2 + (u18+y18+1)**2+(t18)**2 + (u18)**2+(2*z18+1)**2 + (r19
)**2+(L19)**2 + (s19)**2+(i)**2 + (t19)**2+(2**s19)**2 + ((1+t
19)**s19)**2+(v19*t19**(r19+1)+u19*t19**r19+w19)**2 + (w19+x19
+1)**2+(t19**r19)**2 + (u19+y19+1)**2+(t19)**2 + (u19)**2+(2*z
19+1)**2 + (r20)**2+(L20)**2 + (s20)**2+(i)**2 + (t20)**2+(2**
s20)**2 + ((1+t20)**s20)**2+(v20*t20**(r20+1)+u20*t20**r20+w20
)**2 + (w20+x20+1)**2+(t20**r20)**2 + (u20+y20+1)**2+(t20)**2
+ (u20)**2+(2*z20+1)**2 + (r21)**2+(L21)**2 + (s21)**2+(i)**2
+ (t21)**2+(2**s21)**2 + ((1+t21)**s21)**2+(v21*t21**(r21+1)+u
21*t21**r21+w21)**2 + (w21+x21+1)**2+(t21**r21)**2 + (u21+y21+
1)**2+(t21)**2 + (u21)**2+(2*z21+1)**2 + (r22)**2+(EXPRESSION_
IS_ATOM)**2 + (s22)**2+(i)**2 + (t22)**2+(2**s22)**2 + ((1+t22
)**s22)**2+(v22*t22**(r22+1)+u22*t22**r22+w22)**2 + (w22+x22+1
)**2+(t22**r22)**2 + (u22+y22+1)**2+(t22)**2 + (u22)**2+(2*z22
+1)**2 + (r23)**2+(ALIST_SEARCH)**2 + (s23)**2+(i)**2 + (t23)*
*2+(2**s23)**2 + ((1+t23)**s23)**2+(v23*t23**(r23+1)+u23*t23**
r23+w23)**2 + (w23+x23+1)**2+(t23**r23)**2 + (u23+y23+1)**2+(t
23)**2 + (u23)**2+(2*z23+1)**2 + (r24)**2+(L24)**2 + (s24)**2+
(i)**2 + (t24)**2+(2**s24)**2 + ((1+t24)**s24)**2+(v24*t24**(r
```

4.5. The Arithmetization of EVAL: End of Right-Hand Side

```
e.SOURCE.X'00'+ge.X'00'.SOURCE) + 2*(t1780)*(2**s1780) + 2*((1
+t1780)**s1780)*(v1780*t1780**(r1780+1)+u1780*t1780**r1780+w17
80) + 2*(w1780+x1780+1)*(t1780**r1780) + 2*(u1780+y1780+1)*(t1
780) + 2*(u1780)*(2*z1780+1) + 2*(r1781)*(ge.SOURCE.X'00'+ge.X
'00'.SOURCE) + 2*(s1781)*(2*eq.SOURCE.X'00'+i) + 2*(t1781)*(2*
*s1781) + 2*((1+t1781)**s1781)*(v1781*t1781**(r1781+1)+u1781*t
1781**r1781+w1781) + 2*(w1781+x1781+1)*(t1781**r1781) + 2*(u17
81+y1781+1)*(t1781) + 2*(u1781)*(2*z1781+1) + 2*(r1782)*(ge.SO
URCE2.C'(') + 2*(s1782)*(i) + 2*(t1782)*(2**s1782) + 2*((1+t17
82)**s1782)*(v1782*t1782**(r1782+1)+u1782*t1782**r1782+w1782)
+ 2*(w1782+x1782+1)*(t1782**r1782) + 2*(u1782+y1782+1)*(t1782)
 + 2*(u1782)*(2*z1782+1) + 2*(r1783)*(256*ge.SOURCE2.C'(') + 2
*(s1783+128*i)*(256*i+char.SOURCE2) + 2*(t1783)*(2**s1783) + 2
*((1+t1783)**s1783)*(v1783*t1783**(r1783+1)+u1783*t1783**r1783
+w1783) + 2*(w1783+x1783+1)*(t1783**r1783) + 2*(u1783+y1783+1)
*(t1783) + 2*(u1783)*(2*z1783+1) + 2*(r1784+128*i)*(256*i+char
.SOURCE2) + 2*(s1784)*(256*ge.SOURCE2.C'('+255*i) + 2*(t1784)*
(2**s1784) + 2*((1+t1784)**s1784)*(v1784*t1784**(r1784+1)+u178
4*t1784**r1784+w1784) + 2*(w1784+x1784+1)*(t1784**r1784) + 2*(
u1784+y1784+1)*(t1784) + 2*(u1784)*(2*z1784+1) + 2*(r1785)*(ge
.C'('.SOURCE2) + 2*(s1785)*(i) + 2*(t1785)*(2**s1785) + 2*((1+
t1785)**s1785)*(v1785*t1785**(r1785+1)+u1785*t1785**r1785+w178
5) + 2*(w1785+x1785+1)*(t1785**r1785) + 2*(u1785+y1785+1)*(t17
85) + 2*(u1785)*(2*z1785+1) + 2*(r1786)*(256*ge.C'('.SOURCE2)
+ 2*(s1786+char.SOURCE2)*(256*i+128*i) + 2*(t1786)*(2**s1786)
+ 2*((1+t1786)**s1786)*(v1786*t1786**(r1786+1)+u1786*t1786**r1
```

$786+w1786) + 2*(w1786+x1786+1)*(t1786**r1786) + 2*(u1786+y1786$
$+1)*(t1786) + 2*(u1786)*(2*z1786+1) + 2*(r1787+char.SOURCE2)*($
$256*i+128*i) + 2*(s1787)*(256*ge.C'('.SOURCE2+255*i) + 2*(t178$
$7)*(2**s1787) + 2*((1+t1787)**s1787)*(v1787*t1787**(r1787+1)+u$
$1787*t1787**r1787+w1787) + 2*(w1787+x1787+1)*(t1787**r1787) +$
$2*(u1787+y1787+1)*(t1787) + 2*(u1787)*(2*z1787+1) + 2*(r1788)*$
$(eq.SOURCE2.C'(') + 2*(s1788)*(i) + 2*(t1788)*(2**s1788) + 2*($
$1+t1788)**s1788)*(v1788*t1788**(r1788+1)+u1788*t1788**r1788+w$
$1788) + 2*(w1788+x1788+1)*(t1788**r1788) + 2*(u1788+y1788+1)*($
$t1788) + 2*(u1788)*(2*z1788+1) + 2*(r1789)*(2*eq.SOURCE2.C'(')$
$+ 2*(s1789)*(ge.C'('+ge.C'('.SOURCE2) + 2*(t1789)*(2*$
$*s1789) + 2*((1+t1789)**s1789)*(v1789*t1789**(r1789+1)+u1789*t$
$1789**r1789+w1789) + 2*(w1789+x1789+1)*(t1789**r1789) + 2*(u17$
$89+y1789+1)*(t1789) + 2*(u1789)*(2*z1789+1) + 2*(r1790)*(ge.SO$
$URCE2.C'('+ge.C'('.SOURCE2) + 2*(s1790)*(2*eq.SOURCE2.C'('+i)$
$+ 2*(t1790)*(2**s1790) + 2*((1+t1790)**s1790)*(v1790*t1790**(r$
$1790+1)+u1790*t1790**r1790+w1790) + 2*(w1790+x1790+1)*(t1790**$
$r1790) + 2*(u1790+y1790+1)*(t1790) + 2*(u1790)*(2*z1790+1) + 2$
$*(r1791)*(ge.SOURCE2.X'00') + 2*(s1791)*(i) + 2*(t1791)*(2**s1$
$791) + 2*((1+t1791)**s1791)*(v1791*t1791**(r1791+1)+u1791*t179$
$1**r1791+w1791) + 2*(w1791+x1791+1)*(t1791**r1791) + 2*(u1791+$
$y1791+1)*(t1791) + 2*(u1791)*(2*z1791+1) + 2*(r1792)*(256*ge.S$
$OURCE2.X'00') + 2*(s1792+0*i)*(256*i+char.SOURCE2) + 2*(t1792)$
$*(2**s1792) + 2*((1+t1792)**s1792)*(v1792*t1792**(r1792+1)+u17$
$92*t1792**r1792+w1792) + 2*(w1792+x1792+1)*(t1792**r1792) + 2*$
$(u1792+y1792+1)*(t1792) + 2*(u1792)*(2*z1792+1) + 2*(r1793+0*i$
$)*(256*i+char.SOURCE2) + 2*(s1793)*(256*ge.SOURCE2.X'00'+255*i$
$) + 2*(t1793)*(2**s1793) + 2*((1+t1793)**s1793)*(v1793*t1793**$
$(r1793+1)+u1793*t1793**r1793+w1793) + 2*(w1793+x1793+1)*(t1793$
$**r1793) + 2*(u1793+y1793+1)*(t1793) + 2*(u1793)*(2*z1793+1) +$
$2*(r1794)*(ge.X'00'.SOURCE2) + 2*(s1794)*(i) + 2*(t1794)*(2**$
$s1794) + 2*((1+t1794)**s1794)*(v1794*t1794**(r1794+1)+u1794*t1$
$794**r1794+w1794) + 2*(w1794+x1794+1)*(t1794**r1794) + 2*(u179$
$4+y1794+1)*(t1794) + 2*(u1794)*(2*z1794+1) + 2*(r1795)*(256*ge$
$.X'00'.SOURCE2) + 2*(s1795+char.SOURCE2)*(256*i+0*i) + 2*(t179$
$5)*(2**s1795) + 2*((1+t1795)**s1795)*(v1795*t1795**(r1795+1)+u$
$1795*t1795**r1795+w1795) + 2*(w1795+x1795+1)*(t1795**r1795) +$
$2*(u1795+y1795+1)*(t1795) + 2*(u1795)*(2*z1795+1) + 2*(r1796+c$
$har.SOURCE2)*(256*i+0*i) + 2*(s1796)*(256*ge.X'00'.SOURCE2+255$
$*i) + 2*(t1796)*(2**s1796) + 2*((1+t1796)**s1796)*(v1796*t1796$
$**(r1796+1)+u1796*t1796**r1796+w1796) + 2*(w1796+x1796+1)*(t17$
$96**r1796) + 2*(u1796+y1796+1)*(t1796) + 2*(u1796)*(2*z1796+1)$
$+ 2*(r1797)*(eq.SOURCE2.X'00') + 2*(s1797)*(i) + 2*(t1797)*(2$
$**s1797) + 2*((1+t1797)**s1797)*(v1797*t1797**(r1797+1)+u1797*$
$t1797**r1797+w1797) + 2*(w1797+x1797+1)*(t1797**r1797) + 2*(u1$
$797+y1797+1)*(t1797) + 2*(u1797)*(2*z1797+1) + 2*(r1798)*(2*eq$
$.SOURCE2.X'00') + 2*(s1798)*(ge.SOURCE2.X'00'+ge.X'00'.SOURCE2$
$) + 2*(t1798)*(2**s1798) + 2*((1+t1798)**s1798)*(v1798*t1798**$
$(r1798+1)+u1798*t1798**r1798+w1798) + 2*(w1798+x1798+1)*(t1798$
$**r1798) + 2*(u1798+y1798+1)*(t1798) + 2*(u1798)*(2*z1798+1) +$
$2*(r1799)*(ge.SOURCE2.X'00'+ge.X'00'.SOURCE2) + 2*(s1799)*(2*$
$eq.SOURCE2.X'00'+i) + 2*(t1799)*(2**s1799) + 2*((1+t1799)**s17$
$99)*(v1799*t1799**(r1799+1)+u1799*t1799**r1799+w1799) + 2*(w17$
$99+x1799+1)*(t1799**r1799) + 2*(u1799+y1799+1)*(t1799) + 2*(u1$
$799)*(2*z1799+1)$

PART II

PROGRAM SIZE, HALTING PROBABILITIES, RANDOMNESS, & METAMATHEMATICS

Having done the bulk of the work necessary to encode the halting probability Ω as an exponential diophantine equation, we now turn to theory. In Chapter 5 we trace the evolution of the concepts of program-size complexity. In Chapter 6 we define these concepts formally and develop their basic properties. In Chapter 7 we study the notion of a random real and show that Ω is a random real. And in Chapter 8 we develop incompleteness theorems for random reals.

CONCEPTUAL DEVELOPMENT

The purpose of this chapter is to introduce the notion of program-size complexity. We do this by giving a smoothed-over story of the evolution of this concept, giving proof sketches instead of formal proofs, starting with program size in LISP. In Chapter 6 we will start over, and give formal definitions and proofs.

5.1. Complexity via LISP Expressions

Having gone to the trouble of defining a particularly clean and elegant version of LISP, one in which the definition of LISP in LISP really is equivalent to running the interpreter, let's start using it to prove theorems! The usual approach to program-size complexity is rather abstract, in that no particular programming language is directly visible. Eventually, we shall have to go a little bit in this direction. But we can start with a very straightforward concrete approach, namely to consider the size of a LISP expression measured by the number of characters it has. This will help to build our intuition before we are forced to use a more abstract approach to get stronger theorems. The path we shall follow is similar to that in my first paper [CHAITIN (1966,1969a)], except that there I used Turing machines instead of LISP.

So we shall now study, for any given LISP object, its program-size complexity, which is the size of the smallest program (i.e., S-expression) for calculating it. As for notation, we shall use H_{LISP} ("information content measured using LISP"), usually abbreviated in this chapter by omitting the subscript for LISP. And we write $|S|$ for the size in characters of an S-expression S. Thus

$$H_{\text{LISP}}(x) \quad \equiv \quad \min_{x \,=\, \text{value}(p)} \ |p|\,.$$

Thus the *complexity* of an S-expression is the size of the smallest S-expression that evaluates to it,[10] the complexity of a function is the complexity of the simplest S-expression that defines it,[11] and the complexity of an r.e. set of S-expressions is the complexity of the simplest partial function that is defined iff its argument is an S-expression in the r.e. set.

We now turn from the size of programs to their probabilities. In the probability measure on the programs that we have in mind, the probability of a k-character program is 128^{-k}. This is the natural choice since our LISP "alphabet" has 128 characters (see Figure 6), but let's show that it works.

Consider the unit interval. Divide it into 128 intervals, one for each 7-bit character in the LISP alphabet. Divide each interval into 128 subintervals, and each subinterval into 128 subsubintervals, etc. Thus an S-expression with k characters corresponds to a piece of the unit interval that is 128^{-k} long. Now let's consider programs that are syntactically valid, i.e., that have parentheses that balance. Since no extension of such a program is syntactically valid, it follows that if we sum the lengths of the intervals associated with character strings that have balanced parentheses, no subinterval is counted more than once, and thus this sum is between 0 and 1, and defines in a natural manner the probability that an S-expression is syntactically valid.

In fact, we shall now show that the probability of a syntactically correct LISP S-expression is 1, if we adopt the convention that the invalid S-expression ")" consisting just of a right parenthesis actually denotes the empty list "( )". I.e., in Conway's terminology [CONWAY (1986)], "LISP has no syntax," except for a set of measure zero. For if one flips 7 coins for each character, eventually the number of right parentheses will overtake the number of left parentheses, with probability one. This is similar to the fact that heads versus tails will cross the origin infinitely often, with probability one. I.e., a symmetrical random walk on a line will return to the origin with probability one. For a more detailed explanation, see Appendix B.

Now let's select from the set of all syntactically correct programs, which has measure 1, those that give a particular result. I.e., let's consider $P_{\text{LISP}}(x)$

---

[10] Self-contained S-expression; i.e., the expression is evaluated in an empty environment, and all needed function definitions must be made locally within it.

[11] The expressions may evaluate to different function definitions, as long as these definitions compute the same function.

defined to be the probability that an S-expression chosen at random evaluates to x. In other words, if one tosses 7 coins per character, what is the chance that the LISP S-expression that one gets evaluates to x?

Finally, we define Ω_{LISP} to be the probability that an S-expression "halts", i.e., the probability that it has a value. If one tosses 7 coins per character, what is the chance that the LISP S-expression that one gets halts? That is the value of Ω_{LISP}.

Now for an upper bound on LISP complexity. Consider the S-expression

    ('x)

which evaluates to

    x.

This shows that

$$H(x) \leq |x| + 3.$$

The complexity of an S-expression is bounded from above by its size + 3.

Now we introduce the important notion of a *minimal program*. A minimal program is a LISP S-expression having the property that no smaller S-expression has the same value. It is obvious that there is at least one minimal program for any given LISP S-expression, i.e., at least one p with $|p| = H_{\text{LISP}}(x)$ which evaluates to x. Consider the S-expression

    (⊕q)

where q is a minimal program for p, and p is a minimal program for x. This expression evaluates to x, and thus

$$|p| = H(x) \leq 3 + |q| = 3 + H(p),$$

which shows that if p is a minimal program, then

$$H(p) \geq |p| - 3.$$

It follows that all minimal programs p, and there are infinitely many of them, have the property that

$$|\ H(p) - |p|\ | \leq 3.$$

I.e., LISP minimal programs are algorithmically incompressible, at least if one is programming in LISP.

Minimal programs have three other fascinating properties:

1. Large minimal programs are "normal", that is to say, each of the 128
    characters in the LISP character set appears in it with a relative
    frequency close to $1/128$. The longer the minimal program is, the closer
    the relative frequencies are to $1/128$.
2. There are few minimal programs for a given object; minimal programs
    are essentially unique.
3. In any formal axiomatic theory, it is possible to exhibit at most a finite
    number of minimal programs. In other words, there is a version of
    Gödel's incompleteness theorem for minimal programs: to prove that a
    program is minimal is extremely hard.

Let's start by showing how to prove (3). We derive a contradiction
from the assumption that a formal theory enables one to prove that
infinitely many programs are minimal. For if this were the case, we could
define a LISP function f as follows: given the positive integer k as
argument as a list of k 1's, look for the first proof in the formal theory that
an S-expression p is a minimal program of size greater than $2k$, and let p be
the value of $f(k)$. Then it is easy to see that

$$2k - 3 \quad < \quad |p| - 3 \quad \le \quad H(p) \quad = \quad H(f(k)) \quad \le \quad k + O(1),$$

which gives a contradiction for k sufficiently large. For a more refined
version of this result, see Theorem LB in Section 8.1.

How are (1) and (2) established? Both make use of the following
asymptotic estimate for the number of LISP S-expressions of size n, which
is demonstrated in Appendix B:

$$S_n \quad \sim \quad \frac{1}{2\sqrt{\pi}} \; k^{-1.5} \; 128^{n-2}$$

$$\text{where} \quad k \quad \equiv \quad \frac{n}{128} .$$

The reason this estimate is fundamental, is that it implies the following.
Consider the set X of S-expressions of a given size. If we know that a
specific S-expression x in X must be contained in a subset of X that is less
than a fraction of 128^{-n} of the total size of the set X, then there is a
program for that improbable S-expression x that has $n - O(\log n)$ fewer
characters than the size of x.

Then (1) follows from the fact that most S-expressions are normal, and
(2) follows from the observation that at most 128^{-k} of the S-expressions of

size n can have the same value as 128^k other S-expressions of the same size. For more details on how to prove (2), see CHAITIN (1976b).

Now we turn to the important topic of the subadditivity of program-size complexity.

Consider the S-expression

(pq)

where p is a minimal program for the function f, and q is a minimal program for the data x. This expression evaluates to $f(x)$. This shows that

$$H(f(x)) \leq H(f) + H(x) + 2$$

because two characters are added to programs for f and x to get a program for $f(x)$.

Consider the S-expression

$(,p(,q()))$

where p and q are minimal programs for x and y, respectively. This expression evaluates to the pair (xy), and thus

$$H(x, y) \equiv H((xy)) \leq H(x) + H(y) + 8$$

because 8 characters are added to p and q to get a program for (xy). Considering all programs that calculate x and y instead of just the minimal ones, we see that

$$P(x, y) \equiv P((xy)) \geq 2^{-8} P(x) P(y).$$

We see that LISP programs are self-delimiting syntactically, because parentheses must balance. Thus they can be concatenated, and the semantics of LISP also helps to make it easy to build programs from subroutines. In other words, in LISP algorithmic information is subadditive. This is illustrated beautifully by the following example: Consider the M-expression

$\leftarrow (Ex) \rightarrow \circ x() , \bar{\ast} \uparrow x (E \downarrow x) \quad (E'(L))$

where L is a list of expressions to be evaluated, which evaluates to the list of values of the elements of the list L. I.e., E is what is known in normal LISP as EVLIS. This works syntactically because expressions can be concatenated because they are delimited by balanced parentheses, and it works semantically because we are dealing with pure functions and there are no side-effects of evaluations. This yields the following remarkable inequality:

$$H_{\text{LISP}}(x_1, x_2, \ldots, x_n) \leq \sum_{k=1}^{n} H_{\text{LISP}}(x_k) + c.$$

What is remarkable here is that c is independent of n. This is better than we will ultimately be able to do with our final, definitive complexity measure, self-delimiting binary programs, in which c would have to be about $H(n) \approx \log_2 n$, in order to be able to specify how many subroutines there are.

Let $B(n)$ be the maximum of $H_{\text{LISP}}(x)$ taken over all finite binary strings x of size n, i.e., over all x that are a list consisting only of 0's and 1's, with n elements altogether. Then it can be shown from the asymptotic estimate for the number of S-expressions of a given size that

$$B(n) = \frac{n}{7} + O(\log n).$$

Another important consequence of this asymptotic estimate for the number of S-expressions of a given size is that Ω_{LISP} is normal. More precisely, if the real number Ω_{LISP} is written in any base b, then all digits will occur with equal limiting frequency $1/b$. To show this, one needs the following

Theorem: The LISP program-size complexity of the first $7n$ bits of Ω_{LISP} is greater than $n - c$. Proof: Given the first $7n$ bits of Ω_{LISP} in binary, we could in principle determine all LISP S-expressions of size $\leq n$ that have a value, and then all the values, by evaluating more and more S-expressions for more and more time until we find enough that halt to account for the first $7n$ bits of Ω. Thus we would know each S-expression of complexity less than or equal to n. This is a finite set, and we could then pick an S-expression $P(n)$ that is not in this set, and therefore has complexity greater than n. Thus there is a computable partial function P such that

$$2 + H_{\text{LISP}}(P) + H_{\text{LISP}}(\Omega_{7n}) \geq H_{\text{LISP}}(P(\Omega_{7n})) > n$$

for all n, where Ω_{7n} denotes the first $7n$ bits of the base-two numeral for Ω, which implies the assertion of the theorem. The 2 is the number of parentheses in

(Pq)

where q is a minimal program for Ω_{7n}. Hence,

$$H_{\text{LISP}}(\Omega_{7n}) \quad \geq \quad n - H_{\text{LISP}}(P) - 2.$$

5.2. Complexity via Binary Programs

The next major step in the evolution of the concept of program-size complexity was the transition from the concreteness of using a real programming language to a more abstract definition in which

$$B(n) = n + O(1),$$

a step already taken at the end of CHAITIN (1969a). This is easily done, by deciding that programs will be bit strings, and by interpreting the start of the bit string as a LISP S-expression defining a function, which is evaluated and then applied to the rest of the bit string as data to give the result of the program. The binary representation of S-expressions that we have in mind uses 7 bits per character and is described in Figure 6. So now the complexity of an S-expression will be measured by the size in bits of the shortest program of this kind that calculates it. I.e., we use a universal computer U that produces LISP S-expressions as output when it is given as input programs which are bit strings of the following form:

program$_U$ =
(self-delimiting LISP program for function definition f) binary data d.

Since there is one 7-bit byte for each LISP character, we see that

$$H_U(x) \quad = \quad \min_{x = f(d)} \left[7 \, H_{\text{LISP}}(f) + |d| \right].$$

Here "$|d|$" denotes the size in bits of a bit string d.

Then the following convenient properties are immediate:

1. There are at most 2^n bit strings of complexity n, and less than 2^n strings of complexity less than n.
2. There is a constant c such that all bit strings of length n have complexity less than $n + c$. In fact, $c = 7$ will do, because the LISP function ' (QUOTE) is one 7-bit character long.
3. Less than 2^{-k} of the bit strings of length n have $H < n - k$. And more than $1 - 2^{-k}$ of the bit strings of length n have $n - k \leq H < n + c$. This follows immediately from (1) and (2) above.

This makes it easy to prove statistical properties of random strings, but this convenience is bought at a cost. Programs are no longer self-delimiting. Thus the halting probability Ω can no longer be defined in a natural way, because if we give measure 2^{-n} to n-bit programs, then the halting probability diverges, since now for each n there are at least $2^n/c$ n-bit programs that halt. Also the fundamental principle of the subadditivity of algorithmic information

$$H(x, y) \leq H(x) + H(y) + c$$

no longer holds.

5.3. Complexity via Self-Delimiting Binary Programs

The solution is to modify the definition yet again, recovering the property that no valid program is an extension of another valid program that we had in LISP. This was done in CHAITIN (1975b). So again we shall consider a bit string program to start with a (self-delimiting) LISP function definition f that is evaluated and applied to the rest d of the bit string as data.

But we wish to eliminate f with the property that they produce values when applied to d and e if e is an extension of d. To force f to treat its data as self-delimiting, we institute a watch-dog policy that operates in stages. At stage k of applying f to d, we simultaneously consider all prefixes and extensions of d up to k bits long, and apply f to d and to these prefixes and extensions of d for k time steps. We only consider f of d to be defined if f of d can be calculated in time k, and none of the prefixes or extensions of d that we consider at stage k gives a value when f is applied to it for time k. This watch-dog policy achieves the following. If f is self-delimiting, in that $f(d)$ is defined implies $f(e)$ is not defined if e is an extension of d, then nothing is changed by the watch-dog policy (except it slows things down). If however f does not treat its data as self-delimiting, the watch-dog will ignore $f(e)$ for all e that are prefixes or extensions of a d which it has already seen has the property that $f(d)$ is defined. Thus the watch-dog forces f to treat its data as self-delimiting.

The result is a "self-delimiting universal binary computer," a function $V(p)$ where p is a bit string, with the following properties:
1. If $V(p)$ is defined and p' is an extension of p, then $V(p')$ is not defined.
2. If $W(p)$ is any computable partial function on the bit strings with the property in (1), then there is a bit string prefix w such that for all p,

$V(wp) = W(p)$. In fact, w is just a LISP program for W, converted from characters to binary.

3. Hence $H_V(x) \leq H_W(x) + 7\, H_{\mathrm{LISP}}(W)$.

Now we get back most of the nice properties we had before. For example, we have a well-defined halting probability Ω_V again, resulting from assigning the measure 2^{-n} to each n-bit program, because no extension of a program that halts is a program that halts, i.e., no extension of a valid program is a valid program. And information content is subadditive again:

$$H_V(x, y) \quad \leq \quad H_V(x) + H_V(y) + c.$$

However, it is no longer the case that $B_V(n)$, the maximum of $H_V(x)$ taken over all n-bit strings x, is equal to $n + O(1)$. Rather we have

$$B_V(n) \quad = \quad n + H_V(n) + O(1),$$

because in general the best way to calculate an n-bit string in a self-delimiting manner is to first calculate its length n in a self-delimiting manner, which takes $H_V(n)$ bits, and to then read the next n bits of the program, for a total of $H_V(n) + n$ bits. $H_V(n)$ is usually about $\log_2 n$.

A complete LISP program for calculating Ω_V in the limit from below

$$\omega_k \quad \leq \quad \omega_{k+1} \quad \rightarrow \quad \Omega_V$$

is given in Section 5.4. ω_k, the kth lower bound on Ω_V, is obtained by running all programs up to k bits in size on the universal computer U of Section 5.2 for time k. More precisely, a program p contributes measure

$$2^{-|p|}$$

to ω_k if $|p| \leq k$ and (Up) can be evaluated within depth k, and there is no prefix or extension q of p with the same property, i.e., such that $|q| \leq k$ and (Uq) can be evaluated within depth k.

However as this is stated we will not get $\omega_k \leq \omega_{k+1}$, because a program may contribute to ω_k and then be barred from contributing to ω_{k+1}. In order to fix this the computation of ω_k is actually done in stages. At stage $j = 0, 1, 2, \ldots, k$ all programs of size $\leq j$ are run on U for time j. Once a program is discovered that halts, no prefixes or extensions of it are considered in any future stages. And if there is a "tie" and two programs that halt are discovered at the same stage and one of them is an extension of the other, then the smaller program wins and contributes to ω_k.

ω_{10}, the tenth lower bound on Ω_V, is actually calculated in Section 5.4, and turns out to be 127/128. The reason we get this value, is that to calculate ω_{10}, every one-character LISP function f is applied to the remaining bits of a program that is up to 10 bits long. Of the 128 one-character strings f, only "(" fails to halt, because it is syntactically incomplete; the remaining 127 one-character possibilities for f halt because of our permissive LISP semantics and because we consider ")" to mean "()".

5.4. Omega in LISP

LISP Interpreter Run

```
[
   Make a list of strings into a prefix-free set
   by removing duplicates.  Last occurrence is kept.
]
∇ (ρx)
[ ~-equiv: are two bit strings prefixes of each other ? ]
← (~xy)  →∘x1  →∘y1  →=↑x↑y  (~↓x↓y)  0
[ is x ~-equivalent to a member of l ? ]
← (εxl)  →∘l0  →(~x↑l)  1  (εx↓l)
[ body of ρ follows: ]
→∘xx ← r (ρ↓x)  →(ε↑xr)  r  ,↑xr
```

ρ:
```
            (∇(x)(('(∇(~)(('(∇(ε)(→(∘x)x(('(∇(r)(→(ε(↑x)r)r(,(
            ↑x)r))))(ρ(↓x))))))))('(∇(xl)(→(∘l)0(→(~x(↑l))1(εx(↓
            l)))))))))))('(∇(xy)(→(∘x)1(→(∘y)1(→(=(↑x)(↑y))(~(↓x
            )(↓y))0)))))))
```

```
[
   K th approximation to Omega for given U.
]
∇ (ωK)
← (∪xy)  →∘xy  ,↑x(∪↓xy)                    [ concatenation (set union) ]
← (B)
← k □(,"∇,(),□'k())                              [ write k & its value ]
← s (ρ(∪(Hk)s))      [ add to s programs not ~-equiv which halt ]
← s □(,"∇,(),□'s())                              [ write s & its value ]
→=kK (|s)                            [ if k = K, return measure of set s ]
← k ,1k                                              [ add 1 to k ]
  (B)
← k ()                                      [ initialize k to zero ]
← s ()                        [ initialize s to empty set of programs ]
  (B)
```

ω:
```
            (∇(K)(('(∇(∪)(('(∇(B)(('(∇(k)(('(∇(s)(B)))())))())())
            ))('(∇()(('(∇(k)(('(∇(s)(('(∇(s)(→(=kK)(|s)(('(∇(k
            )(B)))(,1k)))))(□((,∇(,()(,(□('s))()))))))))))(ρ(∪(H
            k)s)))))(□((,∇(,()(,(□('k))())))))))))))))('(∇(xy)(→
            (∘x)y(,(↑x)(∪(↓x)y)))))))
```

```
[
   Subset of computer programs of size up to k
   which halt within time k when run on U.
]
∇ (Hk)
[ quote all elements of list ]
← (Qx) →∘xx ,,"',↑x()(Q↓x)
[ select elements of x which have property P ]
← (Sx) →∘xx →(P↑x) ,↑x(S↓x)  (S↓x)
[ property P
   is that program halts within time k when run on U ]
← (Px) =0∘♠k(Q,U,x())
[ body of H follows:
   select subset of programs of length up to k ]
(S(Xk))
```

H: (∇(k)(('(∇(Q)(('(∇(S)(('(∇(P)(S(Xk))))('(∇(x)(=0(∘
                   (♠k(Q(,U(,x()))))))))))))))('(∇(x)(→(∘x)x(→(P(↑x))(,(
                   ↑x)(S(↓x)))(S(↓x)))))))))))('(∇(x)(→(∘x)x(,(,'(,(↑x)
                   ()))(Q(↓x)))))))))

```
[
   Produce all bit strings of length less than or equal to k.
   Bigger strings come first.
]
∇ (Xk)
→∘k '(())
← (Zy) →∘y '(())  ,,0↑y ,,1↑y (Z↓y)
(Z(X↓k))
```

X: (∇(k)(→(∘k)('(()))(('(∇(Z)(Z(X(↓k)))))('(∇(y)(→(∘y
)('(()))(,(,0(↑y))(,(,1(↑y))(Z(↓y))))))))))))))

```
∇ (|x)    [ | calculates measure of set of programs ]
[ S = sum of three bits ]
← (Sxyz) =x=yz
[ C = carry of three bits ]
← (Cxyz) →x→y1z→yz0
[ + = addition (left-aligned base-two fractions)
   returns carry followed by sum ]
← (+xy) →∘x,0y →∘y,0x ← z (+↓x↓y) ,(C↑x↑y↑z) ,(S↑x↑y↑z) ↓z
[ | = change bit string to 2**-length of string
   example: (111) has length 3, becomes 2**-3 = (001) ]
← (|x) →∘x'(1) ,0(|↓x)
[ / = given list of strings,
   form sum of 2**-length of strings ]
← (/x)
     →∘x'(0)
     ← y (+(|↑x)(/↓x))
     ← z →↑y ▯'(overflow) 0        [ if carry out, overflow ! ]
     ↓y                            [ remove carry ]
[ body of definition of measure of a set of programs follows:]
```

```
← s (/x)
,↑s ,. ↓s                              [ insert binary point ]

|:          (∇(x)((' (∇(S)(('(∇(C)(('(∇(+)(('(∇(|)(('(∇(/)(('(∇
            (s)(,(↑s)(,.(↓s)))))(/x))))('(∇(x)(→(∘x)('(0))(('(
            ∇(y)(('(∇(z)(↓y)))(→(↑y)(□('(overflow)))0))))(+(|(
            ↑x))(/(↓x)))))))))))('(∇(x)(→(∘x)('(1))(,0(|(↓x))))
            )))))('(∇(xy)(→(∘x)(,0y)(→(∘y)(,0x)(('(∇(z)(,(C(↑x
            )(↑y)(↑z))(,(S(↑x)(↑y)(↑z))(↓z)))))(+(↓x)(↓y))))))
            ))))('(∇(xyz)(→x(→y1z)(→yz0)))))))))('(∇(xyz)(=x(=yz
            ))))))
```



```
[
  If k th bit of string x is 1 then halt, else loop forever.
  Value, if has one, is always 0.
]
∇ (0xk)  →=0∘□k (0↓x↓k)                                    [ else ]
         →∘x (0xk)   [ string too short implies bit = 0, else ]
         →↑x 0 (0xk)

0:          (∇(xk)(→(=0(∘(□k)))(0(↓x)(↓k))(→(∘x)(0xk)(→(↑x)0(0
            xk)))))
```


[[[*Universal Computer*]]]

∇ (Us)

```
[
  Alphabet:
]
← A '"
(((((((((leftparen)(rightparen))(AB))((CD)(EF)))(((GH)(IJ))((KL
)(MN))))((((OP)(QR))((ST)(UV)))(((WX)(YZ))((ab)(cd)))))(((((ef
)(gh))((ij)(kl)))(((mn)(op))((qr)(st))))((((uv)(wx))((yz)(01))
)(((23)(45))((67)(89))))))((((((¢.)(<+))((|&)(!$)))(((*;)(¬-))
((/,)(%_))))((((>?)(∧¨))((∨:)(#@)))((('=)("~))((↑↓)(≤⌈)))))(((
((∟→)(□⊃))((⊂○)(←⁻)))(((∩∪)(⊥≥))((∘α)(εⁱ))))((((ρω)(×\))((÷∇)(
∆τ)))(((≠φ)(⍉⍢))((⍋⍝)(⊛⍎))))))))
[
  Read 7-bit character from bit string.
  Returns character followed by rest of string.
  Typical result is (A 1111 000).
]
← (Cs)
→∘↓↓↓ ↓↓↓s (Cs)     [ undefined if less than 7 bits left ]
← (Rx) ↑↓x          [ 1 bit: take right half ]
← (Lx) ↑x           [ 0 bit: take left half ]

'
  (→↑s R L
  (→↑↓s R L
  (→↑↓↓s R L
  (→↑↓↓↓s R L
  (→↑↓↓↓↓s R L
  (→↑↓↓↓↓↓s R L
  (→↑↓↓↓↓↓↓s R L
```

```
  A)))) )))
↓↓↓↓ ↓↓↓s
[
  Read zero or more s-exp's until get to a right parenthesis.
  Returns list of s-exp's followed by rest of string.
  Typical result is ((AB) 1111 000).
]
← (Ls)
← c (Cs)                           [ c = read char from input s ]
→=↑c'(right paren) ,()↓c                        [ end of list ]
← d (Es)                           [ d = read s-exp from input s ]
← e (L↓d)                     [ e = read list from rest of input ]
   ,,↑d↑e↓e                          [ add s-exp to list ]
[
  Read single s-exp.
  Returns s-exp followed by rest of string.
  Typical result is ((AB) 1111 000).
]
← (Es)
← c (Cs)                           [ c = read char from input s ]
→=↑c'(right paren) ,()↓c    [ invalid right paren becomes () ]
→=↑c'(left  paren) (L↓c)        [ read list from rest of input ]
c                        [ otherwise atom followed by rest of input ]

                        [ end of definitions; body of U follows: ]

← x (Es)   [ split bit string into function followed by data ]
⍦ ,↑x,,"',↓x()()     [ apply unquoted function to quoted data ]

U:              (∇(s)(('(∇(A)(('(∇(C)(('(∇(L)(('(∇(E)(('(∇(x)(⍦(,(
                ↑x)(,(,'(,(↓x)()))(()))))))(Es))))('(∇(s)(('(∇(c)(→(
                =(↑c)('(rightparen)))(,()(↓c))(→(=(↑c)('(leftparen
                )))(L(↓c))c))))(Cs)))))))('(∇(s)(('(∇(c)(→(=(↑c)('
                (rightparen)))(,()(↓c))(('(∇(d)(('(∇(e)(,(,(↑d)(↑e
                ))(↓e))))(L(↓d)))))(Es)))))(Cs))))))('(∇(s)(→(∘(↓
                (↓(↓(↓(↓(↓s)))))))(Cs)(('(∇(R)(('(∇(L)(,((→(↑s)RL)
                ((→(↑(↓s))RL)((→(↑(↓(↓s)))RL)((→(↑(↓(↓(↓s))))RL)((
                →(↑(↓(↓(↓(↓s)))))RL)((→(↑(↓(↓(↓(↓(↓s))))))RL)((→(↑
                (↓(↓(↓(↓(↓(↓s)))))))RL)A)))))))(↓(↓(↓(↓(↓(↓(↓s)))
                )))))('(∇(x)(↑x))))))('(∇(x)(↑(↓x))))))))))('(((
                (((((leftparen)(rightparen))(AB))((CD)(EF)))(((GH)
                (IJ))((KL)(MN))))((((OP)(QR))((ST)(UV)))(((WX)(YZ)
                )((ab)(cd)))))((((((ef)(gh))((ij)(kl)))(((mn)(op))(
                (qr)(st))))((((uv)(wx))((yz)(01)))(((23)(45))((67)
                (89))))))(((((((¢.)(<+))((|&)(!$)))(((*;)(¬-))((/,)
                (%_))))((((>?)(∧¨))((v:)(#∂)))((('=)("~))((↑↓)(≤⌈)
                ))))(((((L→)(⎕⊃))((⊂∘)(←⁻)))(((∩∪)(⊥≥))((∘α)(∈ι)))
                )((((ρω)(×\))((÷∇)(∆⊤)))(((≠φ)(⍀⍫))((∆⍦)(⊛⍢)))))))
                )))
```



```
[ Omega ! ]
(ω'(1111 111 111))

expression  (ω('(1111111111)))
display     k
```

```
display      ()
display      s
display      ()
display      k
display      (1)
display      s
display      ()
display      k
display      (11)
display      s
display      ()
display      k
display      (111)
display      s
display      ()
display      k
display      (1111)
display      s
display      ()
display      k
display      (11111)
display      s
display      ()
display      k
display      (111111)
display      s
display      ()
display      k
display      (1111111)
display      s
display      ()
display      k
display      (11111111)
display      s
display      ()
display      k
display      (111111111)
display      s
display      ()
display      k
display      (1111111111)
display      (000)
display      (100)
display      (010)
display      (110)
display      (001)
display      (101)
display      (011)
display      (111)
display      (00)
display      (10)
display      (01)
display      (11)
display      (0)
display      (1)
display      ()
display      s
```

display   ((1000000) (0100000) (1100000) (0010000) (1010000) (011
0000) (1110000) (0001000) (1001000) (0101000) (1101000)
(0011000) (1011000) (0111000) (1111000) (0000100) (1000
100) (0100100) (1100100) (0010100) (1010100) (0110100) (
1110100) (0001100) (1001100) (0101100) (1101100) (00111
00) (1011100) (0111100) (1111100) (0000010) (1000010) (0
100010) (1100010) (0010010) (1010010) (0110010) (111001
0) (0001010) (1001010) (0101010) (1101010) (0011010) (10
11010) (0111010) (1111010) (0000110) (1000110) (0100110
) (1100110) (0010110) (1010110) (0110110) (1110110) (000
1110) (1001110) (0101110) (1101110) (0011110) (1011110)
(0111110) (1111110) (0000001) (1000001) (0100001) (1100
001) (0010001) (1010001) (0110001) (1110001) (0001001) (
1001001) (0101001) (1101001) (0011001) (1011001) (01110
01) (1111001) (0000101) (1000101) (0100101) (1100101) (0
010101) (1010101) (0110101) (1110101) (0001101) (100110
1) (0101101) (1101101) (0011101) (1011101) (0111101) (11
11101) (0000011) (1000011) (0100011) (1100011) (0010011
) (1010011) (0110011) (1110011) (0001011) (1001011) (010
1011) (1101011) (0011011) (1011011) (0111011) (1111011)
(0000111) (1000111) (0100111) (1100111) (0010111) (1010
111) (0110111) (1110111) (0001111) (1001111) (0101111) (
1101111) (0011111) (1011111) (0111111) (1111111))

value   (0.1111111)

End of LISP Run

Elapsed time is 38.855583 *seconds.*

CHAPTER 6

PROGRAM SIZE

6.1. Introduction

In this chapter we present a new definition of program-size complexity. $H(A, B/C, D)$ is defined to be the size in bits of the shortest self-delimiting program for calculating strings A and B if one is given a minimal-size self-delimiting program for calculating strings C and D. As is the case in LISP, programs are required to be self-delimiting, but instead of achieving this with balanced parentheses, we merely stipulate that no meaningful program be a prefix of another. Moreover, instead of being given C and D directly, one is given a program for calculating them that is minimal in size. Unlike previous definitions, this one has precisely the formal properties of the entropy concept of information theory.

What train of thought led us to this definition? Following [CHAITIN (1970a)], think of a computer as decoding equipment at the receiving end of a noiseless binary communications channel. Think of its programs as code words, and of the result of the computation as the decoded message. Then it is natural to require that the programs/code words form what is called a "prefix-free set," so that successive messages sent across the channel (e.g. subroutines) can be separated. Prefix-free sets are well understood; they are governed by the Kraft inequality, which therefore plays an important role in this chapter.

One is thus led to define the relative complexity $H(A, B/C, D)$ of A and B with respect to C and D to be the size of the shortest self-delimiting program for producing A and B from C and D. However, this is still not quite right. Guided by the analogy with information theory, one would like

$$H(A, B) = H(A) + H(B/A) + \Delta$$

to hold with an error term Δ bounded in absolute value. But, as is shown in the Appendix of CHAITIN (1975b), $|\Delta|$ is unbounded. So we stipulate instead that $H(A, B/C, D)$ is the size of the smallest self-delimiting program that produces A and B when it is given *a minimal-size self-delimiting program* for C and D. We shall show that $|\Delta|$ is then bounded.

For related concepts that are useful in statistics, see RISSANEN (1986).

6.2. Definitions

In this chapter, $\Lambda = $ LISP () is the empty string. {Λ, 0, 1, 00, 01, 10, 11, 000, ... } is the set of finite binary strings, ordered as indicated. Henceforth we say "string" instead of "binary string;" a string is understood to be finite unless the contrary is explicitly stated. As before, $|s|$ is the length of the string s. The variables p, q, s, and t denote strings. The variables c, i, k, m, and n denote non-negative integers. $\#(S)$ is the cardinality of the set S.

Definition of a Prefix–Free Set

A prefix-free set is a set of strings S with the property that no string in S is a prefix of another.

Definition of a Computer

A computer C is a computable partial function that carries a program string p and a free data string q into an output string $C(p, q)$ with the property that for each q the domain of $C(., q)$ is a prefix-free set; i.e., if $C(p, q)$ is defined and p is a proper prefix of p', then $C(p', q)$ is not defined. In other words, programs must be self-delimiting.

Definition of a Universal Computer

U is a universal computer iff for each computer C there is a constant $\text{sim}(C)$ with the following property: if $C(p, q)$ is defined, then there is a p' such that $U(p', q) = C(p, q)$ and $|p'| \leq |p| + \text{sim}(C)$.

Theorem

There is a universal computer U.

Proof

U first reads the binary representation of a LISP S-expression f from the beginning of its program string p, with 7 bits per character as specified in Figure 6. Let p' denote the remainder of the program string p. Then U proceeds in stages. At stage t, U applies for t time units the S-expression f that it has read to two arguments, the rest of the program string p', and the free data string q. And U also applies f for t time units to each string of size less than or equal to t and the free data string q. More precisely, "U applies f for time t to x and y" means that U uses the LISP primitive function $\imath$ to evaluate the triple $(f\,('x)\,('y))$, so that the unquoted function definition f is evaluated before being applied to its arguments, which are quoted. If $f(p', q)$ yields a value before any f(a prefix or extension of p', q) yields a value, then $U(p, q) = f(p', q)$. Otherwise $U(p, q)$ is undefined, and, as before, in case of "ties", the smaller program wins. It follows that U satisfies the definition of a universal computer with

$$\text{sim}(C) \ = \ 7\,H_{\text{LISP}}(C).$$

Q.E.D.

We pick this particular universal computer U as the standard one we shall use for measuring program–size complexities throughout the rest of this book.

Definition of Canonical Programs, Complexities, and Probabilities
(a) The canonical program.

$$s^* \ \equiv \ \min_{U(p,\,\Lambda)=s} p\,.$$

I.e., s^* is the shortest string that is a program for U to calculate s, and if several strings of the same size have this property, we pick the one that comes first when all strings of that size are ordered from all 0's to all 1's in the usual lexicographic order.
(b) Complexities.

$$H_C(s) \ \equiv \ \min_{C(p,\,\Lambda)=s} |p| \qquad (\text{may be } \infty),$$

$$H(s) \ \equiv \ H_U(s),$$

$$H_C(s/t) \ \equiv \ \min_{C(p,\,t^*)=s} |p| \qquad (\text{may be } \infty),$$

$$H(s/t) \ \equiv \ H_U(s/t),$$

$$H_C(s{:}t) \ \equiv \ H_C(t) - H_C(t/s),$$

$$H(s:t) \quad \equiv \quad H_U(s:t).$$

(c) Probabilities.

$$P_C(s) \quad \equiv \quad \sum_{C(p, \Lambda)=s} 2^{-|p|},$$

$$P(s) \quad \equiv \quad P_U(s),$$

$$P_C(s/t) \quad \equiv \quad \sum_{C(p, t^*)=s} 2^{-|p|},$$

$$P(s/t) \quad \equiv \quad P_U(s/t),$$

$$\Omega \quad \equiv \quad \sum_{U(p, \Lambda) \text{ is defined}} 2^{-|p|}.$$

Remark on Omega

Note that the LISP program for calculating Ω in the limit from below that we gave in Section 5.4 is still valid, even though the notion of "free data" did not appear in Chapter 5. Section 5.4 still works, because giving a LISP function only one argument is equivalent to giving it that argument and the empty list Λ as a second argument.

Remark on Nomenclature

The names of these concepts mix terminology from information theory, from probability theory, and from the field of computational complexity. $H(s)$ may be referred to as the algorithmic information content of s or the program-size complexity of s, and $H(s/t)$ may be referred to as the algorithmic information content of s relative to t or the program-size complexity of s given t. Or $H(s)$ and $H(s/t)$ may be termed the algorithmic entropy and the conditional algorithmic entropy, respectively. $H(s:t)$ is called the mutual algorithmic information of s and t; it measures the degree of interdependence of s and t. More precisely, $H(s:t)$ is the extent to which knowing s helps one to calculate t, which, as we shall see in Theorem I9, also turns out to be the extent to which it is cheaper to calculate them together than to calculate them separately. $P(s)$ and $P(s/t)$ are the algorithmic probability and the conditional algorithmic probability of s given t. And Ω is of course the halting probability of U (with null free data).

Theorem I0

$$H(s) \quad \leq \quad H_C(s) + \text{sim}(C), \tag{a}$$

$$H(s/t) \quad \leq \quad H_C(s/t) + \text{sim}(C), \tag{b}$$

$$s^* \quad \neq \quad \Lambda, \tag{c}$$

$$s \quad = \quad U(s^*, \Lambda), \tag{d}$$

$$H(s) \quad = \quad |s^*|, \tag{e}$$

$$H(s) \quad \neq \quad \infty, \tag{f}$$

$$H(s/t) \quad \neq \quad \infty, \tag{g}$$

$$0 \quad \leq \quad P_C(s) \quad \leq \quad 1, \tag{h}$$

$$0 \quad \leq \quad P_C(s/t) \quad \leq \quad 1, \tag{i}$$

$$1 \quad \geq \quad \sum_s P_C(s), \tag{j}$$

$$1 \quad \geq \quad \sum_s P_C(s/t), \tag{k}$$

$$P_C(s) \quad \geq \quad 2^{-H_C(s)}, \tag{l}$$

$$P_C(s/t) \quad \geq \quad 2^{-H_C(s/t)}, \tag{m}$$

$$0 \quad < \quad P(s) \quad < \quad 1, \tag{n}$$

$$0 \quad < \quad P(s/t) \quad < \quad 1, \tag{o}$$

$$\#\Big(\{s : H_C(s) < n\}\Big) \quad < \quad 2^n, \tag{p}$$

$$\#\Big(\{s : H_C(s, t) < n\}\Big) \quad < \quad 2^n, \tag{q}$$

$$\#\left(\left\{s : P_C(s) > \frac{n}{m}\right\}\right) \quad < \quad \frac{m}{n}, \tag{r}$$

$$\#\left(\left\{s : P_C(s/t) > \frac{n}{m}\right\}\right) \quad < \quad \frac{m}{n}. \tag{s}$$

Proof

These are immediate consequences of the definitions. Q.E.D.

Extensions of the Previous Concepts to Tuples of Strings

We have defined the program-size complexity and the algorithmic probability of individual strings, the relative complexity of one string given another, and the algorithmic probability of one string given another. Let's extend this from individual strings to tuples of strings: this is easy to do because we have used LISP to construct our universal computer U, and the ordered list $(s_1 s_2 \ldots s_n)$ is a basic LISP notion. Here each s_k is a string, which is defined in LISP as a list of 0's and 1's. Thus, for example, we can define the relative complexity of computing a triple of strings given another triple of strings:

$$H(s_1, s_2, s_3 / s_4, s_5, s_6) \quad \equiv \quad H(\,(s_1 s_2 s_3)\,/\,(s_4 s_5 s_6)\,).$$

$H(s, t) \equiv H((st))$ is often called the joint information content of s and t.

Extensions of the Previous Concepts to Non–Negative Integers

We have defined H and P for tuples of strings. This is now extended to tuples each of whose elements may either be a string or a non-negative integer n. We do this by identifying n with the list consisting of n 1's, i.e., with the LISP S-expression (111...111) that has exactly n 1's.

6.3. Basic Identities

This section has two objectives. The first is to show that H satisfies the fundamental inequalities and identities of information theory to within error terms of the order of unity. For example, the information in s about t is nearly symmetrical. The second objective is to show that P is approximately a conditional probability measure: $P(t/s)$ and $P(s, t)/P(s)$ are within a constant multiplicative factor of each other.

The following notation is convenient for expressing these approximate relationships. $O(1)$ denotes a function whose absolute value is less than or equal to c for all values of its arguments. And $f \simeq g$ means that the functions f and g satisfy the inequalities $cf \geq g$ and $f \leq cg$ for all values of their arguments. In both cases c is an unspecified constant.

Theorem I1

$$H(s, t) \quad = \quad H(t, s) + O(1), \tag{a}$$

$$H(s/s) \;=\; O(1), \tag{b}$$

$$H(H(s)/s) \;=\; O(1), \tag{c}$$

$$H(s) \;\leq\; H(s, t) + O(1), \tag{d}$$

$$H(s/t) \;\leq\; H(s) + O(1), \tag{e}$$

$$H(s, t) \;\leq\; H(s) + H(t/s) + O(1), \tag{f}$$

$$H(s, t) \;\leq\; H(s) + H(t) + O(1), \tag{g}$$

$$H(s{:}t) \;\geq\; O(1), \tag{h}$$

$$H(s{:}t) \;\leq\; H(s) + H(t) - H(s, t) + O(1), \tag{i}$$

$$H(s{:}s) \;=\; H(s) + O(1), \tag{j}$$

$$H(\Lambda{:}s) \;=\; O(1), \tag{k}$$

$$H(s{:}\Lambda) \;=\; O(1). \tag{l}$$

Proof

These are easy consequences of the definitions. The proof of Theorem I1(f) is especially interesting, and is given in full below. Also, note that Theorem I1(g) follows immediately from Theorem I1(f,e), and Theorem I1(i) follows immediately from Theorem I1(f) and the definition of $H(s{:}t)$.

Now for the proof of Theorem I1(f). We claim (see the next paragraph) that there is a computer C with the following property. If

$$U(p, s^*) \;=\; t \quad \text{and} \quad |p| \;=\; H(t/s)$$

(i.e., if p is a minimal-size program for calculating t from s^*), then

$$C(s^*p, \Lambda) \;=\; (s, t).$$

By using Theorem I0(e,a) we see that

$$H_C(s, t) \;\leq\; |s^*p| \;=\; |s^*| + |p| \;=\; H(s) + H(t/s),$$

and

$$H(s, t) \;\leq\; H_C(s, t) + \operatorname{sim}(C) \;\leq\; H(s) + H(t/s) + O(1).$$

It remains to verify the claim that there is such a computer. C does the following when it is given the program s^*p and the free data Λ. First C pretends to be U. More precisely, C generates the r.e. set

$V = \{v:U(v, \Lambda) \text{ is defined}\}$. As it generates V, C continually checks whether or not that part r of its program that it has already read is a prefix of some known element v of V. Note that initially $r = \Lambda$. Whenever C finds that r is a prefix of a $v \in V$, it does the following. If r is a proper prefix of v, C reads another bit of its program. And if $r = v$, C calculates $U(r, \Lambda)$, and C's simulation of U is finished. In this manner C reads the initial portion s^* of its program and calculates s.

Then C simulates the computation that U performs when given the free data s^* and the remaining portion of C's program. More precisely, C generates the r.e. set $W = \{w:U(w, s^*) \text{ is defined}\}$. As it generates W, C continually checks whether or not that part r of its program that it has already read is a prefix of some known element w of W. Note that initially $r = \Lambda$. Whenever C finds that r is a prefix of a $w \in W$, it does the following. If r is a proper prefix of w, C reads another bit of its program. And if $r = w$, C calculates $U(r, s^*)$, and C's second simulation of U is finished. In this manner C reads the final portion p of its program and calculates t from s^*. The entire program has now been read, and both s and t have been calculated. C finally forms the pair (s, t) and halts, indicating this to be the result of the computation. Q.E.D.

Remark

The rest of this section is devoted to showing that the "$\leq$" in Theorem I1(f) and I1(i) can be replaced by "$=$." The arguments used have a strong probabilistic as well as an information-theoretic flavor.

Theorem I2

(Extended Kraft inequality condition for the existence of a prefix-free set).

Hypothesis. Consider an effectively given list of finitely or infinitely many "requirements"

$$\{ (s_k, n_k) : k = 0,1,2, \dots \}$$

for the construction of a computer. The requirements are said to be "consistent" if

$$1 \geq \sum_k 2^{-n_k},$$

and we assume that they are consistent. Each requirement (s_k, n_k) requests that a program of length n_k be "assigned" to the result s_k. A computer C is said to "satisfy" the requirements if there are precisely as many programs p of length n such that $C(p, \Lambda) = s$ as there are pairs (s, n) in the list of requirements. Such a C must have the property that

$$P_C(s) = \sum_{s_k = s} 2^{-n_k}$$

and

$$H_C(s) = \min_{s_k = s} n_k \,.$$

Conclusion. There are computers that satisfy these requirements. Moreover, if we are given the requirements one by one, then we can simulate a computer that satisfies them. Hereafter we refer to the particular computer that the proof of this theorem shows how to simulate as the one that is "determined" by the requirements.

Proof

(a) First we give what we claim is the definition of a particular computer C that satisfies the requirements. In the second part of the proof we justify this claim.

As we are given the requirements, we assign programs to results. Initially, all programs for C are available. When we are given the requirement (s_k, n_k) we assign *the first available program* of length n_k to the result s_k (first in the usual ordering $\Lambda, 0, 1, 00, 01, 10, 11, 000, \dots$). As each program is assigned, it and all its prefixes and extensions become unavailable for future assignments. Note that a result can have many programs assigned to it (of the same or different lengths) if there are many requirements involving it.

How can we simulate C? As we are given the requirements, we make the above assignments, and we simulate C by using the technique that was given in the proof of Theorem I1(f), reading just that part of the program that is necessary.

(b) Now to justify the claim. We must show that the above rule for making assignments never fails, i.e., we must show that it is never the case that all programs of the requested length are unavailable.

A geometrical interpretation is necessary. Consider the unit interval $[0,1) \equiv \{\text{real } x : 0 \leq x < 1\}$. The kth program $(0 \leq k < 2^n)$ of length n corresponds to the interval

$[k2^{-n}, (k + 1)2^{-n})$.

Assigning a program corresponds to assigning all the points in its interval. The condition that the set of assigned programs be prefix-free corresponds to the rule that an interval is available for assignment iff no point in it has already been assigned. The rule we gave above for making assignments is to assign that interval

$[k2^{-n}, (k + 1)2^{-n})$

of the requested length 2^{-n} that is available that has the smallest possible k. Using this rule for making assignments gives rise to the following fact.

Fact. The set of those points in $[0,1)$ that are unassigned can always be expressed as the union of a finite number of intervals

$[k_i 2^{-n_i}, (k_i + 1)2^{-n_i})$

with the following properties: $n_i > n_{i+1}$, and

$(k_i + 1)2^{-n_i} \le k_{i+1}2^{-n_{i+1}}$.

I.e., these intervals are disjoint, their lengths are *distinct* powers of 2, and they appear in $[0,1)$ in order of increasing length.

We leave to the reader the verification that this fact is always the case and that it implies that an assignment is impossible only if the interval requested is longer than the total length of the unassigned part of $[0,1)$, i.e., only if the requirements are inconsistent. Q.E.D.

Note

The preceding proof may be considered to involve a computer memory "storage allocation" problem. We have one unit of storage, and all requests for storage request a power of two of storage, i.e., one-half unit, one-quarter unit, etc. Storage is never freed. The algorithm given above will be able to service a series of storage allocation requests as long as the total storage requested is not greater than one unit. If the total amount of storage remaining at any point in time is expressed as a real number in binary, then the crucial property of the above storage allocation technique can be stated as follows: at any given moment there will be a block of size 2^{-k} of free storage if and only if the binary digit corresponding to 2^{-k} in the base-two expansion for the amount of storage remaining at that point is a 1 bit.

Theorem I3

(Computing H_C and P_C "in the limit").

Consider a computer C.

(a) The set of all true propositions of the form

$$\text{``}H_C(s) \quad \leq \quad n\text{''}$$

is recursively enumerable. Given t^* one can recursively enumerate the set of all true propositions of the form

$$\text{``}H_C(s/t) \quad \leq \quad n\text{''}.$$

(b) The set of all true propositions of the form

$$\text{``}P_C(s) \quad > \quad \frac{n}{m}\text{''}$$

is recursively enumerable. Given t^* one can recursively enumerate the set of all true propositions of the form

$$\text{``}P_C(s/t) \quad > \quad \frac{n}{m}\text{''}.$$

Proof

This is an easy consequence of the fact that the domain of C is an r.e. set. Q.E.D.

Remark

The set of all true propositions of the form

$$\text{``}H(s/t) \quad \leq \quad n\text{''}$$

is not r.e.; for if it were r.e., it would easily follow from Theorems I1(c) and I0(q) that Theorem 5.1(f) of CHAITIN (1975b) is false.

Theorem I4

For each computer C there is a constant c such that

$$H(s) \quad \leq \quad - \log_2 P_C(s) + c, \tag{a}$$

$$H(s/t) \quad \leq \quad - \log_2 P_C(s/t) + c. \tag{b}$$

Proof

First a piece of notation. By lg x we mean the greatest integer less than the base-two logarithm of the real number x. I.e., if $2^n < x \le 2^{n+1}$, then lg $x = n$. Thus

$$2^{\lg x} < x$$

as long as x is positive. E.g., lg $2^{-3.5} = $ lg $2^{-3} = -4$ and lg $2^{3.5} = $ lg $2^4 = 3$.

It follows from Theorem I3(b) that one can eventually discover every lower bound on $P_C(s)$ that is a power of two. In other words, the set of all true propositions

$$T \equiv \{ \text{``} P_C(s) > 2^{-n} \text{''} : P_C(s) > 2^{-n} \}$$

is recursively enumerable. Similarly, given t^* one can eventually discover every lower bound on $P_C(s/t)$ that is a power of two. In other words, given t^* one can recursively enumerate the set of all true propositions

$$T_t \equiv \{ \text{``} P_C(s/t) > 2^{-n} \text{''} : P_C(s/t) > 2^{-n} \}.$$

This will enable us to use Theorem I2 to show that there is a computer D with these properties:

$$\begin{cases} H_D(s) &= - \lg P_C(s) + 1, \\ P_D(s) &= 2^{\lg P_C(s)} \quad < \quad P_C(s), \end{cases} \tag{1}$$

$$\begin{cases} H_D(s/t) &= - \lg P_C(s/t) + 1, \\ P_D(s/t) &= 2^{\lg P_C(s/t)} \quad < \quad P_C(s/t), \end{cases} \tag{2}$$

By applying Theorem I0(a,b) to (1) and (2), we see that Theorem I4 holds with $c = \text{sim}(D) + 2$.

How does the computer D work? First of all, it checks whether the free data that it has been given is Λ or t^*. These two cases can be distinguished, for by Theorem I0(c) it is impossible for t^* to be equal to Λ.

(a) If D has been given the free data Λ, it enumerates T without repetitions and simulates the computer determined by the set of all requirements of the form

$$\begin{aligned} &\{ (s, \ n + 1) : \text{``} P_C(s) > 2^{-n} \text{''} \in T \} \\ &= \{ (s, \ n + 1) : P_C(s) > 2^{-n} \}. \end{aligned} \tag{3}$$

Thus (s, n) is taken as a requirement iff $n \geq - \lg P_C(s) + 1$. Hence the number of programs p of length n such that $D(p, \Lambda) = s$ is 1 if $n \geq - \lg P_C(s) + 1$ and is 0 otherwise, which immediately yields (1).

However, we must check that the requirements (3) on D satisfy the Kraft inequality and are consistent.

$$\sum_{D(p,\,\Lambda)=s} 2^{-|p|} = 2^{\lg P_C(s)} < P_C(s).$$

Hence

$$\sum_{D(p,\,\Lambda)\text{ is defined}} 2^{-|p|} < \sum_s P_C(s) \leq 1$$

by Theorem I0(j). Thus the hypothesis of Theorem I2 is satisfied, the requirements (3) indeed determine a computer, and the proof of (1) and Theorem I4(a) is complete.

(b) If D has been given the free data t^*, it enumerates T_t without repetitions and simulates the computer determined by the set of all requirements of the form

$$\begin{aligned} & \{ (s, n + 1) : \text{``}P_C(s/t) > 2^{-n\text{''}} \in T_t \} \\ = & \{ (s, n + 1) : P_C(s/t) > 2^{-n} \}. \end{aligned} \tag{4}$$

Thus (s, n) is taken as a requirement iff $n \geq - \lg P_C(s/t) + 1$. Hence the number of programs p of length n such that $D(p, t^*) = s$ is 1 if $n \geq - \lg P_C(s/t) + 1$ and is 0 otherwise, which immediately yields (2).

However, we must check that the requirements (4) on D satisfy the Kraft inequality and are consistent.

$$\sum_{D(p,\,t^*)=s} 2^{-|p|} = 2^{\lg P_C(s/t)} < P_C(s/t).$$

Hence

$$\sum_{D(p,\,t^*)\text{ is defined}} 2^{-|p|} < \sum_s P_C(s/t) \leq 1$$

by Theorem I0(k). Thus the hypothesis of Theorem I2 is satisfied, the requirements (4) indeed determine a computer, and the proof of (2) and Theorem I4(b) is complete. Q.E.D.

Theorem I5

For each computer C there is a constant c such that

$$\begin{cases} P(s) \geq 2^{-c}P_C(s), \\ P(s/t) \geq 2^{-c}P_C(s/t). \end{cases} \quad \text{(a)}$$

$$\begin{cases} H(s) = -\log_2 P(s) + O(1), \\ H(s/t) = -\log_2 P(s/t) + O(1). \end{cases} \quad \text{(b)}$$

Proof

Theorem I5(a) follows immediately from Theorem I4 using the fact that

$$P(s) \geq 2^{-H(s)}$$

and

$$P(s/t) \geq 2^{-H(s/t)}$$

(Theorem I0(l,m)). Theorem I5(b) is obtained by taking $C = U$ in Theorem I4 and also using these two inequalities. Q.E.D.

Remark

Theorem I4(a) extends Theorem I0(a,b) to probabilities. Note that Theorem I5(a) is not an immediate consequence of our weak definition of a universal computer.

Theorem I5(b) enables one to reformulate results about H as results concerning P, and vice versa; it is the first member of a trio of formulas that will be completed with Theorem I9(e,f). These formulas are closely analogous to expressions in classical information theory for the information content of *individual* events or symbols [SHANNON and WEAVER (1949)].

Theorem I6

(There are few minimal programs).

$$\#(\{p : U(p, \Lambda) = s \ \& \ |p| \leq H(s) + n\}) \leq 2^{n+O(1)}. \quad \text{(a)}$$

$$\#(\{p : U(p, t^*) = s \ \& \ |p| \leq H(s/t) + n\}) \leq 2^{n+O(1)}. \quad \text{(b)}$$

Proof

This follows immediately from Theorem I5(b). Q.E.D.

Theorem I7

$$P(s) \simeq \sum_t P(s, t).$$

Proof

On the one hand, there is a computer C such that

$$C(p, \Lambda) = s \quad \text{if} \quad U(p, \Lambda) = (s, t).$$

Thus

$$P_C(s) \geq \sum_t P(s, t).$$

Using Theorem I5(a), we see that

$$P(s) \geq 2^{-c} \sum_t P(s, t).$$

On the other hand, there is a computer C such that

$$C(p, \Lambda) = (s, s) \quad \text{if} \quad U(p, \Lambda) = s.$$

Thus

$$\sum_t P_C(s, t) \geq P_C(s, s) \geq P(s).$$

Using Theorem I5(a), we see that

$$\sum_t P(s, t) \geq 2^{-c} P(s).$$

Q.E.D.

Theorem I8

There is a computer C and a constant c such that

$$H_C(t/s) = H(s, t) - H(s) + c.$$

Proof

By Theorems I7 and I5(b) there is a c independent of s such that

$$2^{H(s)-c} \sum_t P(s, t) \leq 1.$$

Given the free data s^*, C computes $s = U(s^*, \Lambda)$ and $H(s) = |s^*|$, and then simulates the computer determined by the requirements

$$\{ (t, |p| - H(s) + c) : U(p, \Lambda) = (s, t) \}$$

Thus for each p such that

$$U(p, \Lambda) = (s, t)$$

there is a corresponding p' such that

$$C(p', s^*) = t$$

and

$$|p'| = |p| - H(s) + c.$$

Hence

$$H_C(t/s) = H(s, t) - H(s) + c.$$

However, we must check that these requirements satisfy the Kraft inequality and are consistent:

$$\sum_{\substack{C(p, s^*) \text{ is defined}}} 2^{-|p|} = \sum_{\substack{U(p, \Lambda)=(s, t)}} 2^{-|p|+H(s)-c}$$

$$= 2^{H(s)-c} \sum_t P(s, t) \leq 1$$

because of the way c was chosen. Thus the hypothesis of Theorem I2 is satisfied, and these requirements indeed determine a computer. Q.E.D.

Theorem I9

$$H(s, t) = H(s) + H(t/s) + O(1), \tag{a}$$

$$H(s{:}t) = H(s) + H(t) - H(s, t) + O(1), \tag{b}$$

$$H(s{:}t) = H(t{:}s) + O(1), \tag{c}$$

$$P(t/s) \simeq \frac{P(s, t)}{P(s)}, \tag{d}$$

$$H(t/s) = \log_2 \frac{P(s)}{P(s, t)} + O(1), \tag{e}$$

$$H(s:t) = \log_2 \frac{P(s, t)}{P(s)P(t)} + O(1). \tag{f}$$

Proof

Theorem I9(a) follows immediately from Theorems I8, I0(b), and I1(f). Theorem I9(b) follows immediately from Theorem I9(a) and the definition of $H(s:t)$. Theorem I9(c) follows immediately from Theorems I9(b) and I1(a). Thus the mutual information $H(s:t)$ is the extent to which it is easier to compute s and t together than to compute them separately, as well as the extent to which knowing s makes t easier to compute. Theorem I9(d,e) follow immediately from Theorems I9(a) and I5(b). Theorem I9(f) follows immediately from Theorems I9(b) and I5(b). Q.E.D.

Remark

We thus have at our disposal essentially the entire formalism of information theory. Results such as these can now be obtained effortlessly:

$$H(s_1) \leq H(s_1/s_2) + H(s_2/s_3) + H(s_3/s_4) + H(s_4) + O(1),$$

$$H(s_1, s_2, s_3, s_4)$$
$$= H(s_1/s_2, s_3, s_4) + H(s_2/s_3, s_4) + H(s_3/s_4) + H(s_4) + O(1).$$

However, there is an interesting class of identities satisfied by our H function that has no parallel in classical information theory. The simplest of these is

$$H(H(s)/s) = O(1)$$

(Theorem I1(c)), which with Theorem I9(a) immediately yields

$$H(s, H(s)) = H(s) + O(1).$$

In words, "a minimal program tells us its size as well as its output." This is just one pair of a large family of identities, as we now proceed to show.

Keeping Theorem I9(a) in mind, consider modifying the computer C used in the proof of Theorem I1(f) so that it also measures the lengths $H(s)$

and $H(t/s)$ of its subroutines s^* and p, and halts indicating $(s, t, H(s), H(t/s))$ to be the result of the computation instead of (s, t). It follows that

$$H(s, t) = H(s, t, H(s), H(t/s)) + O(1)$$

and

$$H(H(s), H(t/s) / s, t) = O(1).$$

In fact, it is easy to see that

$$H(H(s), H(t), H(t/s), H(s/t), H(s, t) / s, t) = O(1),$$

which implies

$$H(H(s:t)/s, t) = O(1).$$

And of course these identities generalize to tuples of three or more strings.

6.4. Random Strings

In this section we begin studying the notion of randomness or algorithmic incompressibility that is associated with the program-size complexity measure H.

Theorem I10
   (Bounds on the complexity of positive integers).

$$\sum_n 2^{-H(n)} \leq 1. \tag{a}$$

Consider a computable total function f that carries positive integers into positive integers.

$$\sum_n 2^{-f(n)} = \infty \quad \Rightarrow \quad H(n) > f(n) \text{ infinitely often.} \tag{b}$$

$$\sum_n 2^{-f(n)} < \infty \quad \Rightarrow \quad H(n) \leq f(n) + O(1). \tag{c}$$

Proof
(a) By Theorem I0(1,j),

$$\sum_n 2^{-H(n)} \quad \le \quad \sum_n P(n) \quad \le \quad 1.$$

(b) If

$$\sum_n 2^{-f(n)}$$

diverges, and

$$H(n) \quad \le \quad f(n)$$

held for all but finitely many values of n, then

$$\sum_n 2^{-H(n)}$$

would also diverge. But this would contradict Theorem I10(a), and thus

$$H(n) \quad > \quad f(n)$$

infinitely often.

(c) If

$$\sum_n 2^{-f(n)}$$

converges, there is an n_0 such that

$$\sum_{n \ge n_0} 2^{-f(n)} \quad \le \quad 1.$$

Thus the Kraft inequality that Theorem I2 tells us is a necessary and sufficient condition for the existence a computer C determined by the requirements

$$\{ (n, f(n)) : n \ge n_0 \}$$

is satisfied. It follows that

$$H(n) \quad \le \quad f(n) + \mathrm{sim}(C)$$

for all $n \ge n_0$. Q.E.D.

Remark

$H(n)$ can in fact be characterized as a minimal function computable in the limit from above that lies just on the borderline between the convergence and the divergence of

$$\sum 2^{-H(n)}.$$

Theorem I11

(Maximal complexity finite bit strings).

$$\max_{|s|=n} H(s) \quad = \quad n + H(n) + O(1). \tag{a}$$

$$\#(\ \{\ s:\ |s|\ =n\ \&\ H(s) \le n + H(n) - k\ \}\ ) \quad \le \quad 2^{n-k+O(1)}. \tag{b}$$

Proof

Consider a string s of length n. By Theorem I9(a),

$$H(s) \quad = \quad H(n, s) + O(1) \quad = \quad H(n) + H(s/n) + O(1).$$

We now obtain Theorem I11(a,b) from this estimate for $H(s)$. There is a computer C such that

$$C(p, |p|*) \quad = \quad p$$

for all p. Thus

$$H(s/n) \quad \le \quad n + \mathrm{sim}(C),$$

and

$$H(s) \quad \le \quad n + H(n) + O(1).$$

On the other hand, by Theorem I0(q), fewer than 2^{n-k} of the s satisfy

$$H(s/n) \quad < \quad n - k.$$

Hence fewer than 2^{n-k} of the s satisfy

$$H(s) \quad < \quad n - k + H(n) + O(1).$$

This concludes the proof of Theorem I11. Q.E.D.

Definition of Randomness (Finite Case)

In the case of finite strings, randomness is a matter of degree. To the question "How random is s?" one must reply indicating how close $H(s)$ is to the maximum possible for strings of its size. A string s is most random if $H(s)$ is approximately equal to $|s| + H(|s|)$. As we shall see in the next chapter, a good cut-off to choose between randomness and non-randomness is $H(s) \approx |s|$.

The natural next step is to define an infinite string to be random if all its initial segments are finite random strings. There are several other possibilities for defining random infinite strings and real numbers, and we study them at length in Chapter 7. To anticipate, the undecidability of the halting problem is a fundamental theorem of recursive function theory. In algorithmic information theory the corresponding theorem is as follows: The base-two representation of the probability Ω that U halts is a random (i.e., maximally complex) infinite string.

RANDOMNESS

Our goal is to use information-theoretic arguments based on the size of computer programs to show that randomness, chaos, unpredictability and uncertainty can occur in mathematics. In this chapter we construct an equation involving only whole numbers and addition, multiplication and exponentiation, with the property that if one varies a parameter and asks whether the number of solutions is finite or infinite, the answer to this question is indistinguishable from the result of independent tosses of a fair coin. In the next chapter, we shall use this to obtain a number of powerful Gödel incompleteness type results concerning the limitations of the axiomatic method, in which entropy/information measures are used.

7.1. Introduction

Following TURING (1937), consider an enumeration $r_1, r_2, r_3, \ldots$ of all computable real numbers between zero and one. We may suppose that r_k is the real number, if any, computed by the kth computer program. Let $.d_{k1}d_{k2}d_{k3} \ldots$ be the successive digits in the decimal expansion of r_k. Following Cantor, consider the diagonal of the array of r_k:

$$r_1 = .d_{11}d_{12}d_{13} \ldots$$
$$r_2 = .d_{21}d_{22}d_{23} \ldots$$
$$r_3 = .d_{31}d_{32}d_{33} \ldots$$

This gives us a new real number with decimal expansion $.d_{11}d_{22}d_{33} \ldots$. Now change each of these digits, avoiding the digits zero and nine. The result is an uncomputable real number, because its first digit is different from the first digit of the first computable real, its second digit is different from the second digit of the second computable real, etc. It is necessary to avoid zero and nine, because real numbers with different digit sequences can be equal to each other if one of them ends with an infinite sequence of zeros and the other ends with an infinite sequence of nines, for example, .3999999... = .4000000.... .

Having constructed an uncomputable real number by diagonalizing over the computable reals, Turing points out that it follows that the halting problem is unsolvable. In particular, there can be no way of deciding if the kth computer program ever outputs a kth digit. Because if there were, one could actually calculate the successive digits of the uncomputable real number defined above, which is impossible. Turing also notes that a version of Gödel's incompleteness theorem is an immediate corollary, because if there cannot be an algorithm for deciding if the kth computer program ever outputs a kth digit, there also cannot be a formal axiomatic system which would always enable one to prove which of these possibilities is the case, for in principle one could run through all possible proofs to decide. Using the powerful techniques which were developed in order to solve Hilbert's tenth problem,[12] it is possible to encode the unsolvability of the halting problem as a statement about an exponential diophantine equation. An exponential diophantine equation is one of the form

$$P(x_1, \ldots, x_m) = P'(x_1, \ldots, x_m),$$

where the variables $x_1, \ldots, x_m$ range over non-negative integers and P and P' are functions built up from these variables and non-negative integer constants by the operations of addition $A + B$, multiplication $A \times B$, and exponentiation A^B. The result of this encoding is an exponential diophantine equation $P = P'$ in $m + 1$ variables $n, x_1, \ldots, x_m$ with the property that

$$P(n, x_1, \ldots, x_m) = P'(n, x_1, \ldots, x_m)$$

has a solution in non-negative integers $x_1, \ldots, x_m$ if and only if the nth computer program ever outputs an nth digit. It follows that there can be no algorithm for deciding as a function of n whether or not $P = P'$ has a solution, and thus there cannot be any complete proof system for settling such questions either.

---

[12] See DAVIS, PUTNAM and ROBINSON (1961), DAVIS, MATIJASEVIC and ROBINSON (1976), and JONES and MATIJASEVIC (1984).

Up to now we have followed Turing's original approach, but now we will set off into new territory. Our point of departure is a remark of COURANT and ROBBINS (1941) that another way of obtaining a real number that is not on the list $r_1, r_2, r_3, \ldots$ is by tossing a coin. Here is their measure-theoretic argument that the real numbers are uncountable. Recall that $r_1, r_2, r_3, \ldots$ are the computable reals between zero and one. Cover r_1 with an interval of length $\varepsilon/2$, cover r_2 with an interval of length $\varepsilon/4$, cover r_3 with an interval of length $\varepsilon/8$, and in general cover r_k with an interval of length $\varepsilon/2^k$. Thus all computable reals in the unit interval are covered by this infinite set of intervals, and the total length of the covering intervals is

$$\sum_{k=1}^{\infty} \frac{\varepsilon}{2^k} = \varepsilon.$$

Hence if we take ε sufficiently small, the total length of the covering is arbitrarily small. In summary, the reals between zero and one constitute an interval of length one, and the subset that are computable can be covered by intervals whose total length is arbitrarily small. In other words, the computable reals are a set of measure zero, and if we choose a real in the unit interval at random, the probability that it is computable is zero. Thus one way to get an uncomputable real with probability one is to flip a fair coin, using independent tosses to obtain each bit of the binary expansion of its base-two representation.

If this train of thought is pursued, it leads one to the notion of a random real number, which can never be a computable real. Following MARTIN-LÖF (1966), we give a definition of a random real using constructive measure theory. We say that a set of real numbers X is a constructive measure zero set if there is an algorithm A which given n generates a (possibly infinite) set of intervals whose total length is less than or equal to 2^{-n} and which covers the set X. More precisely, the covering is in the form of a set C of finite binary strings s such that

$$\sum_{s \in C} 2^{-|s|} \leq 2^{-n}$$

(here $|s|$ denotes the length of the string s), and each real in the covered set X has a member of C as the initial part of its base-two expansion. In other words, we consider sets of real numbers with the property that there is an algorithm A for producing arbitrarily small coverings of the set. Such sets of reals are constructively of measure zero. Since there are only countably many algorithms A for constructively covering measure zero sets, it follows that almost all real numbers are not contained in any set of constructive measure zero. Such reals are called (Martin-Löf) random reals. In fact, if the successive bits of a real number are chosen by coin flipping, with probability one it will not be contained in any set of constructive measure zero, and hence will be a random real number.

Note that no computable real number r is random. Here is how we get a constructive covering of arbitrarily small measure. The covering algorithm, given n, yields the n-bit initial sequence of the binary digits of r. This covers r and has total length or measure equal to 2^{-n}. Thus there is an algorithm for obtaining arbitrarily small coverings of the set consisting of the computable real r, and r is not a random real number. We leave to the reader the adaptation of the argument in FELLER (1970) proving the strong law of large numbers to show that reals in which all digits do not have equal limiting frequency have constructive measure zero.[13] It follows that random reals are normal in Borel's sense, that is, in any base all digits have equal limiting frequency.

Let us consider the real number p whose nth bit in base-two notation is a zero or a one depending on whether or not the exponential diophantine equation

$$P(n, x_1, \overset{'}{\ldots}, x_m) = P'(n, x_1, \ldots, x_m)$$

has a solution in non-negative integers $x_1, \ldots, x_m$. We will show that p is not a random real. In fact, we will give an algorithm for producing coverings of measure $(n + 1)2^{-n}$, which can obviously be changed to one for producing coverings of measure not greater than 2^{-n}. Consider the first N values of the parameter n. If one knows for how many of these values of n, $P = P'$ has a solution, then one can find for which values of $n < N$ there are solutions. This is because the set of solutions of $P = P'$ is recursively enumerable, that is, one can try more and more solutions and eventually find each value of the parameter n for which there is a solution. The only problem is to decide when to give up further searches because all values of $n < N$ for which there are solutions have been found. But if one is told how many such n there are, then one knows when to stop searching for solutions. So one can assume each of the $N + 1$ possibilities ranging from p has all of its initial N bits off to p has all of them on, and each one of these

---

[13]   A self-contained proof is given later. See Theorem R7 in the following section.

assumptions determines the actual values of the first N bits of p. Thus we have determined $N + 1$ different possibilities for the first N bits of p, that is, the real number p is covered by a set of intervals of total length $(N + 1)2^{-N}$, and hence is a set of constructive measure zero, and p cannot be a random real number.

Thus asking whether an exponential diophantine equation has a solution as a function of a parameter cannot give us a random real number. However asking whether or not the number of solutions is infinite can give us a random real. In particular, there is an exponential diophantine equation $Q = Q'$ such that the real number q is random whose nth bit is a zero or a one depending on whether or not there are infinitely many different m-tuples of non-negative integers $x_1, \ldots, x_m$ such that

$$Q(n, x_1, \ldots, x_m) = Q'(n, x_1, \ldots, x_m).$$

The equation $P = P'$ that we considered before encoded the halting problem, that is, the nth bit of the real number p was zero or one depending on whether the nth computer program ever outputs an nth digit. To construct an equation $Q = Q'$ such that q is random, we use instead the halting probability Ω of a universal Turing machine; $Q = Q'$ has finitely or infinitely many solutions depending on whether the nth bit of the base-two expansion of the halting probability Ω is a zero or a one.

$Q = Q'$ is quite a remarkable equation, as it shows that there is a kind of uncertainty principle even in pure mathematics, in fact, even in the theory of whole numbers. Whether or not $Q = Q'$ has infinitely many solutions jumps around in a completely unpredictable manner as the parameter n varies. It may be said that the truth or falsity of the assertion that there are infinitely many solutions is indistinguishable from the result of independent tosses of a fair coin. In other words, these are independent mathematical facts with probability one-half! This is where our search for a probabilistic proof of Turing's theorem that there are uncomputable real numbers leads us, to a dramatic version of Gödel's incompleteness theorem.

7.2. Random Reals

We have seen (Theorem I11) that the most complex n-bit strings x have $H(x) = n + H(n) + O(1)$, and that the number of n-bit strings is halved each time the complexity is reduced by one bit. I.e., there are less than

$$2^{n-k+O(1)}$$

n-bit strings x with $H(x) \leq n + H(n) - k$. With finite bit strings randomness is a question of degree. What is the right place to draw the cut-off between random and non-random for an n-bit string x? Somewhere around $H(x) = n$. Thus minimal programs are right on the boundary, for if $U(p) = s$ and $|p| = H(s)$, then it is easy to see that $H(p) = |p| + O(1)$.

There are two reasons for choosing this cut-off. One is that it permits us to still say that a string is random if any program for calculating it is larger (within $O(1)$) than it is. The other reason, is that it permits us to define an infinite random bit string as one having the property that all its initial segments are finite random bit strings.

Now we show that this complexity-based definition of an infinite random string is equivalent to a definition of randomness that seems to have nothing to do with complexity, Martin-Löf's definition of a random real number using constructive measure theory. To do this, we shall make use of another measure-theoretic definition of randomness due to Solovay, which has the advantage that it does not require a regulator of convergence.

The advantage of this approach is demonstrated by Theorem R7, which asserts that any total recursive scheme for predicting the next bit of an infinite random string from the preceding ones, must fail about half the time. Previously we could only prove this to be the case if (the number of bits predicted among the first n) / log n → ∞; now this works as long as infinitely many predictions are made. So by going from considering the size of LISP expressions to considering the size of self-delimiting programs in a rather abstract programming language, we lose the concreteness of the familiar, but we gain extremely sharp theorems.

Definition [MARTIN-LÖF (1966)]

Speaking geometrically, a real r is Martin-Löf random if it is never the case that it is contained in each set of an r.e. infinite sequence A_i of sets of intervals with the property that the measure[14] of the ith set is always less than or equal to 2^{-i} :

$$\mu(A_i) \leq 2^{-i}. \tag{5}$$

Here is the definition of a Martin-Löf random real r in a more compact notation:

---

[14] I.e., the sum of the lengths of the intervals, being careful to avoid counting overlapping intervals twice.

$$\forall i \left[\mu(A_i) \leq 2^{-i} \right] \implies \neg \forall i \left[r \in A_i \right].$$

An equivalent definition, if we restrict ourselves to reals in the unit interval $0 \leq r \leq 1$, may be formulated in terms of bit strings rather than geometrical notions, as follows. Define a *covering* to be an r.e. set of ordered pairs consisting of a positive integer i and a bit string s,

$$\text{Covering} \quad = \quad \{ (i, s) \},$$

with the property that if $(i, s) \in$ Covering and $(i, s') \in$ Covering, then it is not the case that s is an extension of s' or that s' is an extension of s.[15] We simultaneously consider A_i to be a set of (finite) bit strings

$$\{ s : (i, s) \in \text{Covering} \}$$

and to be a set of real numbers, namely those which in base-two notation have a bit string in A_i as an initial segment.[16] Then condition (5) becomes

$$\mu(A_i) \quad = \quad \sum_{(i, s) \in \text{Covering}} 2^{-|s|} \quad \leq \quad 2^{-i}, \tag{6}$$

where $|s| = $ the length in bits of the string s.

Note

This is equivalent to stipulating the existence of an arbitrary "regulator of convergence" $f \to \infty$ that is computable and nondecreasing such that

$$\mu(A_i) \quad \leq \quad 2^{-f(i)}.$$

---

[15] This is to avoid overlapping intervals and enable us to use the formula (6). It is easy to convert a covering which does not have this property into one that covers exactly the same set and does have this property. How this is done depends on the order in which overlaps are discovered: intervals which are subsets of ones which have already been included in the enumeration of A_i are eliminated, and intervals which are supersets of ones which have already been included in the enumeration must be split into disjoint subintervals, and the common portion must be thrown away.

[16] I.e., the geometrical statement that a point is covered by (the union of) a set of intervals, corresponds in bit string language to the statement that an initial segment of an infinite bit string is contained in a set of finite bit strings.

Definition [SOLOVAY (1975)]

A real r is Solovay random if for any r.e. infinite sequence A_i of sets of intervals with the property that the sum of the measures of the A_i converges

$$\sum \mu(A_i) \; < \; \infty,$$

r is contained in at most finitely many of the A_i. In other words,

$$\sum \mu(A_i) < \infty \;\Rightarrow\; \exists N \; \forall(i > N) \left[r \notin A_i \right].$$

Definition [CHAITIN (1975b)]

A real r is weakly Chaitin random if (the information content of the initial segment r_n of length n of the base-two expansion of r) does not drop arbitrarily far below n: $\liminf H(r_n) - n > -\infty$. In other words,

$$\exists c \; \forall n \left[H(r_n) \geq n - c \right]$$

A real r is Chaitin random if (the information content of the initial segment r_n of length n of the base-two expansion of r) eventually becomes and remains arbitrarily greater than n: $\lim H(r_n) - n = \infty$. In other words,

$$\forall k \; \exists N_k \; \forall(n \geq N_k) \left[H(r_n) \geq n + k \right]$$

Note

All these definitions hold with probability one (see Theorem R5 below).

Theorem R1 [SCHNORR (1974)]

Martin-Löf random $\Longleftrightarrow$ weakly Chaitin random.

Proof ***¬Martin-Löf*** $\Rightarrow$ ***¬(weak Chaitin)***

Suppose that a real number r has the property that

$$\forall i \left[\mu(A_i) \leq 2^{-i} \; \& \; r \in A_i \right].$$

The series

$$\sum 2^n / 2^{n^2} \;=\; \sum 2^{-n^2 + n}$$

$$= \; 2^{-0} + 2^{-0} + 2^{-2} + 2^{-6} + 2^{-12} + 2^{-20} + \cdots$$

obviously converges, and define N so that:

$$\sum_{n \geq N} 2^{-n^2 + n} \leq 1.$$

(In fact, we can take $N = 2$.) Let the variable s range over bit strings, and consider the following inequality:

$$\sum_{n \geq N} \sum_{s \in A_{n^2}} 2^{-\lceil |s| - n \rceil} = \sum_{n \geq N} 2^n \mu(A_{n^2}) \leq \sum_{n \geq N} 2^{-n^2 + n} \leq 1.$$

Thus the requirements

$$\left\{ (s, |s| - n) : s \in A_{n^2} \ \& \ n \geq N \right\}$$

for constructing a computer C such that

$$H_C(s) = |s| - n \quad \text{if } s \in A_{n^2} \ \& \ n \geq N$$

satisfy the Kraft inequality and are consistent (Theorem I2). It follows that

$$s \in A_{n^2} \quad \& \quad n \geq N \quad \Rightarrow \quad H(s) \leq |s| - n + \text{sim}(C).$$

Thus, since $r \in A_{n^2}$ for all $n \geq N$, there will be infinitely many initial segments r_k of length k of the base-two expansion of r with the property that $r_k \in A_{n^2}$ and $n \geq N$, and for each of these r_k we have

$$H(r_k) \leq |r_k| - n + \text{sim}(C).$$

Thus the information content of an initial segment of the base-two expansion of r can drop arbitrarily far below its length.

Proof $\neg$(weak Chaitin) $\Rightarrow \neg$Martin-Löf
Suppose that $H(r_n) - n$ can go arbitrarily negative. There are less than

$$2^{n-k+c}$$

n-bit strings s such that $H(s) < n + H(n) - k$. Thus there are less than

$$2^{n-H(n)-k}$$

n-bit strings s such that $H(s) < n - k - c$. I.e., the probability that an n-bit string s has $H(s) < n - k - c$ is less than

$$2^{-H(n)-k}.$$

Summing this over all n, we get

$$\sum_n 2^{-H(n)-k} \;=\; 2^{-k}\sum_n 2^{-H(n)} \;\leq\; 2^{-k}\,\Omega \;\leq\; 2^{-k},$$

since $\Omega \leq 1$. Thus if a real r has the property that $H(r_n)$ dips below $n - k - c$ for even one value of n, then r is covered by an r.e. set A_k of intervals with $\mu(A_k) \leq 2^{-k}$. Thus if $H(r_n) - n$ goes arbitrarily negative, for each k we can compute an A_k with $\mu(A_k) \leq 2^{-k}$ and $r \in A_k$, and r is not Martin-Löf random. Q.E.D.

Theorem R2 [SOLOVAY (1975)]
Martin-Löf random $\Longleftrightarrow$ Solovay random.

Proof ¬*Martin-Löf* $\Rightarrow$ ¬*Solovay*
We are given that $\forall i\, [\, r \in A_i\,]$ and $\forall i\, [\, \mu(A_i) \leq 2^{-i}\,]$. Thus

$$\sum \mu(A_i) \;\leq\; \sum 2^{-i} \;<\; \infty.$$

Hence $\sum \mu(A_i)$ converges and r is in infinitely many of the A_i and cannot be Solovay random.

Proof ¬*Solovay* $\Rightarrow$ ¬*Martin-Löf*
Suppose

$$\sum \mu(A_i) \;\leq\; 2^c$$

and the real number r is in infinitely many of the A_i. Let

$$B_n \;=\; \{\, x : x \text{ is in at least } 2^{n+c} \text{ of the } A_i \,\}.$$

Then $\mu(B_n) \leq 2^{-n}$ and $r \in B_n$ for all n, so r is not Martin-Löf random. Q.E.D.

Theorem R3
Solovay random $\Longleftrightarrow$ Chaitin random.

Proof ¬*Solovay* $\Rightarrow$ ¬*Chaitin*
Suppose that a real number r has the property that it is in infinitely many A_i, and

$$\sum \mu(A_i) \;<\; \infty.$$

Then there must be an N such that

$$\sum_{i \geq N} \mu(A_i) \leq 1.$$

Hence

$$\sum_{i \geq N} \sum_{s \in A_i} 2^{-|s|} = \sum_{i \geq N} \mu(A_i) \leq 1.$$

Thus the requirements

$$\{ (s, |s|) : s \in A_i \ \& \ i \geq N \}$$

for constructing a computer C such that

$$H_C(s) = |s| \quad \text{if } s \in A_i \ \& \ i \geq N$$

satisfy the Kraft inequality and are consistent (Theorem I2). It follows that

$$s \in A_i \quad \& \quad i \geq N \quad \Rightarrow \quad H(s) \leq |s| + \text{sim}(C),$$

i.e., if a bit string s is in A_i and i is greater than or equal to N, then s's information content is less than or equal to its size in bits $+ \text{sim}(C)$. Thus

$$H(r_n) \leq |r_n| + \text{sim}(C) = n + \text{sim}(C)$$

for infinitely many initial segments r_n of length n of the base-two expansion of r, and it is not the case that $H(r_n) - n \to \infty$.

Proof ¬Chaitin ⟹ ¬Solovay

¬Chaitin says that there is a k such that for infinitely many values of n we have $H(r_n) - n < k$. The probability that an n-bit string s has $H(s) < n + k$ is less than

$$2^{-H(n)+k+c}.$$

Let A_n be the r.e. set of all n-bit strings s such that $H(s) < n + k$.

$$\sum \mu(A_n)$$

$$\leq \sum_n 2^{-H(n)+k+c} = 2^{k+c} \sum 2^{-H(n)} \leq 2^{k+c} \Omega \leq 2^{k+c},$$

since $\Omega \leq 1$. Hence $\Sigma\, \mu(A_n) < \infty$ and r is in infinitely many of the A_n, and thus r is not Solovay random. Q.E.D.

Theorem R4

A real number is Martin-Löf random $\Longleftrightarrow$ it is Solovay random $\Longleftrightarrow$ it is Chaitin random $\Longleftrightarrow$ it is weakly Chaitin random.

Proof

The equivalence of all four definitions of a random real number follows immediately from Theorems R1, R2, and R3. Q.E.D.

Note

That weak Chaitin randomness is coextensive with Chaitin randomness, reveals a complexity gap. I.e., we have shown that if $H(r_n) > n - c$ for all n, necessarily $H(r_n) - n \to \infty$.

Theorem R5

With probability one, a real number r is Martin-Löf/Solovay/Chaitin random.

Proof 1

Since Solovay randomness $\Rightarrow$ Martin-Löf and Chaitin randomness, it is sufficient to show that r is Solovay random with probability one. Suppose

$$\sum \mu(A_i) \;<\; \infty,$$

where the A_i are an r.e. infinite sequence of sets of intervals. Then (this is the Borel–Cantelli lemma [FELLER (1970)])

$$\lim_{N \to \infty} \mu(\bigcup_{i \geq N} A_i) \;\leq\; \lim_{N \to \infty} \sum_{i \geq N} \mu(A_i) \;=\; 0$$

and the probability is zero that a real r is in infinitely many of the A_i. But there are only countably many choices for the r.e. sequence of A_i, since there are only countably many algorithms. Since the union of a countable number of sets of measure zero is also of measure zero, it follows that with probability one r is Solovay random.

Proof 2

We use the Borel–Cantelli lemma again. This time we show that the Chaitin criterion for randomness, which is equivalent to the Martin-Löf and Solovay criteria, is true with probability one. Since for each k,

$$\sum_n \mu(\{r : H(r_n) < n + k\}) \quad \leq \quad 2^{k+c}$$

and thus converges,[17] it follows that for each k with probability one $H(r_n) < n + k$ only finitely often. Thus, with probability one,

$$\lim_{n \to \infty} H(r_n) - n \quad = \quad \infty.$$

Q.E.D.

Theorem R6

Ω is a Martin-Löf/Solovay/Chaitin random real number.[18]

Proof

It is easy to see that Ω can be computed as a limit from below. We gave a LISP program for doing this at the end of Chapter 5. Indeed,

$$\{ p : U(p, \Lambda) \text{ is defined} \} \quad \equiv \quad \{ p_1, p_2, p_3, \dots \}$$

is a recursively enumerable set. Let

$$\omega_n \quad \equiv \quad \sum_{k \leq n} 2^{-|p_k|}.$$

Then $\omega_n < \omega_{n+1} \to \Omega$.

It follows that given Ω_n, the first n bits of the non-terminating base-two expansion of the real number Ω,[19] one can calculate all programs of size not greater than n that halt, then the finite set of all S-expressions x such that $H(x) \leq n$, and finally an S-expression x with $H(x) > n$. For compute ω_k for $k = 1,2,3, \dots$ until ω_k is greater than Ω_n. Then

$$\Omega_n \quad < \quad \omega_k \quad \leq \quad \Omega \quad \leq \quad \Omega_n + 2^{-n},$$

so that all objects with complexity H less than or equal to n are in the set

---

[17] See the second half of the proof of Theorem R3.

[18] Incidentally, this implies that Ω is not a computable real number. Since algebraic numbers are computable, it follows that Ω must be transcendental.

[19] I.e., if there is a choice between ending the base-two expansion of Ω with infinitely many consecutive zeros or with infinitely many consecutive ones (i.e., if Ω is a dyadic rational), then we must choose the infinity of consecutive ones. Of course, it will follow from this theorem that Ω must be an irrational number, so this situation cannot actually occur, *but we don't know that yet!*

$$\{U(p_i, \Lambda) : i \leq k\},$$

and one can calculate this set and then pick an arbitrary object that isn't in it.

Thus there is a computable partial function ψ such that

$$\psi(\Omega_n) \quad = \quad \text{an S-expression } x \text{ with } H(x) > n.$$

But

$$H(\psi(\Omega_n)) \quad \leq \quad H(\Omega_n) + c_\psi .$$

Hence

$$n \quad < \quad H(\psi(\Omega_n)) \quad \leq \quad H(\Omega_n) + c_\psi ,$$

and

$$H(\Omega_n) \quad > \quad n - c_\psi .$$

Thus Ω is weakly Chaitin random, and by Theorem R4 it is Martin-Löf/Solovay/Chaitin random. Q.E.D.

Note

More generally, if X is an infinite r.e. set of S-expressions, then

$$\sum_{x \in X} 2^{-H(x)}$$

and

$$\sum_{x \in X} P(x)$$

are both Martin-Löf/Solovay/Chaitin random reals.

Theorem R7

Ω is unpredictable. More precisely, consider a total recursive prediction function F, which given an arbitrary finite initial segment of an infinite bit string, returns either "no prediction", "the next bit is a 0", or "the next bit is a 1". Then if F predicts infinitely many bits of Ω, it does no better than chance, because in the limit the relative frequency of correct and incorrect predictions both tend to ½.

Proof Sketch

Consider the set A_n of all infinite bit strings for which F makes at least n predictions and the number of correct predictions k among the first n made satisfies

$$\left| \frac{1}{2} - \frac{k}{n} \right| > \varepsilon.$$

We shall show that

$$\mu(A_n) \leq n \, (1 - \varepsilon)^{\text{int}\left[\varepsilon n/2 \right]}.$$

Here $\text{int}[x]$ is the integer part of the real number x. Thus

$$\sum \mu(A_n)$$

essentially converges like a geometric series with ratio less than one. Since Ω satisfies the Solovay randomness criterion, it follows that Ω is in at most finitely many of the A_n. I.e., if F predicts infinitely many bits of Ω, then, for any $\varepsilon > 0$, from some point on the number of correct predictions k among the first n made satisfies

$$\left| \frac{1}{2} - \frac{k}{n} \right| \leq \varepsilon,$$

which was to be proved.

It remains to establish the upper bound on $\mu(A_n)$. This follows from the following upper bound on binomial coefficients:

$$\binom{n}{k} \equiv \frac{n}{1} \frac{n-1}{2} \frac{n-2}{3} \cdots \frac{n-k+1}{k} \leq 2^n \, (1 - \varepsilon)^{\text{int}\left[\varepsilon n/2 \right]}$$

if

$$\left| \frac{1}{2} - \frac{k}{n} \right| > \varepsilon.$$

To prove this, note that the binomial coefficients "n choose k" sum to 2^n, and that the coefficients start small, grow until the middle, and then decrease as k increases beyond $n/2$. Thus the coefficients that we are interested in are obtained by taking the large middle binomial coefficient, which is less than 2^n, and multiplying it by at least εn fractions, each of which is less than unity. In fact, at least $\varepsilon n/2$ of the fractions that the largest binomial coefficient is multiplied by are less than $1 - \varepsilon$. Q.E.D.

Note

Consider an F that always predicts that the next bit of Ω is a 1. Applying Theorem R7, we see that Ω has the property that 0's and 1's both have limiting relative frequency ½. Next consider an F that predicts that each 0 bit in Ω is followed by a 1 bit. In the limit this prediction will be right half the time and wrong half the time. Thus 0 bits are followed by 0 bits half the time, and by 1 bits half the time. It follows by induction that each of the 2^k possible blocks of k bits in Ω has limiting relative frequency 2^{-k}. Thus, to use Borel's terminology, Ω is "normal" in base two.

The question of how quickly relative frequencies approach their limiting values is studied carefully in probability theory [FELLER (1970)]; the answer is known as "the law of the iterated logarithm." The law of the iterated logarithm also applies to the relative frequency of correct and incorrect predictions of bits of Ω. For Feller's proof of the law of the iterated logarithm depends only on the first Borel–Cantelli lemma, which is merely the Martin-Löf/Solovay randomness property of Ω, and on the second Borel–Cantelli lemma, which we shall show that Ω satisfies in Section 8.3.

Theorem R8

There is an exponential diophantine equation

$$L(n, x_1, \ldots, x_m) \;=\; R(n, x_1, \ldots, x_m)$$

which has only finitely many solutions $x_1, \ldots, x_m$ if the nth bit of Ω is a 0, and which has infinitely many solutions $x_1, \ldots, x_m$ if the nth bit of Ω is a 1. I.e., this equation involves only addition $A + B$, multiplication $A \times B$, and exponentiation A^B of non-negative integer constants and variables, the number of different m-tuples $x_1, \ldots, x_m$ of non-negative integers which are solutions of this equation is infinite if the nth bit of the base-two representation of Ω is a 1, and the number of different m-tuples $x_1, \ldots, x_m$ of non-negative integers which are solutions of this equation is finite if the nth bit of the base-two representation of Ω is a 0.

Proof

By combining the definitions of the functions ω and o that were given in Section 5.4, one obtains a LISP definition of a function φ of two variables such that $\varphi(n, k)$ is undefined for all sufficiently large values of k if the nth bit of Ω is a 0, and $\varphi(n, k)$ is defined for all sufficiently large values of k if the nth bit of Ω is a 1. I.e., the definition of $\varphi(n, k)$ loops forever for all sufficiently large values of k if the nth bit of Ω is a 0, and the definition of $\varphi(n, k)$ terminates for all sufficiently large values of k if the nth bit of Ω is a 1.

Now let's plug the LISP expression for $\varphi(n, k)$ into the variable *input.EXPRESSION* in that 900,000-character exponential diophantine equation that is a LISP interpreter that we went to so much trouble to construct in Part I. I.e., we substitute for the variable *input.EXPRESSION* the 8-bit-per-character binary representation (with the characters in reverse order) of an S-expression of the form

$$(\ (' (\nabla (nk) \ldots)) \ (' (11 \ldots 11)) \ (' (11 \ldots 11)) \ ) \tag{7}$$

where there are n 1's in the first list of 1's and k 1's in the second list of 1's. The resulting equation will have a solution in non-negative integers if and only if $\varphi(n, k)$ is defined, and for given n and k it can have at most one solution.

We are almost at our goal; we need only point out that the binary representation of the S-expression (7) can be written in closed form as an algebraic function of n and k that only uses $+$, $\times$, $-$, and exponentiation. This is easy to see; the essential step is that the binary representation of a character string consisting only of 1's is just the sum of a geometric series with multiplier 256. Then, proceeding as in Chapter 2, we eliminate the minus signs and express the fact that s is the binary representation of the S-expression (7) with given n and k by means of a few exponential diophantine equations. Finally we fold this handful of equations into the left-hand side and the right-hand side of our LISP interpreter equation, using the same "sum of squares" trick that we did in Chapter 2.

The result is that our equation has gotten a little bigger, and that the variable *input.EXPRESSION* has been replaced by three new variables s, n and k and a few new auxiliary variables. This new monster equation has a solution if and only if $\varphi(n, k)$ is defined, and for given n and k it can have at most one solution. Recall that $\varphi(n, k)$ is defined for all sufficiently large values of k if and only if the nth bit of the base-two representation of Ω is a 1. Thus our new equation has infinitely many solutions for a given value of n if the nth bit of Ω is a 1, and it has finitely many solutions for a given value of n if the nth bit of Ω is a 0. Q.E.D.

INCOMPLETENESS

Having developed the necessary information-theoretic formalism in Chapter 6, and having studied the notion of a random real in Chapter 7, we can now begin to derive incompleteness theorems.

The setup is as follows. The axioms of a formal theory are considered to be encoded as a single finite bit string, the rules of inference are considered to be an algorithm for enumerating the theorems given the axioms, and in general we shall fix the rules of inference and vary the axioms. More formally, the rules of inference F may be considered to be an r.e. set of propositions of the form

"Axioms $\mid-_F$ Theorem".

The r.e. set of theorems deduced from the axiom A is determined by selecting from the set F the theorems in those propositions which have the axiom A as an antecedent. In general we'll consider the rules of inference F to be fixed and study what happens as we vary the axioms A. By an n-bit theory we shall mean the set of theorems deduced from an n-bit axiom.

8.1. Incompleteness Theorems for Lower Bounds on Information Content

Let's start by rederiving within our current formalism an old and very basic result, which states that even though most strings are random, one can never prove that a specific string has this property.

As we saw when we studied randomness, if one produces a bit string s by tossing a coin n times, 99.9% of the time it will be the case that

$H(s) \approx n + H(n)$. In fact, if one lets n go to infinity, with probability one $H(s) > n$ for all but finitely many n (Theorem R5). However,

Theorem LB [CHAITIN (1974a,1974b,1975a,1982b)]

Consider a formal theory all of whose theorems are assumed to be true. Within such a formal theory a specific string cannot be proven to have information content more than $O(1)$ greater than the information content of the axioms of the theory. I.e., if "$H(s) \geq n$" is a theorem only if it is true, then it is a theorem only if $n \leq H(\text{axioms}) + O(1)$. Conversely, there are formal theories whose axioms have information content $n + O(1)$ in which it is possible to establish all true propositions of the form "$H(s) \geq n$" and of the form "$H(s) = k$" with $k < n$.

Proof

The idea is that if one could prove that a string has no distinguishing feature, then that itself would be a distinguishing property. This paradox can be restated as follows: There are no uninteresting numbers (positive integers), because if there were, the first uninteresting number would *ipso facto* be interesting! Alternatively, consider "the smallest positive integer that cannot be specified in less than a thousand words." We have just specified it using only fourteen words.

Consider the enumeration of the theorems of the formal axiomatic theory in order of the size of their proofs. For each positive integer k, let $s*$ be the string in the theorem of the form "$H(s) \geq n$" with $n > H(\text{axioms}) + k$ which appears first in the enumeration. On the one hand, if all theorems are true, then

$$H(\text{axioms}) + k \quad < \quad H(s*).$$

On the other hand, the above prescription for calculating $s*$ shows that

$$s* \quad = \quad \psi(\text{axioms}, H(\text{axioms}), k) \qquad (\psi \text{ partial recursive}),$$

and thus

$$H(s*) \quad \leq \quad H(\text{axioms}, H(\text{axioms}), k) + c_\psi$$
$$\leq \quad H(\text{axioms}) + H(k) + O(1).$$

Here we have used the subadditivity of information $H(s, t) \leq H(s) + H(t) + O(1)$ and the fact that $H(s, H(s)) \leq H(s) + O(1)$. It follows that

$$H(\text{axioms}) + k \quad < \quad H(s*) \quad \leq \quad H(\text{axioms}) + H(k) + O(1),$$

and thus

$$k \quad < \quad H(k) + O(1).$$

However, this inequality is false for all $k \geq k_0$, where k_0 depends only on the rules of inference. A contradiction is avoided only if s^* does not exist for $k = k_0$, i.e., it is impossible to prove in the formal theory that a specific string has H greater than $H(\text{axioms}) + k_0$.

Proof of Converse

The set T of all true propositions of the form "$H(s) \leq k$" is recursively enumerable. Choose a fixed enumeration of T without repetitions, and for each positive integer n, let s^* be the string in the last proposition of the form "$H(s) \leq k$" with $k < n$ in the enumeration. Let

$$\Delta \quad = \quad n - H(s^*) \quad > \quad 0.$$

Then from s^*, $H(s^*)$, and Δ we can calculate $n = H(s^*) + \Delta$, then all strings s with $H(s) < n$, and then a string s_n with $H(s_n) \geq n$. Thus

$$n \quad \leq \quad H(s_n) \quad = \quad H(\psi(s^*, H(s^*), \Delta)) \qquad (\psi \text{ partial recursive}),$$

and so

$$n \quad \leq \quad H(s^*, H(s^*), \Delta) + c_\psi \quad \begin{matrix} \leq \\ \leq \end{matrix} \quad \begin{matrix} H(s^*) + H(\Delta) + O(1) \\ n + H(\Delta) + O(1) \end{matrix} \qquad (8)$$

using the subadditivity of joint information and the fact that a program tells us its size as well as its output. The first line of (8) implies that

$$\Delta \quad \equiv \quad n - H(s^*) \quad \leq \quad H(\Delta) + O(1),$$

which implies that Δ and $H(\Delta)$ are both bounded. Then the second line of (8) implies that

$$H(s^*, H(s^*), \Delta) \quad = \quad n + O(1).$$

The triple $(s^*, H(s^*), \Delta)$ is the desired axiom: it has information content $n + O(1)$, and by enumerating T until all true propositions of the form "$H(s) \leq k$" with $k < n$ have been discovered, one can immediately deduce all true propositions of the form "$H(s) \geq n$" and of the form "$H(s) = k$" with $k < n$. Q.E.D.

Note

Here are two other ways to establish the converse, two axioms that solve the halting problem for all programs of size $\leq n$:

1. Consider the program p of size $\leq n$ that takes longest to halt. It is easy to see that $H(p) = n + O(1)$.

2. Consider the number h_n of programs of size $\leq n$ that halt. Solovay has shown[20] that

$$h_n = 2^{n-H(n)+O(1)},$$

from which it is easy to show that $H(h_n) = n + O(1)$.

Restating Theorem LB in terms of the halting problem, we have shown that if a theory has information content n, then there is a program of size $\leq n + O(1)$ that never halts, but this fact cannot be proved within the theory. Conversely, there are theories with information content $n + O(1)$ that enable one to settle the halting problem for all programs of size $\leq n$.

8.2. Incompleteness Theorems for Random Reals: First Approach

In this section we begin our study of incompleteness theorems for random reals. We show that any particular formal theory can enable one to determine at most a finite number of bits of Ω. In the following sections (8.3 and 8.4) we express the upper bound on the number of bits of Ω which can be determined, in terms of the axioms of the theory; for now, we just show that an upper bound exists. We shall not use any ideas from algorithmic information theory until Section 8.4; for now (Sections 8.2 and 8.3) we only make use of the fact that Ω is Martin-Löf random.

If one tries to guess the bits of a random sequence, the average number of correct guesses before failing is exactly 1 guess! Reason: if we use the fact that the expected value of a sum is equal to the sum of the expected values, the answer is the sum of the chance of getting the first guess right, plus the chance of getting the first and the second guesses right, plus the chance of getting the first, second and third guesses right, et cetera:

$$\frac{1}{2} + \frac{1}{4} + \frac{1}{8} + \frac{1}{16} + \cdots = 1.$$

---

[20] For a proof of Solovay's result, see Theorem 8 [CHAITIN (1976c)].

Or if we directly calculate the expected value as the sum of (the number right till first failure) × (the probability):

$$0 \times \frac{1}{2} + 1 \times \frac{1}{4} + 2 \times \frac{1}{8} + 3 \times \frac{1}{16} + 4 \times \frac{1}{32} + \cdots$$

$$= 1 \times \sum_{k > 1} 2^{-k} + 1 \times \sum_{k > 2} 2^{-k} + 1 \times \sum_{k > 3} 2^{-k} + \cdots$$

$$= \frac{1}{2} + \frac{1}{4} + \frac{1}{8} + \cdots = 1.$$

On the other hand (see the next section), if we are allowed to try 2^n times a series of n guesses, one of them will always get it right, if we try all 2^n different possible series of n guesses.

Theorem X

Any given formal theory T can yield only finitely many (scattered) bits of (the base-two expansion of) Ω. When we say that a theory yields a bit of Ω, we mean that it enables us to determine its position and its $0/1$ value.

Proof

Consider a theory T, an r.e. set of true assertions of the form
"The nth bit of Ω is 0."
"The nth bit of Ω is 1."
Here n denotes specific positive integers.

If T provides k different (scattered) bits of Ω, then that gives us a covering A_k of measure 2^{-k} which includes Ω: Enumerate T until k bits of Ω are determined, then the covering is all bit strings up to the last determined bit with all determined bits okay. If n is the last determined bit, this covering will consist of 2^{n-k} n-bit strings, and will have measure $2^{n-k}/2^n = 2^{-k}$.

It follows that if T yields infinitely many different bits of Ω, then for any k we can produce by running through all possible proofs in T a covering A_k of measure 2^{-k} which includes Ω. But this contradicts the fact that Ω is Martin-Löf random. Hence T yields only finitely many bits of Ω. Q.E.D.

Corollary X

Since by Theorem R8 Ω can be encoded into an exponential diophantine equation

$$L(n, x_1, \ldots, x_m) = R(n, x_1, \ldots, x_m), \tag{9}$$

it follows that any given formal theory can permit one to determine whether (9) has finitely or infinitely many solutions $x_1, \ldots, x_m$, for only finitely many specific values of the parameter n.

8.3. Incompleteness Theorems for Random Reals: |Axioms|

Theorem A
   If

$$\sum 2^{-f(n)} \leq 1$$

and f is computable, then there is a constant c_f with the property that no n-bit theory ever yields more than $n + f(n) + c_f$ bits of Ω.

Proof
   Let A_k be the event that there is at least one n such that there is an n-bit theory that yields $n + f(n) + k$ or more bits of Ω.

$$\mu(A_k) \leq \sum_n \left[\binom{2^n}{\substack{n\text{-bit} \\ \text{theories}}} \binom{2^{-\lceil n+f(n)+k \rceil}}{\substack{\text{probability that yields} \\ n + f(n) + k \text{ bits of } \Omega}} \right]$$

$$= 2^{-k} \sum_n 2^{-f(n)} \leq 2^{-k}$$

since

$$\sum 2^{-f(n)} \leq 1.$$

Hence $\mu(A_k) \leq 2^{-k}$, and $\sum \mu(A_k)$ also converges. Thus only finitely many of the A_k occur (Borel–Cantelli lemma [FELLER (1970)]). I.e.,

$$\lim_{N \to \infty} \mu(\bigcup_{k > N} A_k) \leq \sum_{k > N} \mu(A_k) \leq 2^{-N} \to 0.$$

More detailed proof
   Assume the opposite of what we want to prove, namely that for every k there is at least one n-bit theory that yields $n + f(n) + k$ bits of Ω. From

this we shall deduce that Ω cannot be Martin-Löf random, which is impossible.

To get a covering A_k of Ω with measure $\leq 2^{-k}$, consider a specific n and all n-bit theories. Start generating theorems in each n-bit theory until it yields $n + f(n) + k$ bits of Ω (it doesn't matter if some of these bits are wrong). The measure of the set of possibilities for Ω covered by the n-bit theories is thus

$$\leq \ 2^n \, 2^{-n-f(n)-k} \ = \ 2^{-f(n)-k}.$$

The measure $\mu(A_k)$ of the union of the set of possibilities for Ω covered by n-bit theories with any n is thus

$$\leq \ \sum_n 2^{-f(n)-k} \ = \ 2^{-k} \sum_n 2^{-f(n)} \ \leq \ 2^{-k} \ (\text{since } \sum 2^{-f(n)} \leq 1).$$

Thus Ω is covered by A_k and $\mu(A_k) \leq 2^{-k}$ for every k if there is always an n-bit theory that yields $n + f(n) + k$ bits of Ω, which is impossible. Q.E.D.

Corollary A
   If

$$\sum 2^{-f(n)}$$

converges and f is computable, then there is a constant c_f with the property that no n-bit theory ever yields more than $n + f(n) + c_f$ bits of Ω.

Proof
   Choose c so that

$$\sum 2^{-f(n)} \ \leq \ 2^c.$$

Then

$$\sum 2^{-[f(n)+c]} \ \leq \ 1,$$

and we can apply Theorem A to $f'(n) = f(n) + c$. Q.E.D.

Corollary A2
   Let

$$\sum 2^{-f(n)}$$

converge and f be computable as before. If $g(n)$ is computable, then there is a constant $c_{f,\,g}$ with the property that no $g(n)$-bit theory ever yields more than $g(n) + f(n) + c_{f,\,g}$ bits of Ω. E.g., consider N of the form

$$2^{2^n}.$$

For such N, no N-bit theory ever yields more than $N + f(\text{loglog } N) + c_{f,\,g}$ bits of Ω.

Note

Thus for n of special form, i.e., which have concise descriptions, we get better upper bounds on the number of bits of Ω which are yielded by n-bit theories. This is a foretaste of the way algorithmic information theory will be used in Theorem C and Corollary C2 (Section 8.4).

Lemma for Second Borel–Cantelli Lemma!

For any finite set $\{x_k\}$ of non-negative real numbers,

$$\prod (1 - x_k) \;\le\; \frac{1}{\sum x_k}\; .$$

Proof

If x is a real number, then

$$1 - x \;\le\; \frac{1}{1 + x}\; .$$

Thus

$$\prod (1 - x_k) \;\le\; \frac{1}{\prod (1 + x_k)} \;\le\; \frac{1}{\sum x_k}\; ,$$

since if all the x_k are non-negative

$$\prod (1 + x_k) \;\ge\; \sum x_k\; .$$

Q.E.D.

Second Borel–Cantelli Lemma [FELLER (1970)]

Suppose that the events A_n have the property that it is possible to determine whether or not the event A_n occurs by examining the first $f(n)$ bits of Ω, where f is a computable function. If the events A_n are mutually independent and $\Sigma \, \mu(A_n)$ diverges, then Ω has the property that infinitely many of the A_n must occur.

Proof

Suppose on the contrary that Ω has the property that only finitely many of the events A_n occur. Then there is an N such that the event A_n does not occur if $n \geq N$. The probability that none of the events $A_N, A_{N+1}, \ldots, A_{N+k}$ occur is, since the A_n are mutually independent, precisely

$$\prod_{i=0}^{k}\bigl(1 - \mu(A_{N+i})\bigr) \;\leq\; \cfrac{1}{\left[\displaystyle\sum_{i=0}^{k} \mu(A_{N+i})\right]} \;,$$

which goes to zero as k goes to infinity. This would give us arbitrarily small covers for Ω, which contradicts the fact that Ω is Martin-Löf random. Q.E.D.

Theorem B

If

$$\sum 2^{n-f(n)}$$

diverges and f is computable, then infinitely often there is a run of $f(n)$ zeros between bits 2^n and 2^{n+1} of Ω ($2^n \leq$ bit $< 2^{n+1}$). Hence there are rules of inference which have the property that there are infinitely many N-bit theories that yield (the first) $N + f(\log N)$ bits of Ω.

Proof

We wish to prove that infinitely often Ω must have a run of $k = f(n)$ consecutive zeros between its 2^nth and its 2^{n+1}th bit position. There are 2^n bits in the range in question. Divide this into non-overlapping blocks of $2k$ bits each, giving a total of $\mathbf{int}[2^n/2k]$ blocks, where $\mathbf{int}[x]$ denotes the integer part of the real number x. The chance of having a run of k consecutive zeros in each block of $2k$ bits is

$$\geq \quad \frac{k \, 2^{k-2}}{2^{2k}} \;. \tag{10}$$

Reason:

1. There are $2k - k + 1 \geq k$ different possible choices for where to put the run of k zeros in the block of $2k$ bits.
2. Then there must be a 1 at each end of the run of 0's, but the remaining $2k - k - 2 = k - 2$ bits can be anything.
3. This may be an underestimate if the run of 0's is at the beginning or end of the $2k$ bits, and there is no room for endmarker 1's.
4. There is no room for another $10^k 1$ to fit in the block of $2k$ bits, so we are not overestimating the probability by counting anything twice.

If $2k$ is a power of two, then $\text{int}[2^n/2k] = 2^n/2k$. If not, there is a power of two that is $\leq 4k$ and divides 2^n exactly. In either case, $\text{int}[2^n/2k] \geq 2^n/4k$. Summing (10) over all $\text{int}[2^n/2k] \geq 2^n/4k$ blocks and over all n, we get

$$\geq \sum_n \left[\frac{k \, 2^{k-2}}{2^{2k}} \frac{2^n}{4k} \right] = \frac{1}{16} \sum_n 2^{n-k} = \frac{1}{16} \sum 2^{n-f(n)} = \infty.$$

Invoking the second Borel–Cantelli lemma (if the events A_i are independent and $\sum \mu(A_i)$ diverges, then infinitely many of the A_i must occur), we are finished. Q.E.D.

Corollary B

If

$$\sum 2^{-f(n)}$$

diverges and f is computable and nondecreasing, then infinitely often there is a run of $f(2^{n+1})$ zeros between bits 2^n and 2^{n+1} of Ω ($2^n \leq \text{bit} < 2^{n+1}$). Hence there are infinitely many N-bit theories that yield (the first) $N + f(N)$ bits of Ω.

Proof

Recall the Cauchy condensation test [HARDY (1952)]: if $\phi(n)$ is a nonincreasing function of n, then the series $\sum \phi(n)$ is convergent or divergent according as $\sum 2^n \phi(2^n)$ is convergent or divergent. Proof:

$$\sum \phi(k) \geq \sum [\phi(2^n + 1) + \cdots + \phi(2^{n+1})] \geq \sum 2^n \phi(2^{n+1})$$

$$= \frac{1}{2} \sum 2^{n+1} \phi(2^{n+1}).$$

On the other hand,

$$\sum \phi(k) \quad \le \quad \sum \left[\phi(2^n) + \cdots + \phi(2^{n+1} - 1) \right] \quad \le \quad \sum 2^n \phi(2^n).$$

If

$$\sum 2^{-f(n)}$$

diverges and f is computable and nondecreasing, then by the Cauchy condensation test

$$\sum 2^n \, 2^{-f(2^n)}$$

also diverges, and therefore so does

$$\sum 2^n \, 2^{-f(2^{n+1})}.$$

Hence, by Theorem B, infinitely often there is a run of $f(2^{n+1})$ zeros between bits 2^n and 2^{n+1}. Q.E.D.

Corollary B2

If

$$\sum 2^{-f(n)}$$

diverges and f is computable, then infinitely often there is a run of $n + f(n)$ zeros between bits 2^n and 2^{n+1} of Ω ($2^n \le$ bit $< 2^{n+1}$). Hence there are infinitely many N-bit theories that yield (the first) $N + \log N + f(\log N)$ bits of Ω.

Proof

Take $f(n) = n + f'(n)$ in Theorem B. Q.E.D.

Theorem AB

First a piece of notation. By $\log x$ we mean the integer part of the base-two logarithm of x. I.e., if $2^n \le x < 2^{n+1}$, then $\log x = n$.

(a) There is a c with the property that no n-bit theory ever yields more than $n + \log n + \log\log n + 2 \log\log\log n + c$ (scattered) bits of Ω.
(b) There are infinitely many n-bit theories that yield (the first) $n + \log n + \log\log n + \log\log\log n$ bits of Ω.

Proof

Using the Cauchy condensation test, we shall show below that

$$\sum \frac{1}{n \log n \, (\log\log n)^2} < \infty, \qquad (a)$$

$$\sum \frac{1}{n \log n \, \log\log n} = \infty. \qquad (b)$$

The theorem follows immediately from Corollaries A and B.

Now to use the condensation test:

$$\sum \frac{1}{n^2}$$

behaves the same as

$$\sum 2^n \, \frac{1}{2^{2n}} = \sum \frac{1}{2^n},$$

which converges.

$$\sum \frac{1}{n \, (\log n)^2}$$

behaves the same as

$$\sum 2^n \, \frac{1}{2^n \, n^2} = \sum \frac{1}{n^2},$$

which converges. And

$$\sum \frac{1}{n \log n \, (\log\log n)^2}$$

behaves the same as

$$\sum 2^n \frac{1}{2^n n (\log n)^2} \quad = \quad \sum \frac{1}{n (\log n)^2} \; ,$$

which converges.

On the other hand,

$$\sum \frac{1}{n}$$

behaves the same as

$$\sum 2^n \frac{1}{2^n} \quad = \quad \sum 1,$$

which diverges.

$$\sum \frac{1}{n \log n}$$

behaves the same as

$$\sum 2^n \frac{1}{2^n n} \quad = \quad \sum \frac{1}{n} \; ,$$

which diverges. And

$$\sum \frac{1}{n \log n \; \text{loglog} \; n}$$

behaves the same as

$$\sum 2^n \frac{1}{2^n n \log n} \quad = \quad \sum \frac{1}{n \log n} \; ,$$

which diverges. Q.E.D.

8.4. Incompleteness Theorems for Random Reals: H(Axioms)

Theorem C is a remarkable extension of Theorem R6:

1. We have seen that the information content of knowing the first n bits of Ω is $\geq n - c$.
2. Now we show that the information content of knowing **any** n bits of Ω (their positions and $0/1$ values) is $\geq n - c$.

Lemma C

$$\sum_n \#\{s : H(s) < n\} \, 2^{-n} \leq 1.$$

Proof

$$1 \geq \Omega \geq \sum_s 2^{-H(s)}$$

$$= \sum_n \#\{s : H(s) = n\} \, 2^{-n} = \sum_n \#\{s : H(s) = n\} \, 2^{-n} \sum_{k \geq 1} 2^{-k}$$

$$= \sum_n \sum_{k \geq 1} \#\{s : H(s) = n\} \, 2^{-n-k} = \sum_n \#\{s : H(s) < n\} \, 2^{-n}.$$

Q.E.D.

Theorem C

If a theory has $H(\text{axiom}) < n$, then it can yield at most $n + c$ (scattered) bits of Ω.

Proof

Consider a particular k and n. If there is an axiom with $H(\text{axiom}) < n$ which yields $n + k$ scattered bits of Ω, then even without knowing which axiom it is, we can cover Ω with an r.e. set of intervals of measure

$$\leq \begin{pmatrix} \#\{s : H(s) < n\} \\ \# \text{ of axioms} \\ \text{with } H < n \end{pmatrix} \begin{pmatrix} 2^{-n-k} \\ \text{measure of set of} \\ \text{possibilities for } \Omega \end{pmatrix}$$

$$= \#\{s : H(s) < n\} \, 2^{-n-k}.$$

But by the preceding lemma, we see that

$$\sum_n \#\{s : H(s) < n\} \, 2^{-n-k} = 2^{-k} \sum_n \#\{s : H(s) < n\} \, 2^{-n} \leq 2^{-k}.$$

Thus if even one theory with $H < n$ yields $n + k$ bits of Ω, for any n, we get a cover for Ω of measure $\leq 2^{-k}$. This can only be true for finitely many values of k, or Ω would not be Martin-Löf random. Q.E.D.

Corollary C

No n-bit theory ever yields more than $n + H(n) + c$ bits of Ω.

Proof

This follows immediately from Theorem C and the fact that

$$H(\text{axiom}) \quad \leq \quad |\text{axiom}| + H(|\text{axiom}|) + c,$$

which is an immediate consequence of Theorem I11(a). Q.E.D.

Lemma C2

If $g(n)$ is computable and unbounded, then $H(n) < g(n)$ for infinitely many values of n.

Proof

Define the inverse of g as follows:

$$g^{-1}(n) \quad = \quad \min_{g(k) \,\geq\, n} k.$$

Then it is easy to see that for all sufficiently large values of n:

$$H(g^{-1}(n)) \quad \leq \quad H(n) + O(1) \quad \leq \quad O(\log n) \quad < \quad n \quad \leq \quad g(g^{-1}(n)).$$

I.e., $H(k) < g(k)$ for all $k = g^{-1}(n)$ and n sufficiently large. Q.E.D.

Corollary C2

Let $g(n)$ be computable and unbounded.
For infinitely many n, no n-bit theory yields more than $n + g(n) + c$ bits of Ω.

Proof

This is an immediate consequence of Corollary C and Lemma C2. Q.E.D.

Note

In appraising Corollaries C and C2, the trivial formal systems in which there is always an n-bit axiom that yields the first n bits of Ω should be kept in mind. Also, compare Corollaries C and A, and Corollaries C2 and A2.

In summary,

Theorem D

There is an exponential diophantine equation

$$L(n, x_1, \ldots, x_m) \quad = \quad R(n, x_1, \ldots, x_m) \tag{11}$$

which has only finitely many solutions $x_1, \ldots, x_m$ if the nth bit of Ω is a 0, and which has infinitely many solutions $x_1, \ldots, x_m$ if the nth bit of Ω is a 1. Let us say that a formal theory "settles k cases" if it enables one to prove that the number of solutions of (11) is finite or that it is infinite for k specific values (possibly scattered) of the parameter n. Let $f(n)$ and $g(n)$ be computable functions.

$$\sum 2^{-f(n)} < \infty \quad \Rightarrow$$
all n-bit theories settle $\leq n + f(n) + O(1)$ cases. $\tag{a}$

$$\sum 2^{-f(n)} = \infty \quad \& \quad f(n) \leq f(n+1) \quad \Rightarrow \quad \text{for infinitely many } n,$$
there is an n-bit theory that settles $\geq n + f(n)$ cases. $\tag{b}$

$$H(\text{theory}) < n \quad \Rightarrow \quad \text{it settles} \leq n + O(1) \text{ cases.} \tag{c}$$

$$n\text{-bit theory} \quad \Rightarrow \quad \text{it settles} \leq n + H(n) + O(1) \text{ cases.} \tag{d}$$

$$g \text{ unbounded} \quad \Rightarrow \quad \text{for infinitely many } n,$$
all n-bit theories settle $\leq n + g(n) + O(1)$ cases. $\tag{e}$

Proof

The theorem combines Theorem R8, Corollaries A and B, Theorem C, and Corollaries C and C2. Q.E.D.

CHAPTER 9

CONCLUSION

In conclusion, we see that proving whether particular exponential diophantine equations have finitely or infinitely many solutions, is absolutely intractable (Theorem D). Such questions escape the power of mathematical reasoning. This is a region in which mathematical truth has no discernible structure or pattern and appears to be completely random. These questions are completely beyond the power of human reasoning. Mathematics cannot deal with them.

Nonlinear dynamics [FORD (1983) and JENSEN (1987)] and quantum mechanics have shown that there is randomness in nature. I believe that we have demonstrated in this book that randomness is already present in pure mathematics, in fact, even in rather elementary branches of number theory. This doesn't mean that the universe and mathematics are lawless, it means that sometimes laws of a different kind apply: statistical laws.

More generally, this tends to support what TYMOCZKO (1986) has called a "quasi-empirical" approach to the foundations of mathematics. To quote from CHAITIN (1982b), where I have argued this case at length, "Perhaps number theory should be pursued more openly in the spirit of experimental science!" To prove more, one must sometimes assume more.

I would like to end with a few speculations on the deep problem of the origin of biological complexity, the question of why living organisms are so complicated, and in what sense we can understand them.[21] I.e., how do biological "laws" compare with the laws of physics?[22]

We have seen that Ω is about as random, patternless, unpredictable and incomprehensible as possible; the pattern of its bit sequence defies understanding. However with computations in the limit, which is equivalent to having an oracle for the halting problem,[23] Ω seems quite understandable: it becomes a computable sequence. Biological evolution is the nearest thing to an infinite computation in the limit that we will ever see: it is a computation with molecular components that has proceeded for 10^9 years in parallel over the entire surface of the earth. That amount of computing could easily produce a good approximation to Ω, except that that is not the goal of biological evolution. The goal of evolution is survival, for example, keeping viruses such as those that cause AIDS from subverting one's molecular mechanisms for their own purposes.

This suggests to me a very crude evolutionary model based on the game of matching pennies, in which players use computable strategies for predicting their opponent's next play from the previous ones.[24] I don't think it would be too difficult to formulate this more precisely and to show that prediction strategies will tend to increase in program-size complexity with time.

Perhaps biological structures are simple and easy to understand only if one has an oracle for the halting problem.

---

[21] Compare my previous thoughts on theoretical biology, CHAITIN (1970b) and CHAITIN (1979). There I suggest that mutual information $H(s:t)$ can be used to pick out the highly correlated regions of space that contain organisms. This view is static; here we are concerned with the dynamics of the situation. Incidentally, it is possible to also regard these papers as an extremely abstract discussion of musical structure and metrics between compositional styles.

[22] In CHAITIN (1985a) I examine the complexity of physical laws by actually programming them, and the programs turn out to be amazingly small. I use APL instead of LISP.

[23] See CHAITIN (1977a,1976c).

[24] See the discussion of matching pennies in CHAITIN (1969a).

IMPLEMENTATION NOTES

The programs in this book were run under the VM/CMS time-sharing system on a large IBM 370 main-frame, a 3090 processor. A virtual machine with 4 megabytes of storage was used.

The compiler for converting register machine programs into exponential diophantine equations is a 700-line[25] REXX program. REXX is a very nice and easy to use pattern-matching string processing language implemented by means of a very efficient interpreter.[26]

There are three implementations of our version of pure LISP:

1. The first is in REXX, and is 350 lines of code. This is the simplest implementation of the LISP interpreter, and it serves as an "executable design document."

2. The second is on a simulated register machine. This implementation consists of a 250-line REXX driver that converts M-expressions into S-expressions, remembers function definitions, and does most input and output formating, and a 1000-line 370 Assembler H expression evaluator. The REXX driver wraps each expression in a lambda expression which binds all current definitions, and then hands it to the assembler expression evaluator. The 1000 lines of assembler code includes the register machine simulator, many macro definitions, and the LISP interpreter in register machine language. This is the slowest of the three implementations; its goals are theoretical, but it is fast enough to test and debug.

---

[25] Including comments and blank lines.
[26] See COWLISHAW (1985) and O'HARA and GOMBERG (1985).

3. The third LISP implementation, like the previous one, has a 250-line REXX driver; the real work is done by a 700-line 370 Assembler H expression evaluator. This is the high-performance evaluator, and it is amazingly small: less than 8K bytes of 370 machine language code, tables, and buffers, plus a megabyte of storage for the stack, and two megabytes for the heap, so that there is another megabyte left over for the REXX driver. It gets by without a garbage collector: since all information that must be preserved from one evaluation to another (mostly function definitions) is in the form of REXX character strings, the expression evaluator can be reinitialized after each evaluation. Another reason for the simplicity and speed of this interpreter is that our version of pure LISP is "permissive;" error checking and the production of diagnostic messages are usually a substantial portion of an interpreter.

All the REXX programs referred to above need to know the set of valid LISP characters, and this information is parameterized as a small 128-character file.

An extensive suite of tests has been run through all three LISP implementations, to ensure that the three interpreters produce identical results.

This software is available from the author on request.

THE NUMBER OF S-EXPRESSIONS OF SIZE N

In this appendix we prove the results concerning the number of S-expressions of a given size that were used in Chapter 5 to show that there are few minimal LISP programs and other results. We have postponed the combinatorial and analytic arguments to here, in order not to interrupt our discussion of program size with material of a rather different mathematical nature. However, the estimates we obtain here of the number of syntactically correct LISP programs of a given size, are absolutely fundamental to a discussion of the basic program-size characteristics of LISP. And if we were to discuss another programming language, estimates of the number of different possible programs and outputs of a given size would also be necessary. In fact, in my first paper on program-size complexity [CHAITIN (1966)], I go through an equivalent discussion of the number of different Turing machine programs with n-states and m-tape symbols, but using quite different methods.

Let us start by stating more precisely what we are studying, and by looking at some examples. Let α be the number of different characters in the alphabet used to form S-expressions, not including the left and right parentheses. In other words, α is the number of atoms, excluding the empty list. In fact $\alpha = 126$, but let's proceed more generally. We shall study S_n, the number of different S-expressions n characters long that can be formed from these α atoms by grouping them together with parentheses. The only restriction that we need to take into account is that left and right parentheses must balance for the first time precisely at the end of the expression. Our task is easier than in normal LISP because we ignore blanks and all atoms are exactly one character long, and also because NIL and () are not synonyms.

Here are some examples. $S_0 = 0$, since there are no zero-character S-expressions. $S_1 = \alpha$, since each atom by itself is an S-expression. $S_2 = 1$, because the empty list $()$ is two characters. $S_3 = \alpha$ again:

> (a)

$S_4 = \alpha^2 + 1$:

> (aa)
> $(())$

$S_5 = \alpha^3 + 3\,\alpha$:

> (aaa)
> $(a())$
> $(()a)$
> $((a))$

$S_6 = \alpha^4 + 6\,\alpha^2 + 2$:

> $(aaaa)$
> $(aa())$
> $(a()a)$
> $(a(a))$
> $(()aa)$
> $(()())$
> $((a)a)$
> $((aa))$
> $((()))$

$S_7 = \alpha^5 + 10\,\alpha^3 + 10\,\alpha$:

> $(aaaaa)$
> $(aaa())$
> $(aa()a)$
> $(aa(a))$
> $(a()aa)$
> $(a()())$
> $(a(a)a)$
> $(a(aa))$
> $(a(()))$
> $(()aaa)$
> $(()a())$

```
( ( ) ( ) a )
( ( ) ( a ) )
( ( a ) a a )
( ( a ) ( ) )
( ( a a ) a )
( ( ( ) ) a )
( ( a a a ) )
( ( a ( ) ) )
( ( ( ) a ) )
( ( ( a ) ) )
```

Our main result is that S_n/S_{n-1} tends to the limit $\alpha + 2$. More precisely, the following asymptotic estimate holds:

$$S_n \sim \frac{1}{2\sqrt{\pi}} k^{-1.5} (\alpha + 2)^{n-2}$$

where $k \equiv \dfrac{n}{\alpha + 2}$.

In other words, it is almost, but not quite, the case that each character in an n-character S-expression can independently be an atom or a left or right parenthesis, which would give $S_n = (\alpha + 2)^n$. The difference, a factor of $(\alpha + 2)^{-2} k^{-1.5}/2\sqrt{\pi}$, is the extent to which the syntax of LISP S-expressions limits the multiplicative growth of possibilities. We shall also show that for $n \geq 3$ the ratio S_n/S_{n-1} is never less than α and is never greater than $(\alpha + 2)^2$. In fact, numerical computer experiments suggest that this ratio increases from α to its limiting value $\alpha + 2$. Thus it is perhaps the case that $\alpha \leq S_n/S_{n-1} \leq \alpha + 2$ for all $n \geq 3$.

Another important fact about S_n is that one will always eventually obtain a syntactically valid S-expression by successively choosing characters at random, unless one has the bad luck to start with a right parenthesis. Here it is understood that successive characters are chosen independently with equal probabilities from the set of $\alpha + 2$ possibilities until an S-expression is obtained. This will either happen immediately if the first character is not a left parenthesis, or it will happen as soon as the number of right parentheses equals the number of left parentheses. This is equivalent to the well-known fact that with probability one a symmetrical random walk in one dimension will eventually return to the origin [FELLER (1970)]. Stated in terms of S_n instead of in probabilistic terminology, we have shown that

$$\sum_{n=0}^{\infty} S_n \, (\alpha + 2)^{-n} \; = \; 1 - \frac{1}{\alpha + 2} \, .$$

Moreover, it follows from the asymptotic estimate for S_n that this infinite series converges as $\Sigma \, n^{-1.5}$.

In fact, the asymptotic estimate for S_n stated above is derived by using the well-known fact that the probability that the first return to the origin in a symmetrical random walk in one dimension occurs at epoch $2n$ is precisely

$$\frac{1}{2n-1} \binom{2n}{n} 2^{-2n} \quad \sim \quad \frac{1}{2n \sqrt{\pi n}} \, .$$

This is equivalent to the assertion that if $\alpha = 0$, i.e., we are forming S-expressions only out of parentheses, then

$$S_n \;\; = \;\; \frac{1}{2} \; \frac{1}{2n-1} \binom{2n}{n} \quad \sim \quad \frac{1}{4n \sqrt{\pi n}} \, 2^{2n}.$$

For we are choosing exactly half of the random walks, i.e., those that start with a left parenthesis not a right parenthesis.

Accepting this estimate for the moment (we shall give a proof later) [or see FELLER (1970)], we now derive the asymptotic estimate for S_n for unrestricted α. To obtain an arbitrary n-character S-expression, first decide the number $2k$ ($0 \leq 2k \leq n$) of parentheses that it contains. Then choose which of the n characters will be parentheses and which will be one of the α atoms. There are $n - 2$ choose $2k - 2$ ways of doing this, because the first and the last characters must always be a left and a right parenthesis, respectively. There remain α^{n-2k} choices for the characters that are not parentheses, and one-half the number of ways a random walk can return to the origin for the first time at epoch $2k$ ways to choose the parentheses. The total number of n-character S-expressions is therefore

$$\sum_{0 \leq 2k \leq n} \alpha^{n-2k} \binom{n-2}{2k-2} \left[\frac{1}{2} \, \frac{1}{2k-1} \binom{2k}{k} \right].$$

This is approximately equal to

$$\sum_{0 \leq 2k \leq n} \binom{n}{2k} \left[\frac{2k}{n} \right]^2 \alpha^{n-2k} 2^{2k} \left[\frac{1}{4\sqrt{\pi}\, k^{1.5}} \right].$$

To estimate this sum, compare it with the binomial expansion of $(\alpha + 2)^n$. Note first of all that we only have every other term. The effect of this is to divide the sum in half, since the difference between the two sums, the even terms and the odd ones, is $(\alpha - 2)^n$. I.e., for large n the binomial coefficients approach a smooth gaussian curve, and therefore don't vary much from one term to the next. Also, since we are approaching a gaussian bell-shaped curve, most of the sum is contributed by terms of the binomial a few standard deviations around the mean.[27] In other words, we can expect there to be about twice

$$k \quad = \quad \frac{n}{\alpha + 2} + O(\sqrt{n})$$

parentheses in the n characters. The correction factor between the exact sum and our estimate is essentially constant for k in this range. And this factor is the product of $(2k/n)^2$ to fix the binomial coefficient, which is asymptotic to $4/(\alpha + 2)^2$, and $k^{-1.5}/4\sqrt{\pi}$ due to the random walk of parentheses. Thus our estimate for S_n is essentially every other term, i.e., one-half, of the binomial expansion for $(\alpha + 2)^n$ multiplied by this correction factor:

$$\frac{1}{2} (\alpha + 2)^n \; \frac{4}{(\alpha + 2)^2} \; \frac{1}{4\sqrt{\pi}\, k^{1.5}}$$

with $k = n/(\alpha + 2)$. I.e.,

$$S_n \quad \sim \quad \frac{(\alpha + 2)^{n-2}}{2\sqrt{\pi}\, k^{1.5}},$$

which was to be proved.

Now we turn from asymptotic estimates to exact formulas for S_n, via recurrences.

Consider an n-character S-expression. The head of the S-expression can be an arbitrary $(n - k)$-character S-expression and its tail can be an

---

[27]   Look at the ratios of successive terms [see FELLER (1970) for details].

arbitrary k-character S-expression, where k, the size of the tail, goes from 2 to $n - 1$. There are $S_{n-k} S_k$ ways this can happen. Summing all the possibilities, we get the following recurrence for S_n:

$$S_0 = 0, \quad S_1 = \alpha, \quad S_2 = 1,$$

$$S_n = \sum_{k=2}^{n-1} S_{n-k} S_k \quad (n \geq 3). \tag{12}$$

Thus $S_n \geq \alpha S_{n-1}$ for $n \geq 3$, since one term in the sum for S_n is $S_1 S_{n-1} = \alpha S_{n-1}$.

To proceed, we use the method of generating functions.[28] Note that each of the n characters in an n-character S-expression can be one of the α atoms or a left or right parenthesis, at most $\alpha + 2$ possibilities raised to the power n :

$$S_n \leq (\alpha + 2)^n.$$

This upper bound shows that the following generating function for S_n is absolutely convergent in a neighborhood of the origin

$$F(x) \equiv \sum_{n=0}^{\infty} S_n x^n \quad \left(|x| < \frac{1}{\alpha + 2} \right).$$

The recurrence (12) for S_n and its boundary conditions can then be reformulated in terms of the generating function as follows:

$$F(x) = F(x)^2 - \alpha x F(x) + \alpha x + x^2.$$

I.e.,

$$F(x)^2 + [-\alpha x - 1] F(x) + [\alpha x + x^2] = 0.$$

We now replace the above $(n - 2)$-term recurrence for S_n by a two-term recurrence.[29]

The first step is to eliminate the annoying middle term by completing the square. We replace the original generating function F by a new generating function whose coefficients are the same for all terms of degree 2 or higher:

---

[28] For some of the history of this method, and its use on a related problem, see "A combinatorial problem in plane geometry," Exercises 7-9, Chapter VI, p. 102, POLYA (1954).

[29] I am grateful to my colleague Victor Miller for suggesting the method we use to do this.

$$G(x) \equiv F(x) + \frac{1}{2} (-\alpha x - 1).$$

With this modified generating function, we have

$$G(x)^2 = F(x)^2 + [-\alpha x - 1] F(x) + \frac{1}{4} [-\alpha x - 1]^2$$

$$= -\alpha x - x^2 + \frac{1}{4} [-\alpha x - 1]^2 \equiv P(x),$$

where we introduce the notation P for the second degree polynomial on the right-hand side of this equation. I.e.,

$$G(x)^2 = P(x).$$

Differentiating with respect to x, we obtain

$$2 G(x) G'(x) = P'(x).$$

Multiplying both sides by $G(x)$,

$$2 G(x)^2 G'(x) = P'(x) G(x),$$

and thus

$$2 P(x) G'(x) = P'(x) G(x),$$

from which we now derive a recurrence for calculating S_n from S_{n-1} and S_{n-2}, instead of needing all previous values.

We have

$$G(x)^2 = P(x),$$

that is,

$$G(x)^2 = -\alpha x - x^2 + \frac{1}{4} [-\alpha x - 1]^2.$$

Expanding the square,

$$P(x) = -\alpha x - x^2 + \frac{1}{4} [\alpha^2 x^2 + 2\alpha x + 1].$$

Collecting terms,

$$P(x) = \left[\frac{1}{4} \alpha^2 - 1 \right] x^2 - \frac{\alpha}{2} x + \frac{1}{4}.$$

Differentiating,

$$P'(x) \;=\; \left[\frac{1}{2}\, \alpha^2 - 2 \right] x - \left[\frac{\alpha}{2} \right].$$

We have seen that

$$2\, P(x) \sum (n + 1)\, S_{n+1}\, x^n \;=\; P'(x) \sum S_n\, x^n,$$

where it is understood that the low order terms of the sums have been "modified." Substituting in $P(x)$ and $P'(x)$, and multiplying through by 2, we obtain

$$\left[(\alpha^2 - 4)\, x^2 - 2\, \alpha\, x + 1 \right] \sum (n + 1)\, S_{n+1}\, x^n$$
$$= \left[(\alpha^2 - 4)\, x - \alpha \right] \sum S_n\, x^n.$$

I.e.,

$$\sum \left[(\alpha^2 - 4)\, (n - 1)\, S_{n-1} - 2\, \alpha\, n\, S_n + (n + 1)\, S_{n+1} \right] x^n$$
$$= \sum \left[(\alpha^2 - 4)\, S_{n-1} - \alpha\, S_n \right] x^n.$$

We have thus obtained the following remarkable recurrence for $n \geq 3$:

$$n\, S_n \;=\; -\left[(\alpha^2 - 4)\, (n - 3) \right] S_{n-2} + \left[2\, \alpha\, (n - 1) - \alpha \right] S_{n-1}. \quad (13)$$

If exact rather than asymptotic values of S_n are desired, this is an excellent technique for calculating them.

We now derive $S_n \leq (\alpha + 2)^2\, S_{n-1}$ from this recurrence. For $n \geq 4$ we have, since we know that S_{n-1} is greater than or equal to S_{n-2},

$$S_n \;\leq\; \left[(\alpha^2 + 4) + (2\, \alpha + \alpha) \right] S_{n-1} \;\leq\; \left[(\alpha + 2)^2 \right] S_{n-1}.$$

In the special case that $\alpha = 0$, one of the terms of recurrence (13) drops out, and we have

$$S_n \;=\; 4\, \frac{n - 3}{n}\, S_{n-2}.$$

From this it can be shown by induction that

$$S_{2n} \;=\; \frac{1}{2}\, \frac{1}{2n - 1} \binom{2n}{n} \;=\; \frac{1}{2}\, \frac{1}{2n - 1}\, \frac{(2n)!}{n!\, n!}\,,$$

which with Stirling's formula [see FELLER (1970)]

$$n! \quad \sim \quad \sqrt{2\pi} \; n^{n+\frac{1}{2}} \, e^{-n}$$

yields the asymptotic estimate we used before. For

$$S_{2n} \; = \; \frac{1}{2} \; \frac{1}{2n-1} \; \frac{(2n)!}{n! \, n!} \quad \sim \quad \frac{1}{4n} \; \frac{\sqrt{2\pi} \; (2n)^{2n+\frac{1}{2}} \, e^{-2n}}{\left[\sqrt{2\pi} \; n^{n+\frac{1}{2}} \, e^{-n}\right]^2} \; = \; \frac{1}{4n} \; \frac{2^{2n}}{\sqrt{\pi n}} \; .$$

For large n recurrence (13) is essentially

$$(\alpha^2 - 4) \, S_{n-2} - 2 \, \alpha \, S_{n-1} + S_n \quad = \quad 0 \qquad (\text{``}n \text{ very large''}). \qquad (14)$$

Recurrences such as (14) are well known. See, for example, the discussion of "Recurring series," and "Solution of difference equations," Exercises 15-16, Chapter VIII, pp. 392-393, HARDY (1952). The limiting ratio $S_n/S_{n-1} \;\rightarrow\; \rho$ must satisfy the following equation:

$$(\alpha^2 - 4) - 2 \, \alpha \, x + x^2 \quad = \quad 0.$$

This quadratic equation factors nicely:

$$(x - (\alpha + 2)) \, (x - (\alpha - 2)) \quad = \quad 0.$$

Thus the two roots ρ are:

$$\rho_1 \; = \; \alpha - 2,$$
$$\rho_2 \; = \; \alpha + 2.$$

The larger root ρ_2 agrees with our previous asymptotic estimate for S_n/S_{n-1}.

BIBLIOGRAPHY

Reprints of the author's papers are available on request.

H. ABELSON, G.J. SUSSMAN, and J. SUSSMAN (1985), *Structure and Interpretation of Computer Programs*, Cambridge, Mass.: MIT Press.

G.J. CHAITIN (1966), "On the length of programs for computing finite binary sequences," *Journal of the ACM 13*, pp. 547-569.

G.J. CHAITIN (1969a), "On the length of programs for computing finite binary sequences: statistical considerations," *Journal of the ACM 16*, pp. 145-159.

G.J. CHAITIN (1969b), "On the simplicity and speed of programs for computing infinite sets of natural numbers," *Journal of the ACM 16*, pp. 407-422.

G.J. CHAITIN (1970a), "On the difficulty of computations," *IEEE Transactions on Information Theory 16*, pp. 5-9.

G.J. CHAITIN (1970b), "To a mathematical definition of 'life'," *ACM SICACT News 4*, pp. 12-18.

G.J. CHAITIN (1974a), "Information-theoretic computational complexity," *IEEE Transactions on Information Theory 20*, pp. 10-15. Reprinted in TYMOCZKO (1986).

G.J. CHAITIN (1974b), "Information-theoretic limitations of formal systems," *Journal of the ACM 21*, pp. 403-424.

G.J. CHAITIN (1975a), "Randomness and mathematical proof," *Scientific American 232* (5), pp. 47-52. Also published in the French, Japanese, and Italian editions of *Scientific American*.

G.J. CHAITIN (1975b), "A theory of program size formally identical to information theory," *Journal of the ACM 22*, pp. 329-340.

G.J. CHAITIN (1976a), "A toy version of the LISP language," *Report RC 5924*, Yorktown Heights: IBM Watson Research Center.

G.J. CHAITIN (1976b), "Information-theoretic characterizations of recursive infinite strings," *Theoretical Computer Science 2*, pp. 45-48.

G.J. CHAITIN (1976c), "Algorithmic entropy of sets," *Computers & Mathematics with Applications 2*, pp. 233-245.

G.J. CHAITIN (1977a), "Program size, oracles, and the jump operation," *Osaka Journal of Mathematics 14*, pp. 139-149.

G.J. CHAITIN (1977b), "Algorithmic information theory," *IBM Journal of Research and Development 21,* pp. 350-359, 496.

G.J. CHAITIN and J.T. SCHWARTZ (1978), "A note on Monte Carlo primality tests and algorithmic information theory," *Communications on Pure and Applied Mathematics 31,* pp. 521-527.

G.J. CHAITIN (1979), "Toward a mathematical definition of 'life'," in R.D. LEVINE and M. TRIBUS (1979), *The Maximum Entropy Formalism,* Cambridge, Mass.: MIT Press, pp. 477-498.

G.J. CHAITIN (1982a), "Algorithmic information theory," in *Encyclopedia of Statistical Sciences I,* New York: Wiley, pp. 38-41.

G.J. CHAITIN (1982b), "Gödel's theorem and information," *International Journal of Theoretical Physics 22,* pp. 941-954. Reprinted in TYMOCZKO (1986).

G.J. CHAITIN (1984), "Computing the busy beaver function," *Report RC 10722,* Yorktown Heights: IBM Watson Research Center.

G.J. CHAITIN (1985a), "An APL2 gallery of mathematical physics—a course outline," *Proceedings Japan 85 APL Symposium,* Publication N:GE18-9948-0, IBM Japan, pp. 1-56.

G.J. CHAITIN (1985b), "Randomness and Gödel's theorem," *Report RC 11582,* Yorktown Heights: IBM Watson Research Center.

G.J. CHAITIN (1987), "Incompleteness theorems for random reals," *Advances in Applied Mathematics 8,* pp. 119-146.

J.H. CONWAY (1986), private communication.

R. COURANT and H. ROBBINS (1941), *What is Mathematics?,* Oxford: Oxford University Press.

M.F. COWLISHAW (1985), *The REXX Language,* Englewood Cliffs, NJ: Prentice-Hall.

M. DAVIS, H. PUTNAM and J. ROBINSON (1961), "The decision problem for exponential diophantine equations," *Annals of Mathematics 74,* pp. 425-436.

M. DAVIS (1965), *The Undecidable—Basic Papers on Undecidable Propositions, Unsolvable Problems and Computable Functions,* Hewlett: Raven Press.

M. DAVIS, Y.V. MATIJASEVIC and J. ROBINSON (1976), "Hilbert's tenth problem. Diophantine equations: positive aspects of a negative solution," in *Mathematical Developments Arising from Hilbert Problems,* Providence: American Mathematical Society, pp. 323-378.

M. DAVIS (1978), "What is a computation?," in L.A. STEEN (1978), *Mathematics Today,* New York: Springer, pp. 241-267.

S. FEFERMAN et al. (1986), *Kurt Gödel: Collected Works I: Publications 1929-1936,* New York: Oxford University Press.

W. FELLER (1970), *An Introduction to Probability Theory and Its Applications I,* New York: Wiley.

J. FORD (1983), "How random is a coin toss?," *Physics Today 36 (4),* pp. 40-47.

K. GÖDEL (1931), "On formally undecidable propositions of *Principia mathematica* and related systems I," *Monatshefte für Mathematik und Physik 38,* pp. 173-198. Reprinted in FEFERMAN (1986).

G.H. HARDY (1952), *A Course of Pure Mathematics,* Cambridge: Cambridge University Press.

R.V. JENSEN (1987), "Classical chaos," *American Scientist 75,* pp. 168-181.

J.P. JONES et al. (1976), "Diophantine representation of the set of prime numbers," *American Mathematical Monthly 83,* pp. 449-464.

J.P. JONES and Y.V. MATIJASEVIC (1984), "Register machine proof of the theorem on exponential diophantine representation of enumerable sets," *Journal of Symbolic Logic 49,* pp. 818-829.

M. LEVIN (1974), "Mathematical Logic for Computer Scientists," *Report TR-131,* Cambridge, Mass.: MIT Project MAC.

B.B. MANDELBROT (1982), *The Fractal Geometry of Nature,* San Francisco: Freeman.

P. MARTIN-LÖF (1966), "The definition of random sequences," *Information and Control 9,* pp. 602-619.

J. McCARTHY (1960), "Recursive functions of symbolic expressions and their computation by machine I," *ACM Communications 3,* pp. 184-195.

J. McCARTHY et al. (1962), *LISP 1.5 Programmer's Manual,* Cambridge, Mass.: MIT Press.

J. McCARTHY (1981), "History of LISP," in R.L. WEXELBLAT (1981), *History of Programming Languages,* New York: Academic Press, pp. 173-197, 710-713.

R.P. O'HARA and D.R. GOMBERG (1985), *Modern Programming Using REXX,* Englewood Cliffs, NJ: Prentice-Hall.

G. POLYA (1954), *Induction and Analogy in Mathematics,* Princeton, NJ: Princeton University Press.

J. RISSANEN (1986), "Stochastic complexity and modeling," *Annals of Statistics 14,* pp. 1080-1100.

R. RUCKER (1987), *Mind Tools,* Boston: Houghton Mifflin.

C.P. SCHNORR (1974), private communication.

C.E. SHANNON and W. WEAVER (1949), *The Mathematical Theory of Communication,* Urbana: University of Illinois Press.

R.M. SOLOVAY (1975), private communication.

A.M. TURING (1937), "On computable numbers, with an application to the Entscheidungsproblem," *Proceedings London Mathematical Society 42,* pp. 230-265. Reprinted in DAVIS (1965).

T. TYMOCZKO (1986), *New Directions in the Philosophy of Mathematics,* Boston: Birkhäuser.

J.C. WEBB (1980), *Mechanism, Mentalism, and Metamathematics,* Dordrecht: Reidel.

P.H. WINSTON and B.K.P. HORN (1984), *LISP,* Reading, Mass.: Addison-Wesley.